Language Matters

*Edited by David Cameron
and Richard Simeon*

Language Matters
How Canadian Voluntary Associations Manage French and English

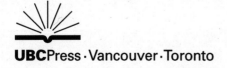

UBCPress · Vancouver · Toronto

20 19 18 17 16 15 14 13 12 11 10 09   5 4 3 2 1

Printed in Canada with vegetable-based inks on FSC-certified ancient-forest-free paper (100 percent post-consumer recycled) that is processed chlorine- and acid-free.

Library and Archives Canada Cataloguing in Publication

Language matters: how Canadian voluntary associations manage French and English / edited by David Robertson Cameron and Richard Simeon.

Includes bibliographical references and index.
ISBN 978-0-7748-1503-1 (bound); ISBN 978-0-7748-1504-8 (pbk.);
ISBN 978-0-7748-1505-5 (e-book)

1. Language policy – Canada. 2. Canada – Languages – Political aspects.
3. Bilingualism – Canada. 4. Associations, institutions, etc. – Canada. I. Cameron, David, 1941- II. Simeon, Richard, 1943-

FC145.B55L26 2009   306.44'971   C2008-907822-5

Canadä

UBC Press gratefully acknowledges the financial support for our publishing program of the Government of Canada through the Book Publishing Industry Development Program (BPIDP), and of the Canada Council for the Arts, and the British Columbia Arts Council.

This book has been published with the help of a grant from the Canadian Federation for the Humanities and Social Sciences, through the Aid to Scholarly Publications Programme, using funds provided by the Social Sciences and Humanities Research Council of Canada.

UBC Press
The University of British Columbia
2029 West Mall
Vancouver, BC V6T 1Z2
604-822-5959 / Fax: 604-822-6083
www.ubcpress.ca

To Stevie Cameron and MaryEtta Cheney

Contents

Preface

Canada today is multinational, multicultural, and multi almost everything. Respecting and accommodating all these dimensions of difference are at once our greatest challenge and greatest opportunity.

Language and religion have defined the primordial lines of cleavage in Canada's historical experience. The Royal Proclamation of 1763, the Quebec Act of 1774, the Constitutional Act of 1791, the 1837 Rebellion in Lower Canada and the Durham Report that followed it, the Act of Union of 1840, Confederation in 1867, the Riel troubles in western Canada, the conscription crises of the two world wars – all of these have demonstrated just how important this cultural duality has been to our national existence.

With the secularization of Canada in the decades following the Second World War, the conflict between Catholic and Protestant has faded into the political background, and language has assumed pre-eminence in defining Canadian duality. How Canadians have responded to language in the postwar period is in important ways a critical template for how Canada has responded to the many other dimensions of Canadian diversity that together compose Canada's reality.

Most analyses of Canada's French-English duality have focused on the political and constitutional dimensions of the relationship. How should powers be distributed between federal and provincial governments? Should Quebec be constitutionally regarded as a "nation" within Canada or as a distinct society? Should there be symmetry or asymmetry in the powers of provinces? And so on.

These are critical questions that engage citizens, parties, and governments in an ongoing constitutional and intergovernmental debate. But there are equally critical questions relating to duality that are posed for groups and associations of citizens in their personal lives. Indeed, what goes on beneath the surface of political debate, in civil society, may be of even more fundamental importance to the future of the country. That is the premise underlying this book.

It presents a set of case studies of important Canadian voluntary associations. Each is engaged in the pursuit of specific objectives of importance to its members; all of them, in doing their work, have had to find ways to recognize and accommodate linguistic difference in their internal lives and in their external relations. Most of them have succeeded – but never without difficulty.

These studies are not designed to be historical accounts but snapshots taken of a variety of organizations at the same moment in time – namely, the concluding years of the twentieth century. Since the research was originally conducted, some of the dynamics we describe may well have changed – we are tracking moving targets – but our intention in this project has been to examine common themes in the lives of these organizations at the same historical moment so that the more general patterns of association can be identified and explained.

In exploring how voluntary associations today manage the complexities of language, our book has the immense advantage of building on the contribution of an earlier work. In the early 1960s, two pioneers of modern social science in Canada, Vincent Lemieux and John Meisel, collaborated in a study commissioned by the Royal Commission on Bilingualism and Biculturalism to investigate how language difference played out in the lives of Canadian voluntary associations. Their work was the inspiration of our own. We revisit many of the associations they examined forty years ago while adding several that did not exist at the time.

And we come to some different conclusions. Their work, conducted in the early to mid-1960s, found many groups that were suffering from intense stress from and in some cases were almost paralyzed by linguistic conflict. Why? These were the early years of the Quiet Revolution. The Québécois were re-creating their national identity in a contemporary idiom. They were demanding both more autonomy for their own social, economic, and political institutions and more voice in Canada-wide institutions – which, as the Royal Commission on Bilingualism and Biculturalism amply demonstrated, did not represent them fully. At the same time, anglophone leaders of national associations were baffled by or resistant to the demands for change. The result was, in many associations, debilitating conflict.

The authors here tell a rather different story. Today linguistic conflict in most of the associations we studied is muted. Most have developed a mutually acceptable accommodation of their language differences. These arrangements take many forms, from the linguistic groups actually going their separate ways to more conventional federal solutions. In the conclusion, we seek to explain how and why these choices were made and the costs and benefits experienced by members of each of the language groups in the working out of these accommodations and in the pursuit of their common goals. The practical ingenuity and problem solving reflected in these accommodations have, we believe, some larger lessons for accommodation in the wider Canadian society.

Acknowledgments

We wish to thank first and foremost our colleagues and contributors to this volume for their commitment to the project and their diligence in helping to bring it to fruition. On their behalf, we want to express our deep appreciation to all those members and leaders of the voluntary associations discussed in this book for their kindness and generosity in providing information and responding to the questions posed to them by the authors. It is their experience we have tried to reflect, and we hope we have done so faithfully.

Many others have helped in this work. Vincent Lemieux and John Meisel, authors of the original monograph that inspired us, have supported this replication of their path-breaking study, and we hope we have kept faith with their vision. Jean Laponce, perhaps the foremost scholar of language and politics anywhere, has provided unstinting encouragement, and we are deeply grateful to Jean for his quiet, constant support. The Government of Canada, through many of its departments and agencies, was the major financial contributor to the research presented in this volume. We are especially grateful to Leslie Seidle for the assistance he offered us in navigating the highways and byways of the federal government. No work of this breadth is published without the help of skilled graduate students. We thank especially Julie Bernier and Luc Turgeon for their skill and insight and Elinor Bray Collins and Dubi Kanengisser for assistance in final editing. Finally, Sari Sherman and Rita O'Brien of the Department of Political Science at U of T provided organizational and administrative support at critical stages of the project, and we are very grateful to them for that.

Acronyms

AFMNB	Association francophone des municipalités du Nouveau-Brunswick
AFMO	Association française des municipalités de l'Ontario
AGA	annual general assembly
AI	Amnesty International
AKFC	Aga Khan Foundation Canada
ALS	amyotrophic lateral sclerosis
AMEQ	Alliance des manufacturiers et exportateurs du Québec
AMO	Association of Municipalities of Ontario
AUCC	Association of Universities and Colleges of Canada
BCNI	Business Council on National Issues
CAUT	Canadian Association of University Teachers
CBIE	Canadian Bureau for International Education
CCA	Canadian Cooperative Association
CCC	Canadian Chamber of Commerce
CCCE	Canadian Council of Chief Executives
CCDM	Chambre de commerce du District de Montréal
CCFC	Christian Children's Fund Canada
CCIC	Canadian Council for International Cooperation
CCMM/BTMM	Chambre de commerce du Montréal métropolitain/ Board of Trade of Metropolitan Montreal
CCPQ	Chambre de commerce de la Province du Québec
CCQ	Chambre de commerce du Québec
CCSD	Canadian Council on Social Development
CEA	Canadian Export Association
CEAs	Canadian executing agencies
CEAD	Centre d'études arabes pour le développement
CEGEPs	Collèges d'enseignement général et professionnel
CEO	chief executive officer
CESO	Canadian Executive Services Overseas

CFA	Canadian Federation of Agriculture
CFCC	Community Funds and Councils of Canada
CFIB	Canadian Federation of Independent Business
CFMM	Canadian Federations of Mayors and Municipalities
CIDA	Canadian International Development Agency
CIDMAA	Centre d'information et de documentation sur la Mozambique et l'Afrique australe
CIHR	Canadian Institutes for Health Research
CMA	Canadian Manufacturers' Association
CME	Canadian Manufacturers and Exporters
COPEM	Comité de promotion économique de Montréal
CPC	Canadian Pork Council
CPQ	Conseil du patronat du Québec
CQDS	Conseil québécois de développement social
CROP	Centre de recherche sur l'opinion publique
CUS	Canadian Union of Students
CUSO	Canadian University Service Overseas
CWC	Canadian Welfare Council
DFC	Dairy Farmers of Canada
EFAI	Éditions francophones d'Amnesty International
ESR	European Student Relief
EUMC	Entraide universitaire mondial du Canada
EUMQ	Entraide universitaire mondiale du Québec
FA	federation agreement
FCEI	Fédération canadienne de l'entreprise indépendante
FCM	Federation of Canadian Municipalities
FIT	Foundation for International Training
FOE	Friends of the Earth
FPLQ	Fédération des producteurs de lait du Québec
FPPQ	Fédération des producteurs de porc du Québec
GATT	General Agreement on Tariffs and Trade
GST	Goods and Services Tax
HEC	École des hautes études commerciales
HOPE	HOPE International Development Agency
HSC/SHC	Huntington Society of Canada/Société Huntington du Canada
HSFC	Heart and Stroke Foundation of Canada
HSFO	Heart and Stroke Foundation of Ontario
IC	International Council
ICC	International Commerce Centre
ICHRDD	International Centre for Human Rights and Democratic Development

ID NGOs	international development non-governmental organizations
IEC	International Executive Committee
IFAP	International Federation of Agricultural Producers
IS	International Secretariat
ISS	International Student Service
KAP	Keystone Agricultural Producers
MBT	Montreal Board of Trade
MP	member of Parliament
NAFTA	North American Free Trade Agreement
NFU	National Farmers Union
NGOs	non-governmental organizations
NHVO	National Volunteer Health Organizations
NSI	North-South Institute
ODA	official development assistance
OECD	Organization for Economic Co-operation and Development
PQ	Parti québécois
SAP	South Asia Partnership – Canada
SHQ	Société Huntington du Québec
SUCO	Solidarité, union, co-operation
UCC	Union catholique des cultivateurs
UGEQ	Union générale des étudiants du Québec
UMNB	Union of Municipalities of New Brunswick
UMPQ	Union des municipalités de la province du Québec
UMQ	Union des municipalités du Québec
UMRCQ	Union des municipalités régionales de comté et des municipalités locales
UNCTAD	United Nations Conference on Trade and Development
UNICEF	United Nations International Children's Emergency Fund (now United Nations Children's Fund)
UPA	Union des producteurs agricole
WRAP	Wild Rose Agricultural Producers Association
WSCF	World Student Christian Federation
WSR	World Student Relief
WTO	World Trade Organization
WUS	World University Service
WUSC	World University Service of Canada
WUSQ	World University Service Quebec
YMCA	Young Men's Christian Association
YWCA	Young Women's Christian Association

Language Matters

1
Language and the Institutions of Civil Society
David Cameron and Richard Simeon

This book examines linguistic dualism in the Canadian voluntary sector. It sets for itself three goals.

- First, it aims to describe the patterns of linguistic association in several Canadian voluntary organizations. Which institutions and practices have they developed to manage their linguistic relationships? And how have these institutions and practices affected their capacity to cooperate in the achievement of common goals?
- Second, it attempts to establish the roles that the external environment and the internal organizational reality play in shaping the linguistic capacities and behaviours of selected voluntary organizations in Canada.
- Third, it seeks to uncover the extent to which and the ways in which the selected voluntary organizations contribute to social cohesion or its absence in a linguistically divided society.

The first goal is descriptive; the second and third are explanatory.

Thus, we ask how well do associations in the Canadian voluntary sector reflect, represent, and accommodate linguistic dualism in their structures, in their practices, and in the work they do? Do they contribute to building a civil society that is able to bridge or transcend the fundamental cleavages that divide Canadian society, or do they deepen the sociolinguistic divisions? Conversely, how significant is the state – federal and provincial – in structuring the patterns of linguistic association in the voluntary organizations of civil society? What impacts do French-English relations at the formal political level have on the groups we examine in the voluntary sector? These are the fundamental questions that underpin this study of a broad variety of associations in the Canadian voluntary sector. We focus on "patterns of linguistic association" in Canadian civil society and their implications both for the lives of these associations and for Canada as a whole.

Citizens, governments, and scholars have in recent decades devoted enormous effort to exploring national unity, the future of Quebec and Canada, and constitutional renewal. But while Canadians have debated a wide range of constitutional and institutional changes that might achieve a lasting political accommodation, they have seldom asked what is going on underneath this superstructure, in civil society, in the world of private, non-governmental associations? Is this world increasingly fragmented and divided along linguistic lines? Has our capacity for discovering the basis of coexistence or accommodation in areas of mutual concern been declining? Or have French- and English-speaking Canadians found the means to work together on the ground in ways that have escaped their political leaders? We believe that there is a rich array of relationships and practices within associations in civil society and that much can be learned from an intensive examination of their internal lives. Each has a distinctive story to tell, and their experiences over the past several decades are both a part of the grand narrative of civil society and a potential source of ideas and innovations for the political community as a whole.

The underlying premise that guides the project is that voluntary associations are central elements in the constitution of "civil society." A vibrant civil society, in turn, is essential to a healthy democratic politics, to building strong communities, and to innovation in public policy. This is because participation in associational life can provide education and experience in the "arts" of democratic participation, compromise, and the like and can help to build strong relationships of trust among citizens and groups. Moreover, effective associations are an essential means for citizens to achieve their collective goals through cooperative action, and they provide channels of communication between citizens and government. What is more, in recent decades, organizations in the voluntary sector have become increasingly important instruments for the achievement of public purposes that previously were regarded as the responsibility of the state; their health, therefore, and their capacity to express the structural values of the country as a whole are for this reason as well a matter of general concern.

In a society deeply divided along ethnic, linguistic, or regional lines, associations in civil society have another vital role. That role is to build linkages or bridges across the dividing lines and thus to help in achieving the accommodations necessary for successful coexistence. Associations that are able to bring members or representatives of the different groups together in face-to-face relationships, and that permit them to cooperate in meeting shared goals, despite linguistic or other such differences, may help to sustain accommodation in the wider political sphere. Conversely, associational patterns in which each group is rooted on one side or the other of the cultural divide, or in which relations between the groups are unequal and conflictual, or in which there is little capacity to pursue common goals are likely to undermine social cohesion. As John Meisel and Vincent Lemieux pointed out in their study many years ago for the Royal Commission on Bilingualism and Biculturalism, it is through their associational linkages that Canadians of different backgrounds "come to grips with one another's preoccupations, priorities, biases and that they attempt to reconcile such differences as may occur between them ... Voluntary associations are a microcosm of ethnic relations in Canada."[1]

Their *Ethnic Relations in Canadian Voluntary Associations* is in fact the inspiration and model for our project.[2] It was carried out in the 1960s for the Royal Commission on Bilingualism and Biculturalism. The pioneering work of these two scholars showed that the capacity of twenty Canadian voluntary associations to build bridges and establish an equal partnership between Canada's two main linguistic groups was limited by the fact that francophones were under-represented in most mixed Canadian voluntary organizations and that their participation in these associations was handicapped by the dominance of English in most important communications and transactions. Francophones therefore sought either a greater voice in national associations or greater autonomy to pursue their goals within the Quebec community, putting major strains on many associations. As Meisel and Lemieux noted, "crises in the relations between the two official-language groups in voluntary associations have frequently coincided with, and could be linked to, prevailing political controversies between Ottawa and the government of Quebec."[3] They found that "there are serious disparities in the degree to which Francophone and Anglophone Canadians benefit from belonging to common associations and to which they participate in their activities; on the whole, Francophones are involved less – and often less effectively ... Most of the difficulties arise essentially from the fact that in many common associations, unilingual Anglophones predominate. A Francophone therefore often finds himself in the position of having to function in the English language if he wishes to benefit from his membership in a countrywide Canadian organization. This imposes obvious penalties and handicaps on members of the official-language minority."[4]

The research we report on in this book returns to many of the issues Meisel and Lemieux addressed almost two generations ago. As we show in the following section of this chapter, the interest in revisiting their work is twofold. First, it allows us to see whether relations between francophones and anglophones within voluntary associations have evolved in the same way and at the same pace as relations between the two linguistic groups in the larger society. Second, it allows us to fill an important gap in our understanding. Although interactions between francophones and anglophones *within Quebec* have been widely studied since the 1960s, surprisingly little has been written on the evolution of interactions between the two linguistic groups at the pan-Canadian level, despite the obvious crucial importance of the issue.

The Political Context

This project is situated within the larger context of the evolution of French-English relations in Canada. How the associations we study deal with language in their own lives and work is profoundly shaped by this context; conversely, how associations manage language in their own affairs will play a part in how Canada as a whole succeeds or fails in maintaining a bilingual society and polity. As Meisel and Lemieux point out, "general conditions prevailing at any given time – quite independently of what is happening to any association – will affect what goes on inside it. This is so particularly with respect to political developments," and in turn "the attitudes that voluntary organizations take towards the problem of finding a satisfactory basis for the creative interaction of the two communities have far-reaching consequences, both because of the example they afford, and because of the influence they exert on their members, the general public, and, in particular, politicians."[5]

The profound cleavage between French and English has lain at the root of some of Canada's most troubled periods, but, prior to Quebec's Quiet Revolution of the early 1960s, conflicts arose out of the friction between two very different ways of life.[6] *Linguistic* conflict was relatively muted. No Quebec political party, for example, included language issues as a part of its platform until well into the 1960s. The reason for the relative absence of linguistic conflict is that francophone Quebec and English Canadian societies remained largely isolated from each other, living within different frameworks of values and inhabiting distinctive socioeconomic structures. Despite some notable exceptions, civil society in Quebec in general was dominated by conservative values and by the church. It was resolutely inward looking, resisting rather than embracing modernizing forces. The rest of Canada – its federal bureaucracy an English-speaking institution,[7] its business community largely anglophone and largely Protestant – had little incentive to engage with French speakers. To the extent that the two language groups did come into contact, the relationships were highly asymmetrical, reflecting the privileged position of the English Canadian minority in Quebec. English was dominant in virtually all areas of shared economic and social life. Prior to the Quiet Revolution, then, francophone and anglophone societies were like ocean liners passing in the night: sharing the same sea but with little need to communicate beyond the flashing signal lights between their governing elites. When major conflict did occur, for example, in the hanging of Louis Riel and in the two conscription crises, it arose out of the collision between two different societies and two discernibly different world views.

The Quiet Revolution fundamentally changed the relationship. At one time, anglophone commentators were inclined to suggest that, "if only

Quebecers could become more like us" (i.e., secular, urban, modern, industrial, bureaucratic), then the bases for conflict would fade away. The irony is that the modernizing revolution undertaken by Quebec in the early 1960s did exactly what the commentators suggested; Quebec did become "more like us." Urbanization, industrialization, and, most important, secularization fundamentally changed the social and economic environment that had sustained the old order.[8] Now, instead of rejecting the activist state as a threat to religious values, Quebec embraced the state as the basic agent of change and *épanouissement*. As Ramsay Cook notes, "the state replaced the Church as the principal institution in the collective lives of Quebecers," and "only the state that French Canadians controlled could be expected to assume the task of making Quebecers *maîtres chez nous:* increasing their control over the economy and making their language the dominant one in public and private institutions" in Quebec.[9] This process of secularization and modernization had the paradoxical consequence of bringing Quebec closer to English Canada and the rest of North America in terms of values, ways of life, and institutional arrangements. Yet, contrary to what some had expected, the result was not a decrease of conflict but an intensification of conflict both within Quebec and between Quebec and the rest of Canada.[10]

Why was this so? In large part, it was because Quebec and the rest of Canada were now no longer ships on different courses passing in the night. Now they were ships on the same course, embracing similar values and aspirations. To shift the metaphor, where once they were playing different games on different fields, now they were playing the same game on the same field. This had a number of consequences. First, it meant that they were now competing for the same things – for control over business enterprises and cultural institutions, for representation at the highest levels of the bureaucracy, and so on. Second, the opportunities and incentives for contact – indeed its necessity – were now greatly increased. Third, there was much greater awareness of the asymmetries and inequalities in these relationships. They were fully documented in the report of the Royal Commission on Bilingualism and Biculturalism and elsewhere. These studies showed that francophones were symbolically excluded from the federal level (e.g., in the country's unilingual currency and its flag, the Red Ensign, which evoked the British connection); that francophones were greatly under-represented at the higher levels of the public service and in senior federal ministerial posts; that the incomes of francophone workers (even those who were bilingual) fell significantly below those of anglophones, especially in Quebec;[11] that the senior management and directors of major corporations in Quebec were overwhelmingly anglophone; and so on.[12] Moreover, other studies demonstrated that, in most of the rest of Canada, the francophone minority populations were declining and that rates of assimilation were high.[13]

It was a time when the terms of engagement between English- and French-speaking Canadians were being renegotiated at every level. Contacts were increasing, but how would they be played out? Both at the societal level and within individual associations, two broad strategies emerged, one led by French-speaking politicians in Ottawa, the other by French-speaking politicians in Quebec. The first might be called the pan-Canadian nation-building project, the second the Quebec nation-building project.

The first was founded on the premise that Canada could be a bilingual country, from sea to sea, or at least that a full provision of bilingual services would mean that people of either language group could feel at home anywhere in the country. At the governmental level, the centrepiece was the Official Languages Act. Where numbers warranted, Ottawa would serve Canadians in both official languages wherever they lived. Francophones would gain higher positions in the public service, and bilingualism among all senior government employees would be strongly encouraged. Special efforts would be made to preserve and protect official language minorities, whether francophones outside Quebec or anglophones within Quebec. Immersion programs in the minority language, an initiative widely supported among middle-class anglophones, would be strongly promoted. The federal government would invest resources in developing student exchange programs and encouraging voluntary associations to provide translation and related services. In general, quite apart from its larger constitutional agenda, this approach attempted to build networks and linkages that would bind francophones and non-francophones more closely together as part of a country-wide community.

The Quebec nation-building strategy responded to the same challenges quite differently. Again, in addition to its constitutional agenda of greater autonomy and perhaps sovereignty for Quebec, its program included Bill 101, the Quebec Language Law, designed to strengthen French as the dominant language within Quebec and to ensure that immigrants would be integrated into the francophone community; the establishment of a strong provincial state with political institutions capable of expressing and serving the Québécois identity; promotion of "Quebec Inc.," a Quebec-based business community closely linked to the provincial state; French-language public television and a wide variety of programs to stimulate arts and culture within the province; and the expansion of a distinct Quebec presence internationally, especially in francophone countries. Quebec leaders set out self-consciously to build a modern but autonomous Quebec-centred civil society, which was seen by many as a prerequisite to the goal of sovereignty.

It was in this fraught social and political context that Meisel and Lemieux conducted their study of associations. The groups they examined were themselves caught up in the stresses of socioeconomic change and in the larger political battles. Francophones in these groups had to choose whether or not to continue to pursue their interests within pan-Canadian associations. Those who did were no longer willing to accept a subordinate status and agitated for greater recognition, greater representation, more effective bilingualism, and the like. Anglophone leaders were often confused and reluctant in their responses. Alternatively, francophones pursued the second strategy, which attenuated their linkages to pan-Canadian civil society and strengthened their engagement in a French-speaking Québécois civil society. This strategy included calls for greater autonomy for the Quebec wings or branches of the given Canadian association; movement toward something like "sovereignty-association," in which an autonomous Quebec association would have a variety of linkages with its English Canadian counterpart; or outright independence – an entirely separate organization. Whichever strategy was followed, the associational milieu analyzed by Meisel and Lemieux was one of considerable tension and dynamism, as both language groups sought to develop new relationships.

A generation later, the fundamental question of the political relationship between Canada and Quebec remains unresolved, but "national unity" has ceased for the time being to be a central, actively debated public concern. Outside Quebec, to the extent that Canadians choose to discuss the matter at all, commitment to a single country that includes Quebec remains strong, but there is little apparent stomach for launching into a new round of formal constitutional talks. Inside Quebec, as well, there is little current inclination to debate the grand issues, but nevertheless among francophone Quebecers identification with Quebec as a national community is strong; it coincides, however, with a continuing belief in a Canadian identity. Political debate about the national question within the province has continued to focus on the alternatives of "renewed federalism" or "sovereignty partnership," with relatively little support for the poles of outright independence or the status quo of the federal system.

But what has been going on beneath the level of formal politics, in civil society? Only a few incomplete indicators point to an answer. Within English-speaking Canada, the primary social change is the broadening of the range of politically relevant identities and the scope of political conflict. In the mid-1960s, social movements such as the women's movement, environmentalism, and issues such as disability and sexual orientation had only just begun to emerge. Since then, Canadian politics has become infused with the politics of identity. The emergent identities cut across the long-standing verities of region and language that have traditionally characterized Canadian life. Moreover, high levels of immigration, coupled with the deracialization of Canadian immigration law, have changed the ethnic face of Canada's large cities. Canadian society is becoming increasingly multicultural and increasingly diverse in ethnic, religious, and cultural terms. Moreover, the claims of Canada's Aboriginal peoples have come to the fore as they mobilize against economic and social discrimination to seek recognition of land claims and treaty rights and to pursue a form of self-government.

After Meisel and Lemieux wrote, these changes began to dominate English-speaking Canadian political discourse. No longer were French-English relations perceived as the only dominant fault line. Managing the Quebec-Canada relationship, while still critical, especially to governmental elites, was now only one of several structural issues confronting Canada. For associations such as those we have studied, the emergence of new issues and identity groups with their own claims for recognition and representation constituted another set of social pressures to which they had to respond. For some, balancing these new commitments with a longer-standing commitment to bilingualism would not be simple.

Quebec society underwent many of the same demographic changes as the rest of Canada in this period. Social movements, such as the feminist movement, were very strong in Quebec. While French-speaking Canadians confronted many of the same issues that their anglophone counterparts addressed elsewhere in Canada, relations between the two linguistic groups in the women's movement were strained, partly because the anglophone movement tended to look to Ottawa for redress (in part a consequence of federal sponsorship of the Charter of Rights and Freedoms), while the Quebec women's movement, like most other "progressive" movements in the province, tended to identify more strongly with the Quebec government. Indeed, it appears that, given the alternatives of either forming alliances across language groups or forming alliances and networks across identity groups within a single linguistic milieu, the latter predominated in most cases. While Quebecers remained deeply divided in their preferred constitutional option, the decades of Quebec institution and network building were forging an ever more cohesive and far-reaching Quebec-based civil society, in which linkages and associations across the language frontier and outside Quebec were playing less and less of a role in the lives of Quebecers. This is, of course, not to deny that very important relationships with the rest of the country continued to exist, but the impression remains that Quebecers increasingly participated in them as self-conscious members of a fully distinct and integrated society, a French-speaking national community within Canada.

For associational life, these developments in Quebec meant that many of the issues that Meisel and Lemieux considered remain alive today. A diversity of arrangements continues to characterize linguistic patterns. In a number of cases, the level of tension associated with an asymmetrical arrangement has declined as both sides have come to reasonably settled understandings, which, if not celebrated, are at least accepted. In other cases, Quebec wings of pan-Canadian associations have gained greater autonomy or even full independence. Again, they may well cooperate frequently with their anglophone counterparts but now as autonomous entities.

Hence the paradox. Quebec and the rest of Canada are in many respects much more alike as societies than they were in the past, yet the level of segmentation between the two communities remains high. What Donald Smiley argued in 1992 remains broadly true today: "The ongoing territorial separation of the two language groups means that on a day-to-day basis most citizens of one are not in contact with members of the other."[14] In fact, when one looks at the books and the newspapers Canadians read, the television they watch, and the music they listen to, one is entitled to conclude that the "two solitudes" are still very much alive.[15]

As Harvey Lazar and Tom McIntosh have recently noted, this diagnosis, relating to Canadian popular culture, largely holds true at the level of civil society as well: "Turning to the connections between Quebec and the rest of Canada, it is our sense that the political chasm is as wide as ever. Economic connections remain thick, but there is little cross-pollination in culture. Connections within civic society are uneven. In labour they are formal but not strong. French-speaking Quebecers generally do not move to other regions of Canada. Business ties between English- and French-speaking Canadians are substantial but many of the pan-Canadian social movements are poorly represented or not represented at all in Quebec, where Quebec-based groups have entirely separate organizations."[16]

But this is an incomplete picture. While we know much about some aspects of the relationship, we know very little about others. There is considerable public opinion data on attitudes and values, though much less on interactions between the two language groups and the feelings members have about each other. There is a virtually endless literature on political relationships and the related constitutional debates. What is missing – apart from the pioneering but now dated study of Meisel and Lemieux – is deeper information on whether and how English and French Canadians work out their day-to-day relationships as they seek to pursue common goals in the voluntary sector. This is a critical part of the larger puzzle; the observation of Raymond Breton in *Les frontières culturelles et la cohésion du Canada* (1981) remains true today: "L'intéraction sociale des Canadiens français et des Canadiens anglais, tant sur le plan de la masse que sur celui de l'élite, a fait l'objet de peu d'études systématiques."[17]

The premise underlying the present volume is twofold. First, it is our belief that patterns of associational life can be expected to reflect and respond to the changing social and political context that we have just described. Our individual case studies will explore how various associations do so. In this sense, the voluntary associations are the dependent variables. But, second, we assume that voluntary associations, as a central part of civil society, can also help to shape it. Looked at from this perspective, voluntary associations may be understood as independent variables.

Beyond this, it is possible that the examination of relationships within these associations will help us to point to some of the ways in which civil society in Canada is likely to evolve in the future. Indeed, as we examine how associations deal with the accommodation of linguistic difference, we may learn some lessons that can not only be applied to other associations facing the same challenges but also serve as reference points for Canadians seeking a lasting political accommodation.

Theoretical Background

Underpinning this exploration is a large question of great theoretical and practical interest. What is it that holds the constituent groups in divided societies such as Canada together? Most simply put, where is the glue? As we noted at the outset, a starting point for this inquiry is the hypothesis that a large part of the answer must lie in the character of a country's civil society. We approach our work with the following questions in mind. What is the relationship between political institutions and the nature and structure of civil society? Does it matter what kind of organizations and associations exist in the voluntary sector? What are the grounds of social cohesion? In what sense and in what form is it necessary? What – at the level of civil society – are the terms of coexistence between the constituent groups in divided societies? In this enterprise, the question of coexistence and cohesion in divided societies arises at two levels. First, in the case studies, we explore the sources of cohesion or division within individual associations; in the last chapter, we reflect on the implications of these experiences for society and government in Canada as a whole.

Let us now examine four differing theoretical approaches to the question of how social cohesion can be achieved in divided societies. First is the "contact thesis." Most crudely stated, it argues that, the more members of differing cultural groups engage in face-to-face relationships ("contact"), the more likely it is that they will develop positive feelings toward each other.[18] "To know you is to love you." At the societal level, promoting contact (as with student exchanges and the like) will result in greater harmony and unity. But as Donald Forbes, Canada's leading student of the contact hypothesis,[19] insists, "linkages (or contacts) among individuals with different social norms (languages, cultures, values, etc.), while they may in a sense knit a society together, tend also, and more strongly, to divide it into self-consciously opposed identity groups ... Linkages within and between such groups can be a basis for wider conflicts rather than benign cooperation."[20] More contact, then, may lead to increased respect and acceptance or to greater prejudice and rejection, depending on the circumstances in which it occurs. It can lead to greater awareness of differences, for example, in cultural styles or substantive interests but not necessarily greater acceptance of these differences. In the minds of the minority, it may engender greater fears of assimilation. The alternative to "to know you is to love you" is "good fences make good neighbours."

It is worth underlining two implications. First, whether contact leads to harmony or division will depend greatly on the nature of the contact: whether the individuals in contact possess equality of status; whether there is "co-operative or competitive" interdependence in the pursuit of common goals; and whether contact itself has broad support in the wider society and among those in authority.[21] Second, we should not expect contact in itself to dissolve all conflict. Rather, "the conflicts will be managed by practical devices."[22] At the societal level, this management includes political arrangements such as brokerage parties, federalism, and language laws. At the group level, it means the role of analogous devices such as patterns of representation, language use, and so on.

Certain hypotheses flow from this analysis. We would expect harmonious relationships within an association to be stronger when its members come together as equals, when they gain mutual benefit from the exchange, and when there is strong normative support for the linkages in the relevant environment. Similarly, they will be stronger when the constitutional arrangements within a group – both structural and procedural – provide proportionate recognition, accommodation, and representation to both cultures.

A second and somewhat more recent theoretical approach is found in the burgeoning literature on "social capital." Social capital theory in a sense extends the logic of the contact hypothesis by positing the social benefits that are assumed to arise out of the relationships of trust and reciprocity created by associational life, by contact; social capital is composed of social linkages, which are held to build social trust and mutual understanding, leading to greater cooperation and reduced conflict.

Social capital is widely understood to be subdivisible into two forms: "bridging" and "bonding." Bonding capital is the glue that holds communities and associations of similar people together, that maintains their solidarity and commitment, often at the expense of the potential links with people outside the group. Bridging capital is composed of the networks and interrelationships that bring into association and mutual respect people who are different from one another and groups that are diverse. Where bonding capital consolidates solidarity in a context of relative uniformity, bridging capital fosters unity in a context of pluralism. Clearly, there is a place for both forms in any society, but the bridging version is of particular importance in maintaining social cohesion in pluralistic societies and is often crucial to stability in divided societies.

Robert Putnam, the most prominent exponent of social capital theory, speaks of bonding (or exclusive) social capital as "a kind of sociological superglue."[23] This form of associational life can be problematic in a country characterized by deep linguistic, cultural, or religious divisions. Indeed, it leads us to think of a country not as a single civil society but as two or more distinct or separate civil societies. Each may be rich in social capital in many ways – and hence build strong trust among its own members – but the danger is that they will exist in isolation, defining themselves and their identities in opposition to the "other" and thus perpetuating and deepening conflict. Here there are echoes of the contingent or contextual reality of the contact hypothesis as highlighted by Forbes. As Breton puts it, "increasing social capital solely within ethnic or racial boundaries without forming any 'bridges' between groups may be a source of conflict, hence the importance of cross-community activities and structures to ensure that social participation and interpersonal relationships extend beyond ethnic boundaries."[24]

The social capital approach requires cross-cutting aggregation (bridging capital), but the presence of two or more major linguistic groups will tend to favour language-based aggregation and segregation along linguistic lines (bonding capital) most of the time. In cases where groups aggregate across linguistic lines, asymmetry will usually prevail since language groups rarely have the same power and status. The idea of bridging capital suggests that in such societies it is essential that there be some shared level of identity and common values and that it is critical to sustain networks that will bring members of the different communities together in relationships of mutual trust. "Frequent interaction among a diverse set of people," says Putnam, "tends to produce a norm of generalized reciprocity. Civic engagement and social capital entail mutual obligation and responsibility for action." He further claims that, "the more we connect with other people, the more we trust them."[25] In his study of communal conflict between Hindus and Muslims in India, Ashutosh Varshney found that the conflict was minimized and contained in cities where local associations of traders and other business-people bridged religious lines. "Vigorous associational life acts as a ... constraint on the polarizing strategies of political elites."[26] As Deepa Narayan puts it, "social cohesion requires not just high social capital within groups. It also requires dense, though not necessarily strong, cross cutting ties among groups."[27]

This perspective suggests that we should assess our associations in terms of their success in bringing large numbers of francophone and anglophone Canadians together in face-to-face meetings based on equality, trust, and mutual understanding. As we shall see, this ideal is seldom met. Three sets of factors militate against it. First, there are enormous distances in Canada, which mean that a relatively small proportion of British Columbians and Quebecers will ever have the opportunity to sustain face-to-face contact. Their relationships will be mediated by others; they will mainly be indirect and second hand. Second, language differences are a profound barrier to communication, and bilingualism is not widespread. At the national level in 1996, 41 percent of francophones were bilingual, while just 9 percent of anglophones were bilingual.[28] In 1996, the rate of bilingualism in Quebec was 38 percent (the highest rate in Canada), while the national average rate of bilingualism was 17 percent.[29] Almost 34 percent of francophones in Quebec were bilingual, while less than 7 percent of anglophones outside Quebec were bilingual.[30] All provinces except Quebec and New Brunswick were well below the national average of 17 percent. For instance, Ontario's rate was 11.6 percent, British Columbia's 6.7 percent, Alberta's 6.7 percent, and Manitoba's 9.4 percent.[31] Only a small minority of anglophones and a larger minority of francophones are capable of full communication in the other language. Third, most of the associations we studied – and, indeed, most pan-Canadian associations – are not mass membership organizations with high degrees of member participation. Rather, they are increasingly specialized, with power highly concentrated in a small elected leadership and in professional staffs. In most, the rank and file are not so much "members" as "volunteers" or "contributors."[32] This reality limits the capacity of associations to support close links between individuals across the cultural divide.

The third approach to understanding cohesion in divided societies places much less emphasis on mass engagement in civil society. It argues that close contacts among individual citizens are not necessary – or perhaps even desirable. Segmented, isolated civil societies can still cohere as long as there is overarching cooperation among the elites.[33] It is they rather than individual members who must cooperate in mutual trust. In some ways, this "elite accommodation" approach, associated with Arend Lijphart, directly contradicts the civil society approach. In other ways, however, the disagreement is simply about the level at which accommodation will take place. Two hypotheses relevant to our study flow from our consideration of the elite accommodation approach. The first is that the success of cross-group accommodation within an association depends largely on the commitment of its elites to a harmonious relationship. The second is that in most groups the relationship between anglophones and francophones will be an indirect one, mediated through the interaction of small, bilingual elites.[34] Where this approach falls down, however, is that it does not help us to predict whether or not the elites will be committed to maintaining the relationship, the essential precondition of the elite accommodation model.

The search for the grounds of commitment leads us to suggest a fourth approach to understanding the accommodation of language within groups, one that owes much to a public choice approach to understanding political behaviour. It argues that successful accommodation will depend on how leaders and activists in the group weigh the costs and benefits of further cooperation. Divided societies may function and even prosper as long as the benefits of doing so clearly outweigh the costs. With this in mind, we need to pay attention to the role that cooperation plays in contributing to the participants' success in meeting their basic goals – from combatting heart disease to promoting international human rights. The benefits of cooperation in turn will depend on a number of factors, including the nature of the interest involved, the cost of cooperation, and what it takes to access the resources required to achieve group goals. In some cases, the incentives to work together will be very strong, in others less so or non-existent.

There are unavoidable costs associated with bilingualism and linguistic accommodation, and they will fall both on individual members of linguistic groups and on the groups themselves. The burden of these costs may be distributed symmetrically or asymmetrically. They are partly financial in the obvious sense of the need to pay for translations of publications and websites and to provide simultaneous translations at meetings.[35] But they are also psychological and personal. There are two dimensions: the cost of language acquisition and the communication disadvantage that one always has to bear when one's native language is not used in most transactions. The implications of having a mother tongue different from that of the majority are uncovered in the following quotation from Phillippe Van Parijs, even though he is speaking about the consequences of having a mother tongue different from the official language: "Having a mother tongue different from the one adopted as the official language puts one at a multiple disadvantage. People in that position have to bear the heavy cost of acquiring proficiency in a foreign language. They are handicapped, relative to natives of the official language, in economic and political competition. Most seriously perhaps, their self-respect is under pressure as a result of the subordinate, inferior status given to something as deeply associated with themselves (in other people's eyes and their own) as their mother tongue."[36]

These kinds of costs fall on both language groups, of course, but they tend to be borne most heavily by the members of the minority community. As Jean Laponce has demonstrated, there is a powerful tendency toward linguistic homogeneity in any group unless there are strong countervailing factors: "As a general rule ... languages in contact, to the extent they cannot ignore each other, will show stratification. Further, except when the object is to forbid rather than to facilitate communications, the dominant language will tend to become the only language."[37] Generally, "the minority is more conscious of being a minority – and thus different – than the dominant group is of being dominant," just as "the left-handed is more conscious of being left-handed than the right-handed individual is."[38] He adds that "asymmetrical power sharing between two language groups results in the dominant group having the power to decide how the burden of bilingualism will be borne." Occasionally, the dominant group will decide to assume most of the costs, but more frequently the dominant group shifts the cost of bilingualism onto the ethnic minority.[39] In national or Canada-wide associations, most of the accommodations to achieve linguistic harmony will necessarily be made by francophones.[40] To reduce this burden, the minority-language group will often diminish contact with the majority-language group by means of territorial concentration or – in the voluntary sector – by separate and distinct unilingual associations.

The associations we studied display considerable variety in membership and participation of the two linguistic groups in their lives and activities. The form and extent of francophone participation, given the inherent tendency toward asymmetry, depends on two sets of factors: the benefits francophones gain from the relationship (and their consequent willingness to bear the costs) and the extent to which associational practices help to minimize or equalize the costs (e.g., through translation). Net benefits for both groups may well be highest when the organizational form provides for maximum autonomy for each language group, but this may be at the price of less intense, and perhaps less effective, cooperation on shared goals.[41]

We believe that this approach is a powerful challenge to those who emphasize contact, shared identities, or mutual goodwill. Instead, it suggests that each group will weigh the costs and benefits of continued association and act accordingly. Several hypotheses also flow from this perspective. The greater the interdependence between the groups, and the more necessary it is to achieve mutual goals, the larger the incentive to cooperate. Groups can coexist and interact effectively independently of shared identities or values; they can do so because they see themselves as linked communities of fate. They cooperate not because they love each other but because they need each other.

Each of these theoretical approaches, we believe, has something to contribute to our account of associational life in Canada and its voice in the country's grand narrative. We might characterize the contributions each makes by proceeding in reverse order from the sequence in which they have been presented above. What might be called the political economy of linguistic association – our fourth approach – provides an excellent way of explaining why English- and especially French-speaking Canadians would take the trouble of associating together in pursuit of shared objectives. Why bear the costs of cross-language association? The existence of common interests is foundational. In the absence of such interests, there is no reason to associate, but the mere existence of common interests cannot in itself explain association.

To explain the coming together of members of the two language communities in a joint enterprise, one must look to the pattern of incentives and constraints generated by the wider political environment in which they function. The larger the gains from cooperation, the greater the willingness to invest efforts and resources in promoting accommodation. The larger the gains, the more willing are both anglophones and francophones to bear the costs and make the necessary compromises. In developing their formal and informal structures and practices, each group will push for arrangements that minimize the costs to them while at the same time not losing the benefits that come from working together. The structural asymmetry that marks relations between French and English means that the calculus is different for each of the two groups; since the costs borne by the participating French-speaking Canadians will almost always be higher than those for participating English-speaking Canadians, the benefits from association must be clearer and more marked. The calculus will also vary depending on the issues in which the groups are engaged. For example, if it is one that, under the Constitution, falls unambiguously within provincial jurisdiction, then there is less need for cross-group cooperation; the reverse holds true for matters clearly lying within federal jurisdiction. If economic interests are central to success, and they cut across group lines, then again cooperation is facilitated.

If the political economy of linguistic association helps to explain *why* groups form across the language divide, it does not in itself help us to understand *how* they go about it. For an answer to that question, it is useful to turn to the consociational model. As we will see, the way in which our voluntary associations organize themselves is chiefly via elite accommodation. Relatively small groups of associational leaders and professional staffs, broadly representative of the two linguistic communities, assume the responsibility of running the organization at the pan-Canadian level and make specific arrangements to accommodate French and English in their headquarters and in their services to the regional organizations and rank-and-file membership. Among this elite, especially among the professional staff, one typically finds a substantially higher level of bilingualism than exists in the membership as a whole, and often one also finds an investment in a set of carefully elaborated linguistic practices that permit unilingual board members and other actors to function satisfactorily at the peak of the organization in a two-language environment. Within effectively functioning pan-Canadian voluntary associations, it is often the institution itself that assumes the burden of bilingualism, through the production of documents in both languages, through the linguistic capacities of its professional staff, and at times through simultaneous translation.

If these theoretical approaches help to explain why and how voluntary organizations form and function across the language divide, one is still left with the need to understand what – beyond the bare calculus of cost and benefit – accounts for those pan-Canadian associations that come together and stay together. What explains institutional momentum and the desire, when confronted with crises and challenges, to make things work? Here we think it is useful to appeal to the first and second theoretical approaches we discussed above, namely the contact hypothesis and social capital theory. In those associations that continue to operate on a pan-Canadian basis, that do not fragment or collapse, that do not radically reconfigure themselves as separate operations, there seems to be evidence of the contact hypothesis functioning in its benign form. The associational leadership's experience of working together on practical problems, of jointly pursuing common objectives, appears in many of the cases we studied to produce sentiments of mutual regard and mutual comprehension. Collaboration in these cases appears to foster – to move to the notion of social capital – the growth of trust and feelings of reciprocity. Consistent with the social capital model, the elite accommodators are invested in the relationship and in the successful pursuit of their common enterprise. Calculations of interest are clothed over time with sentiments of mutual regard, of loyalty, even of affection; a culture of accommodation and colleagueship is formed that offers incentives, beyond pure interest, to manage and nurture the relationship. This, at any rate, is what can be observed in some of the best-functioning pan-Canadian associations we studied. In some other cases, on the other hand, the conditions of continuity have not existed, and the organization has folded or been transformed; even there, at least in circumstances in which French and English successor organizations are created out of the collapse of a pan-Canadian institution, relations between them are frequently good, although, consistent with our theory, the connections that exist are much more narrowly calculated on the basis of self-interest.

Design of the Study

Each of the following chapters focuses on the "patterns of association" found in a particular organization or set of organizations. We define these patterns as the organizational forms and practices that have been developed to represent and manage linguistic dualism within each association. With each of the associations, we use "the same slice of history." We examine them during the period running roughly from the mid-1960s to the mid- to late 1990s. The decade of the 1960s saw the advent of the Quiet Revolution in Quebec and the operation of the federal Royal Commission on Bilingualism and Biculturalism. It was also the period when John Meisel and Vincent Lemieux were completing the study upon which our book builds. In the three decades that followed, Canada went through a tumultuous struggle to accommodate its French- and English-language communities, and it is within the context of this dynamic historical period that we examine the linguistic lives and practices of our voluntary associations. We begin by providing a general profile of each group: its mission, its history, its organizational structure, its resources, and so on. We then situate each group within the larger context of voluntary agencies in its sector.

The body of each chapter examines critical dimensions of internal group life. We look at language use, both in the public face of the association and in its internal communications. We look at how linguistic dualism is reflected in representation on boards, executives, committees, and other decision-making bodies and in the formal and informal practices of group governance. Here we address questions such as what are the burdens and costs of bilingualism, and who bears them? What are the friction points, and how well have they been addressed? Are there pressures for major changes either in formal rules or in informal practices? Have there been critical turning points when linguistic tension came to a head or the organization made fundamental changes in structure or practice? To what extent do these associations provide opportunities for positive, mutually supportive relationships between French- and English-speaking Canadians? How do they balance the need to reflect Canadian dualism against the need to respond to other dimensions of Canadian diversity, including regionalism and multiculturalism? We conclude each case study with some reflections on how these associations might better accommodate and build bridges in their own life and work and with some thoughts about the implications of their experiences for the larger question of building bridging capital in Canada.

Our basic dependent variables throughout these studies are the nature and quality of the relationships and interactions between language groups within the association. To what extent are they characterized by mutual trust and confidence or by distrust and avoidance? To what extent is there cooperation or conflict? To what extent is there mutual recognition and equality in the relationship? And how well are the groups able to collaborate in meeting their shared goals?

We do not presume that any single model or set of practices provides an "ideal" model for the relationship. Indeed, our cases demonstrate a rich array of forms and practices. In some cases, there is a single national association composed of individual members or local chapters. Others, following the larger Canadian pattern, are federations, with an overarching national association and ten provincial associations, exercising different degrees of autonomy. Yet others are "confederal," with the national body being a creature of the provincial associations. All these forms seek to integrate francophones and anglophones into a single organizational structure. In another group of associations, however, distinct francophone and anglophone organizations may coexist, either with both going their own, largely separate, ways or cooperating on shared goals through various forms of "sovereignty-association." Each form is likely to develop different dynamics with respect to membership, representation, language use, and so on and to encounter different sorts of challenges. Unitary associations, for example, may be paralyzed by linguistic conflict or may marginalize members of the minority language group. More separated groups might find it hard to cooperate or, on the other hand, they may find that removing the language "block" facilitates cooperation and trust.

Finally, we are interested in what explains the patterns we have found. First is the larger social and political context. The internal lives of associations do not exist in isolation from trends in the society in which they are embedded. Heightened linguistic tension at the national level is likely to be reflected in the debates within associations. A trend toward decentralization, asymmetry, or secession in pan-Canadian politics will be reflected at the group level. Hence, we locate the evolution of each group within the broader political context.

A second set of explanations we explore lies in the relationship of the groups we have studied to the federal and provincial aspects of the Canadian state. Associations interact with the state in many ways: it can be the source of funds and support, the object of pressure and lobbying for goals important to the groups, and so on. The state in turn depends on associations in civil society to achieve many of its goals. Groups can help to deliver services through partnership arrangements; they can be a vehicle through which governments communicate to citizens. And they can be instruments through which governments attain larger societal goals – including the building of civil society. In the period covered in these studies, both the federal and the Quebec governments were involved in nation-building projects. As part of this strategy, both worked to strengthen their own linkages with associations by building them into their own policy networks, by providing financial support, and, in the federal case, by encouraging greater bilingual capacity in Canada-wide associations. More generally, group structure and dynamics will also be affected by the extent to which the issues the group is concerned with lie primarily within federal, provincial, or shared jurisdiction. "Bien qu'elles soient indépendantes, les associations bénévoles sont sensibles aux modifications de l'environnement politique dans lequel elles fonctionnent, surtout si leurs objectifs sont controversables et consistent à influencer la politique de l'État."[42]

The third set of explanations for patterns of association lies within the groups themselves. Much will depend on the nature of the group's goals and the extent to which achieving them depends on cooperation across language groups. The more this is so, the more the group will be prepared to meet the inevitable costs associated with bilingualism, and the more its members will work at accommodation. How and how well they manage this depend greatly on another factor: the leadership's commitment to the bilingual goal and their willingness to deploy the resources needed to achieve it.

The subsequent chapters weave all three sets of explanations together. Seven case studies are presented here. They are in no sense a random sample of the tens of thousands of voluntary associations that exist in Canada. They have been chosen to represent a number of specific sectors.[43]

- In Chapter 2, William Coleman and Tim Mau explore English-French relations in Canada's comprehensive business associations.
- Grace Skogstad, in Chapter 3, examines linguistic relations in Canada's key farm organizations.
- Chapter 4 looks at a too-often neglected dimension of the public sector, specifically municipal associations, notably the Canadian Federation of Municipalities. This study is distinctive in that the organizations represented are governments rather than civil society associations. Don Stevenson and Richard Gilbert are responsible for this study.
- Richard Simeon, in Chapter 5, addresses language practices in the health sector, reporting specifically on the experiences of the Heart and Stroke Foundations of Canada and the Huntington Societies of Canada and Quebec.
- Jane Jenson and Rachel Laforest study the Canadian Council on Social Development in Chapter 6.
- Cathy Blacklock, in Chapter 7, introduces an international dimension, reflecting on the experience of the World University Service of Canada.
- Finally, in Chapter 8, our second study devoted to the world of international non-governmental organizations (NGOs), Michel Duquette and Sylvie Dugas offer an account of the history of Amnesty International.

These diverse associations demonstrate a wide variety of organizational forms – federal, confederal, sovereignty-association, separated. All have undergone important changes in their continuing search for accommodation over the period studied. Such changes over time can be particularly well documented in the three case studies that replicate those conducted by Meisel and Lemieux: the studies of business, agriculture, and municipalities.

We approach this project both as citizens and as scholars. As scholars, we believe that the pages that follow will contribute to the growing literature on civil society, civic engagement, and social capital. Too few studies in this area have explored what affects the ability of associations to build effective bridges between groups in societies, like Canada, that are characterized by deep cultural cleavages. As citizens, we believe that there is much to be learned from the experiences of these non-governmental associations. The rich variety of ways they have found accommodation will provide lessons for citizens and policy makers as they seek accommodation on the larger constitutional plane.

2

French-English Relations in Comprehensive Business Associations

William Coleman and Tim Mau

Business leaders in Canada share some deep-seated beliefs in the virtues of free enterprise and private ownership. They argue that the longer-term interests of all Canadians will be best served if markets are left unfettered and unregulated. In the present globalizing period, they have also come to share a common belief in the long-term opportunities for growth and wealth creation that come with free trade between nations. These beliefs reflect the very special position that business firms occupy in a market economy embedded in a society with a liberal democratic political system.[1] In some societies, the commitment of business leaders to this kind of free enterprise ideology is overridden by commitments to ethnic or religious communities that exist within those societies. The history of French-English relations in Canada, however, does not fit this kind of pattern. Generally speaking, business leaders in Canada have found that the common interests they possess as a social class are more important than the interests that might divide them as members of one of Canada's two linguistic families. The findings in this study provide further evidence of this long-standing feature of the Canadian business community.

Any attempt to study linguistic relations within Canada's system of business associations is bound to be a complex task. A study of this system based on data collected in the early to mid-1980s found over 600 "nationally relevant" business associations active in Canada.[2] It also indicated that this number had grown at a fairly constant rate since the beginning of the Second World War. Hence, it is reasonable to assume that the number is even higher today. To obtain a snapshot of the characteristics of linguistic relations in these business associations today, we follow the lead of John Meisel and Vincent Lemieux in their study for the Royal Commission on Bilingualism and Biculturalism.[3] They chose to focus on the principal associations at the time that sought to represent the *general interests* of business as whole, namely those in the chamber of commerce system. Since their study, the ranks of these "comprehensive" business associations have expanded to include the

Canadian Council of Chief Executives (CCCE), Canadian Federation of Independent Business (CFIB), Conseil du patronat du Québec (CPQ), and Canadian Manufacturers and Exporters (CME). Accordingly, this study follows the spirit of the earlier one by including these newer associations as well.

The study begins with a historical overview of the development of comprehensive business associations in Canada. It then turns to core issues of the study, French-English relations within these associations, by revisiting the findings of Meisel and Lemieux and then examining contemporary linguistic relations. In finding a pattern of continued relative harmony across the linguistic divide, the study examines next as potential "turning points" the merger of the Montreal Board of Trade and the Chambre de commerce du District de Montréal in 1992 and the activities of each of the comprehensive associations in the constitutional arena. We argue that these events reinforce the ongoing pattern of business leaders finding common ground as a class rather than being divided based on nationality.

Comprehensive Business Associations: Historical Overview

When Meisel and Lemieux conducted their study of the relationships between the Canadian Chamber of Commerce (CCC) and the Chambre de commerce de la Province du Québec (CCPQ) (now Chambre de commerce du Québec [CCQ]) in the 1960s, the universe of groups representing the general interests of the business community was less complex than it is today. The chamber of commerce system dominated the scene, with the Canadian Manufacturers' Association (CMA) serving as a complementary group. Although the CMA represented industrial firms only, secondary industry had been sufficiently important in the Canadian economy through the first half of the twentieth century that the CMA was bound to be an important national voice for business.

Almost from the time that Meisel and Lemieux were writing, this universe began to change. A new comprehensive peak association, the Conseil du patronat du Québec, was conceived in Quebec in 1966 and became active in 1969 to respond to the growing conflict between business and labour and the radicalization of the nationalist movement. A year later John Bulloch, a schoolteacher and the son of a politically outspoken Toronto tailor, formed the Canadian Council on Fair Taxation to protest a federal white paper on tax reform.[4] After the movement contributed to a successful routing of the proposals, Bulloch asked its participants whether a more permanent voice for small business was needed. When they agreed, Bulloch set up the Canadian Federation of Independent Business, which had become the country's largest direct-membership business association within a decade.

Five years later the chief executives of the country's largest corporations decided they needed their own voice that would adopt a less strident position on key national issues than was characteristic of the Canadian chamber and the CMA at the time. The unruly response of the labour movement to wage and price controls in 1975 reinforced this perception, leading to the creation of the Business Council on National Issues (BCNI) in 1976. In 2001, the BCNI changed its name to Canadian Council of Chief Executives. The final change to the landscape of general business associations came in the mid-1990s. With the advent of the Canada-US Free Trade Agreement and the North American Free Trade Agreement (NAFTA), the idea of a protected manufacturing sector at the centre of Macdonald's National Policy in the late nineteenth century was finally dead. With branch plants of US firms either closing or restructuring, it no longer made much sense to have manufacturers and exporters represented in separate associations. The CMA thus entered into a merger with the Canadian Export Association (CEA) in May 1996, creating the Alliance of Manufacturers and Exporters Canada. The alliance changed its name to Canadian Manufacturers and Exporters in 2000.

French-English Relations and Associational Structures
Table 2.1 lists the principal general business associations in Canada, the dates they were founded, and the type of structure they had assumed in 2001, the time of the study. These structures are important because they shape how the respective groups accommodate French and English businesses in their respective organizations. The categories in Table 2.1 are defined as follows.[5]

- *Unitary.* There is no differentiation along territorial lines.
- *Unitary with regional subunits.* This is a unitary organization that has created a number of regional branch organizations. The branches depend on the central organization for resources, staff, and direction. They do not have a separate constitution, and members belong to the national body.
- *Unitary association with regional subunits, one or more of which enjoys an enhanced status.* This status might involve the relevant subunit having responsibility for dealing on its own with related governments.
- *Federal association.* Regional organizations have sufficient autonomy to be called associations in their own right. They employ their own staff members, administer their own budgets, and may have their own constitutions. Members, however, belong to the association as a whole and thus are simultaneously members of the regional and the national associations. They pay one set of dues.
- *Confederal association.* This arrangement features territorial associations that are virtually independent in their own right. Their constitutions may differ significantly from that of the national association to which they belong. Distinct from federal associations, business firms belong directly to the subterritorial association, and it is this latter organization, in turn, that belongs to the broader body.

- *Affiliation arrangements.* Although independent organizations in their own right, these subterritorial associations affiliate themselves to a related association with a more comprehensive territorial domain. This affiliation arrangement facilitates exchanges of information between the two organizations and perhaps occasional political cooperation. But the subterritorial bodies do not "belong" to the more comprehensive body, nor are they subject in any way to its authority. Business persons or firms may choose to belong to one or both of these associations. Belonging to one does not bring any formal membership tie to the other, however, as in the confederal arrangement.

Comprehensive Business Associations: Institutional Evolution

The confederal form taken by the chamber of commerce system arises out of its historical pattern of development. Chambers of commerce or boards of trade emerged first at the local level, and only later, as the provincial and federal governments became more interventionist in society, did they join together to create more territorially comprehensive associations. The first such local organization occurred in the eighteenth century when a group of merchants in Halifax formed an organization to promote trade. The Committee of Trade founded in Quebec City in 1807 signalled the beginning of the chamber of commerce system in Quebec. It was followed in 1822 by the Committee of Trade of Montreal, which was incorporated as the Montreal Board of Trade (MBT) in 1842.

Given the relative strength of English and French business in Quebec in the nineteenth century, it is not completely surprising that the MBT tended to be dominated by the English-speaking business elite. In the charged atmosphere of the Riel Rebellion in 1885 and the formation of Honoré Mercier's Parti national in the same period, French-speaking businesses concluded that they needed their own voice. Under the leadership of Joseph-Xavier Perrault, the Chambre de commerce du District de Montréal (CCDM) was founded in 1887. In a letter to the local business journal, *Le moniteur du commerce,* Perrault explained why he thought such an organization was needed:

> Because our fellow English-speaking citizens form the large majority of the members at the board, they carry out all their discussions in English, and they monopolize all the important positions. That is the principal obstacle.
>
> There is a simple remedy for this problem, and that is to set up a French-speaking chamber of commerce in which all the central questions will be dealt with in our own language and from the point of view of the interests of the large mass of the population of Montreal and of the province of Quebec.

Table 2.1

Comprehensive business associations in Canada

Association	Date of founding	Structural type
Canadian Chamber of Commerce	1926	Mixed* confederation; provincial chambers in British Columbia, Alberta, Saskatchewan, Manitoba, Ontario, Quebec, and Atlantic provinces; affiliation with the BCNI
Chambre de commerce du Québec	1909	Mixed* confederation
Chambre de commerce du Montréal métropolitain/ Board of Trade of Metropolitan Montreal, created by a *merger of*	1992	Unitary
• Montreal Board of Trade	(1822) 1842	
• Chambre de commerce du district de Montréal	1887	
Canadian Council of Chief Executives**	1976	Unitary
Canadian Federation of Independent Business	1971	Unitary with regional subunits; British Columbia and Yukon, Alberta and Northwest Territories, Saskatchewan, Manitoba, Ontario, Quebec, New Brunswick and Prince Edward Island, Nova Scotia and Newfoundland; regional vice-presidents: British Columbia, Prairies, Ontario, Quebec, Atlantic
Canadian Manufacturers and Exporters, originally known as the Alliance of Manufacturers and Exporters Canada, created by a *merger of*	1996	Federation; provincial associations in British Columbia, Alberta, Saskatchewan-Manitoba, Ontario, Quebec, New Brunswick-Prince Edward Island, Nova Scotia, and Newfoundland; affiliation with the BCNI
• Canadian Manufacturers' Association	1871	
• Canadian Export Association	1943	
Alliance des manufacturiers et exportateurs du Québec	1995	Unitary
Conseil du patronat du Québec	1969	Confederation; affiliation with the BCNI

* Mixed means that the association has a basic confederal form but also accepts firms as direct members of the association.
** The Canadian Council of Chief Executives was known as the Business Council on National Issues (BCNI) until 2001.

> We have our own bankers, our own wholesalers, our own retailers, our own brokers, our own entrepreneurs, our own industrialists, and our own businessmen, all of them at the heights of their fields and whose influence must be felt in the settlement of all the questions that are of interest to them. It is time that we take the position that belongs to us here in Montreal.[6]

From that point until 1992, as we show below, two chamber units, one primarily English and the other primarily French, coexisted in Montreal, all the while competing for members and for the ear of government. A year after the formation of the Chambre de Montréal, the Board of Trade responded by translating its constitution, bylaws, and annual report into French.

From the point of view of the individual business, therefore, the local chamber of commerce or board of trade was the primary membership organization. In 1909, the various local chambers in Quebec, following the lead of the Chambre de Montréal, formed a provincial chamber of commerce. For many years, the provincial chamber occupied the same offices as the Chambre de Montréal and was serviced by that chamber's secretariat. When the Canadian Chamber of Commerce was founded in 1926, it, too, was a confederation of local chambers. Provincial chambers did not belong to the national chamber, although their elected chief executive officers came to serve on its Board of Directors. Local chambers in Quebec, therefore, could choose to become members of the provincial chamber, the national chamber, or both. What is distinctive about the chamber system, therefore, is that the local business community, whether francophone, anglophone, or both, is the principal organizational unit. We should also note that, beginning in the postwar period, both the provincial and the national chambers came to enrol corporations directly as members. These corporate members are quite important in that they contribute the vast majority of the dues collected by these associations. This financial arrangement may reduce the likelihood of financial disputes between the federal and the provincial chambers.

The principle of territorial organization differed in the CMA. That association adopted a federal structure such that individual manufacturing firms simultaneously became members of a provincial association or division and the national association. Such a structure probably fit better than a confederal one since its membership included large industrial firms, with branch plants in several provinces. The CEA, the eventual merger partner of the CMA, had a unitary structure. At the time, all of the political action related to international trade took place in Ottawa, so the CEA had little incentive to organize territorial subunits. When the two merged to form the Alliance of Manufacturers and Exporters Canada in 1996, the new association took the federal form that had been characteristic of the CMA. What is important about this form is that the individual business person is conscious of joining the national association directly; he or she is directly a member of that association. It is her or his association. This identification of the individual business with the national association makes the linguistic representation of that national association all the more important. In contrast, individual business persons in the chamber system are most conscious of being members of their local chambers.

The structure of the CCCE is distinctive not only in its unitary character but also in that chief executive officers *as individuals* belong to the association. In each of the other associations, the *business* or the *firm* is the member of the association, and an individual participates in the capacity of being the owner of the business or a senior manager. The CCCE also considers its remit to be national politics only. It is unusual for the association to intervene at the provincial level unless the matter relates to the Canadian Constitution, as we see below. For these reasons, a unitary structure is hardly surprising.

The CFIB also worked with a unitary structure, with the difference that it has created branches at the provincial level. A Quebec branch was relatively late to form, established only in 1982, a decade after the establishment of the association itself. Despite the fact that the association's first salesperson in the province was an anglophone, the association immediately attracted interest from small businesses in Quebec. After the association upgraded the position of its chief Quebec spokesperson to vice-president, installed a very dynamic person in that position, and gave him more resources than his predecessors had, membership grew even more quickly, to the point that 20 percent of the association's members now come from Quebec. The Quebec branch takes responsibility for all direct lobbying and contacts with the provincial government in Quebec. Nevertheless, the Quebec unit is a branch office of the CFIB, and thus members join the CFIB and not a separate Quebec association, as is the situation with the chamber of commerce system or with the CME. If one assumes that the linguistic representation of the national body is more important in a federal association than it is in a confederal one, a point made above, then such representation becomes still more crucial in a unitary one. The CFIB has faced this fact directly when dealing with its Quebec members.

When members put the symbol of the association on the enterprise's door, as often occurs with the CFIB (or Fédération canadienne de l'entreprise indépendante [FCEI], as it is known in French), they are displaying a symbol featuring a red maple leaf and a name with the word *Canadian*. Indirectly, this property of the association has caused political ripples, particularly when the association has been dealing with a Parti québécois (PQ) government. Some Quebec members have even wondered whether it would help membership recruitment and lobbying in the province if the association were to change its name.

Finally, the Conseil du patronat du Québec has a European-style peak association structure. Its voting members included over seventy business associations representing most sectors of the Quebec economy in 2001. In this respect, it represented the business community broadly, including sectors where francophones are dominant and others where anglophones or allophones have the largest firms. It acts as a unitary association in Quebec, having no territorial divisions in the province. It is also an "affiliate member" of the CCCE. An affiliate member is allocated a seat on the Policy Committee of the CCCE, that association's equivalent of a board of directors. Whether or not the seat is actually occupied depends on the initiative of the president of the council. The CCCE reported that the CPQ has not made much active use of that position in recent years.

French-English Relations in Comprehensive Business Associations

The relationship between Canada's two official language communities within comprehensive business associations has not been a subject of systematic study to date. The most comprehensive analysis of this situation is to be found in the study of the relationships between the Canadian Chamber of Commerce and the Chambre de commerce de la Province du Québec carried out by Meisel and Lemieux over three decades ago. This study showed that the two linguistic communities coexisted relatively harmoniously within the chamber system in Canada, facilitated by the confederal organizational form of the two organizations. The authors did worry at the end of their study whether this institutional structure would be able to accommodate the increasing tensions between francophones and anglophones that were developing throughout the 1960s. Subsequently, further analysis by Lemieux suggested that the chamber structure was fairly robust in accommodating both language groups.[7] The analysis that follows shows that the pattern of harmony found in the 1960s has continued into the present. Such harmony, we argue, is secured by the growth of institutional bilingualism within national-level associations, while Quebec associations have edged toward the official unilingualism demanded under the Charte de la langue française. Before carrying out the analysis of the contemporary relationships, however, we provide a summary of the findings of Meisel and Lemieux that will serve as a baseline for our analysis.

The Meisel-Lemieux Study: French-English Relations in the Mid- to Late 1960s

As we noted above, the universe of comprehensive business associations has expanded somewhat since the Meisel and Lemieux study was conducted in the late 1960s. This new complexity must be incorporated into our analysis if any meaningful assessment of current French-English relations within associations seeking to represent and defend the general interests of business is to be provided. Although Meisel and Lemieux concentrated their study on the relationships between the Canadian chamber and the provincial chamber in Quebec, it does provide us with a baseline upon which we can build an evaluation of the relationship between francophones and anglophones in general business interest associations in the late 1990s.

Meisel and Lemieux described relations between the two organizations in the 1960s as "reasonably good, although not particularly close or cordial."[8] No sharp conflicts between the CCC and the CCPQ over any of the national body's major activities (helping local chambers, dispensing propaganda, lobbying, and meeting with other groups) were identified. The authors concluded that the confederal organizational structure of the Canadian chamber facilitated maintenance of harmonious relations. It permitted the CCC and CCPQ to maintain a set of formal relationships, without one association infringing on the autonomy of the other. The direct membership of local chambers in the national chamber rather than through the CCPQ as an intermediary helped to avoid a situation where francophone interests would be represented primarily by the CCPQ within the chamber system. Rather, the CCPQ could concern itself principally with the general interests of business as a whole within Quebec. Francophone interests thus entered the national system through local chambers, with the CCDM clearly playing a large role.

The national chamber had already taken several key steps to improve the recognition and accommodation of francophones by the mid-1960s. There were problems, to be sure, particularly with respect to a lower rate of participation of francophones at the CCC annual general meeting and their under-representation on the Board of Directors and the Executive Committee. Nonetheless, Meisel and Lemieux argued that the situation had improved appreciably with the creation of the French Department Advisory Committee in 1955.[9] For example, the CCC made a conscious effort to add francophones to its staff, and by the mid-1960s all major publications were available in both languages. Moreover, translation services were eventually provided at the annual general meeting, which had the effect of increasing participation by members from the francophone chambers.

Even with these changes, however, the participation of the local Quebec chambers in the activities of the CCC remained lower than that of their counterparts outside Quebec. Several reasons for the under-representation of francophones at the various annual general meetings were given.

- These meetings were often held far from Quebec.
- The local chambers in Quebec were preoccupied with problems different from those of local chambers in the other provinces.
- Francophone delegates were not as prepared to discuss the policy resolutions as their anglophone counterparts.

- They were not adequately represented in the national body's decision-making process.

Meisel and Lemieux noted that there was a persistent pattern of under-representation on the board and executive of the CCC. Three main reasons were offered as an explanation. First, the meetings of these bodies were conducted in English, and there were few francophones who could speak the language well enough to participate fully. Second, many francophones were intimidated by the fact that many anglophone members represented larger and more influential corporations. Finally, many francophones were more parochial in their views and lacked the kind of knowledge of the country as a whole needed to address pan-Canadian economic problems.[10] They concluded that improved incorporation of francophones in central decision-making organs was a high priority.

Meisel and Lemieux concluded their study on a speculative note. They warned that tension between the CCPQ and the CCC could arise in the future if the former was not able to temper its strongly nationalist leanings with the primary objective of promoting and enhancing the free enterprise system in Quebec. It may be difficult, they suggested, to "remain both a loyal Québec nationalist and an adherent of the free enterprise system."[11] They worried about a scenario whereby a fervently nationalist Quebec chamber would urge the local members to boycott the national organization, a step that would ultimately sour relations between the CCC and the CCPQ.

The Dawn of the Millennium: A New Era in French-English Relations?

Now that we have provided an overview of linguistic relations in the chamber of commerce system in the late 1960s, we can evaluate where progress has been made and, more important, where advancements might still have been necessary at the time of data collection (2000-1). As an outgrowth of the Meisel and Lemieux study, our discussion in this section will naturally begin with an examination of the CCC, the CCQ, and the Chambre de commerce du Montréal métropolitain/Board of Trade of Metropolitan Montreal (CCMM/ BTMM). We will then give due consideration to French-English relations within the other key business interest associations, namely the CFIB, CCCE, CPQ, and CME. Table 2.2 presents a summary of the different forms of communication and language use of the various business interest associations in 2001, while Table 2.3 charts the linguistic representation of francophones on boards of directors and executive committees and as delegates at annual general meetings in the late 1990s.

These tables show some general patterns both in approaches to communication and in the representation of the respective language groups. National-level associations tended to communicate with their members in both official languages and to provide their services in the members' official language of

Table 2.2

Communications and language use, 2001

	Publications	Website	Annual general meeting	Board of directors meetings	Executive committee meetings	Other committees and language of work	Language of service
Canadian Chamber of Commerce	Generally available in both languages	Fully bilingual	Simultaneous translation available	No translation services; English is principal language	No translation services; English is principal language	No translation services; English is principal language	Fully bilingual
Chambre de commerce du Québec	Prepared in French; available in English on demand	French	No translation available; French is principal language	No translation available; French is working language	No translation available; French is working language	No translation available; French is working language	Normally French is language of service
Chambre de commerce du Montréal métropolitain/ Board of Trade of Metropolitan Montreal	Fully bilingual	Fully bilingual	No translation available; functions in both languages at choice of member	No translation available; functions in both languages at choice of member	No translation available; functions in both languages at choice of member	No translation available; functions in both languages at choice of member	Fully bilingual
Canadian Council of Chief Executives	Fully bilingual	No website available yet	No translation available; generally functions in English	No translation available; generally functions in English	No translation available; generally functions in English	No translation available; generally functions in English	Fully bilingual, but offers few services

▼ *Table 2.2*

	Publications	Website	Annual general meeting	Board of directors meetings	Executive committee meetings	Other committees and language of work	Language of service
Canadian Federation of Independent Business	Federal-level publications are fully bilingual	Fully bilingual	No translation available; generally functions in English	No translation available; generally functions in English	Not applicable	No committees	Bilingual staff available in national and Ottawa offices
Fédération canadienne de l'entreprise indépendante–Bureau du Québec	Principally in French	No autonomous website	Not applicable	Not applicable	Not applicable	No committees	Functions principally in French
Canadian Manufacturers and Exporters	Principally in English	Principal site in English with link to Quebec site	Translation available when in Quebec or Ottawa	No translation available; functions in English	No translation available; functions in English	No translation available; functions in English	Limited services in French at national office; French available in Ottawa office
Alliance des manufacturiers et exportateurs du Québec	Principally in French	Mostly French; some links to English documents in publications section	Not applicable	No translation available; functions principally in French	No translation available; functions principally in French	No translation available; functions principally in French	Normally French is language of service; English available on demand
Conseil du patronat du Québec	Fully bilingual	French only, but English portion under construction	No translation available; functions principally in French	No translation available; functions principally in French	No translation available; functions principally in French	No translation available; functions principally in French	Fully bilingual

choice. Otherwise, English was the principal internal working language at annual meetings and meetings of executive bodies and association committees. The Canadian chamber departed from this pattern in retaining simultaneous translation at annual general meetings. The CME also differed from the other bodies in failing to meet their level of bilingualism either in official communications or in association services. With the notable exception of the CFIB, francophones still tended to be under-represented at annual meetings and on executive bodies of national-level associations.

Quebec associations conformed to overall developments in the province over the past three decades in using French as their principal language of work and in the provision of communications and services. All were prepared, however, to offer communications and services in English on the demand of their members. Two associations departed somewhat from this pattern; both the CPQ and the CCMM/BTMM were fully bilingual in communication and other member services. An examination of representation on executive bodies showed that anglophones were probably under-represented in Quebec groups. The exception to this pattern was the CCMM/BTMM, where anglophones were fully represented on the Board of Directors and, as we see below, in committees.

This division of labour coincides with what appeared to be relatively harmonious linguistic relations within general business associations. Ethnic tensions did not appear to be a serious problem for any of these groups, with the possible exception of the CME. One of our informants offered a plausible explanation to account for this harmony: "Mais je peux dire que c'est symptomatique d'une espèce de tendance à Montréal – peut-être juste depuis les années 90. Les gens commencent à dire 'on est bilingue ici.' Il y a une grosse communauté anglophone et il y a des gens qui parlent d'autres langues." Bilingualism here means that francophones operating at the national level are comfortable working in English and that anglophones active in the Quebec associations are more and more capable of working in French.

The Chamber of Commerce System
In the 1960s, French-English relations were evaluated as relatively harmonious in the chamber of commerce system, a conclusion that is equally applicable today. Over the past three decades, this organization has continued to evolve in a direction that emphasizes institutional bilingualism. Even the relocation of the CCC's head office to Ottawa from Montreal in 1982, a decision that could have fuelled a nationalist backlash in Quebec, proceeded rather smoothly. It was, our informant suggested, a logical and strategic decision to make since the purpose of the CCC had changed over time. No longer was the CCC primarily in the business of doing "missionary work," helping the local chambers with the production of propaganda and the provision of services. Gradually, members of the chamber system were clamouring for

a common voice and a strong advocate; they wanted to present a united front for businesses, large and small, on national issues such as taxation, the debt, and labour laws that had a significant impact on their operations. In moving its head office to Ottawa, the CCC asserted its intention to act as a national body. It also ended a perhaps incorrect perception of being too close to the Montreal Board of Trade, from which it had long rented office space.

The feared tension between the CCC and the CCQ noted by Meisel and Lemieux has never materialized. The relationship between these two associations was more harmonious in the 1990s than in the 1960s. In fact, it was perhaps stronger than that between the CCC and the other provincial chambers because of a unique services agreement that the CCC negotiated with the CCQ. When the CCQ travels throughout Quebec to recruit local chambers as members, it also solicits memberships on behalf of the CCC. Although the local chambers were quick to join the CCQ,[12] many of them, particularly the smaller ones, questioned the benefit of membership in the national association. It was long the responsibility of Michel Bergeron, the CCQ's former manager of member services, to convince them of the merits of joining the CCC. We thus saw a situation where the provincial chamber had worked to build up the representation of Quebec chambers in the national association by actively endorsing and promoting its activities.

The differences in the relationship between the CCC and the CCQ on the one hand and the other provincial chambers on the other noted by Meisel and Lemieux have diminished as the latter have gained more autonomy.[13] The CCC has moved to have all provincial chambers become self-financing, a situation characteristic only of the CCQ in the 1960s. Over the years, there seems to have been a movement toward greater cooperation between the CCC and the CCQ. Whereas contact between the two groups in the past was sporadic at best, in recent years they have been meeting three to four times annually and often collaborate on various studies and publications of mutual interest.

In common with all of the other comprehensive business associations we examined, none of the chamber groups had *formal* rules regarding the relative representation of francophones or anglophones on permanent staff, boards of directors, or executive committees. The CCC and CCMM/BTMM were particularly sensitive to the need to accommodate linguistic duality. The CCC has generally emphasized the hiring of bilingual staff; the most senior staff person at the national chamber has been a bilingual person for many years. In the past few years, the CCC has finally addressed a fundamental shortcoming identified by Meisel and Lemieux, namely the lack of accession of francophones to the position of chair of the Board of Directors, the highest elected position in the national chamber.[14] Nevertheless, the lack of francophone representation in the ongoing activities of the CCC remained problematic. As Table 2.3 reveals, francophones continued to occupy fewer governance positions than their numbers would justify. In addition, the CCC still had not been able to attract a proportionate number of francophone delegates to annual general meetings. As was discovered in the earlier study, the location of the annual meeting is a determining factor. When the meeting place was outside Quebec, attendance by francophones was low. This situation was complicated in the chamber system by timing conflicts with the annual general meeting of the CCQ.

Like the CCC, the CCMM/BTMM was fully bilingual in all of its external communications (website, publications, and customer service). The association stated that 74 percent of its members were francophone and 26 percent anglophone. With 32 percent anglophone and allophone representation on its 1998-99 Board of Directors and 28 percent on its Executive Committee, the association represented the minority communities well. The CCMM/BTMM maintained a more equitable balance in the representation of the two linguistic groups than either the CCC or the CCQ. Such a balance has been deliberately cultivated since the historical merger between the city's French and English Boards of Trade in 1992, an event we examine as a "turning point" below.

Consistent with the general pattern for Quebec associations, the CCQ had French as its language of work, provided documents and services normally in French, and offered a unilingual French web page.[15] This pattern reverses a trend noted by Meisel and Lemieux whereby the communications of the CCPQ had become increasingly bilingual over time.[16] The CCQ did offer its anglophone members (about 20 percent of its membership) services and documents in English on demand.

Such unilingualism in the Quebec-based business interest associations has not resulted in a souring of French-English relations for two principal reasons. First, members from the minority communities in the province are increasingly able to function in French. As was explained in one interview, "en général, nos conseils d'administration se font en langue française ... Mais de façon générale, je dois dire que c'est la presque totalité, c'est en français, puisque c'est la langue que même les anglophones qui viennent connaissent." According to 1996 census data, 94 percent of the Quebec population now has the ability to conduct a conversation in French.[17] Second, all the Quebec associations were capable of interacting, and willing to do so, with their anglophone and allophone members in English. According to the CCQ, it is the client who determines the language of communication. If a member wants a document or service in English, then the request is respected. Therefore, the linguistic practices of general business associations working in Quebec were consistent with the territorial unilingualism mandated by the Charte de la langue française enacted by the PQ government in 1977.

The CCQ recognized that the representation of anglophones in executive bodies was an area where improvement was needed. Historically, an attempt had always been made to have one or two anglophones on the Executive Committee. Two anglophone representatives out of twelve is a reasonable figure, but when there is only one representative, as was the case in 1997-98, the anglophone business viewpoint may not have received due consideration. More troublesome for the CCQ was its lack of success in recruiting anglophone and allophone board members. More than 90 percent of the Board of Directors consisted of francophones in the late 1990s. This imbalance carried over into the annual general meeting, where francophones typically dominated. Yet anglophones were encouraged to attend the annual meeting, and those who wanted to intervene in English had the right to do so.

Canadian Federation of Independent Business
In spite of its origin in Ontario and initial development outside Quebec, the CFIB developed into a national business interest association that respected the spirit of the official bilingualism of the country. As we remarked earlier, the CFIB existed for more than a decade before its Quebec bureau emerged and initially depended on an anglophone salesperson to recruit members. Under the circumstances, it is remarkable that the association has flourished in Quebec. Despite its growing pains, the CFIB had representation in Quebec only slightly below its proportionate place in Canada (18,400 out of 93,000 members or 19.8 percent in 1999), and the annual renewal rates of small businesses in that province had finally equalled those found elsewhere in the country. In fact, in the 1990s, the association grew more in Quebec than in any other province.

Aside from the problems noted above created by inclusion of the word *Canadian* in the association's name, the only possible source of ethnic frustration related to the quality of its French publications. In the early years of the Quebec bureau, most studies and political submissions were written in English and then translated into French, a practice that many people thought affected the overall quality of the documents produced. Translations, it was suggested, always lose some of the meaning and eloquence of the original publication. More recently at the Quebec bureau, everything is written in French, and if a document needs to be produced in both languages it is translated from the French to English.

The CFIB also maintained adequate francophone representation on its Board of Directors and Executive Committee. When coupled with the flexibility of the association in the operation of its Quebec bureau, this practice was a decided asset in terms of tempering any ethnic discontent that might occur. The president in the study period was fully bilingual and worked cooperatively with the Quebec office. Policy undertakings by the Quebec bureau represented the interests and priorities of Quebec businesses. All lobbying decisions directed at the provincial legislature were also made at the provincial level, which means that the Quebec bureau had the authority to act in many areas. If the Quebec bureau (like any other unit of the association) wished to conduct a poll of its members, however, approval had to come from head office, which controlled the budget. This latter facet of associational life distinguished a unitary association with regional subunits like the CFIB from more decentralized organizations like the CCC or CME, where provincial-level units have more budgetary autonomy.

Canadian Council of Chief Executives

The CCCE operates quite differently from the other business interest associations in this study. Membership in the group is restricted to the chief executive officers (CEOs) of the top 150 corporations in Canada and is by invitation only. Given the nature of membership selection, it tended to have a heavy concentration of members from central Canada, where the vast majority of corporate head offices were located at the time of the study. A thirty-five-member Policy Committee, the equivalent of a board of directors, is the governing body of the CCCE. The elected heads of the CCC, CME, and CPQ also have a seat as *ex-officio* members.

Virtually all of the CCCE's publications were bilingual. English was the working language of the group, a practice facilitated by the fact that the CEOs of Canada's leading companies would all speak English given the global importance of English as a language of business and commerce. Efforts were made to recruit francophones to the association's Policy Committee and Executive Committee, but, given the structure and purpose of the association, proportionate linguistic representation was obviously more difficult to achieve. Nonetheless, as Table 2.3 illustrates, the CCCE fared reasonably well in this regard. There were some significant members of the business community in Quebec who were not members of the CCCE, but this void was symptomatic of a pan-Canadian recruitment problem. CEOs of Canada's largest family-owned companies showed less interest in joining the association and in participating in the public policy process. Finally, we note below that the BCNI/CCCE's activities related to the Calgary Declaration were testament to a persistent concern with improving French-English relations in Canada.

Conseil du patronat du Québec

With an affiliate relationship with the CCCE and a strong representation of the largest corporations in the province, the CPQ tended to play an analogous bridging role at the provincial level. Although French was its language of work, the CPQ practised bilingualism in the preparation of its major publications and in the offering of services to its members. Over time, its role evolved to one of concentrating on the broad set of issues related to employer-employee relations in the province. With this more specialized focus, it also saw the relative participation of anglophones and their representation on executive bodies decline. Whereas the association sought a balanced representation in the 1980s and its Board of Governors was split fifty-fifty between anglophones and francophones, Table 2.3 shows that in the late 1990s anglophones were significantly under-represented at the executive level. In this respect, the CPQ followed the pattern found for the CCQ and the Alliance des manufacturiers et exportateurs du Québec (AMEQ).

Canadian Manufacturers and Exporters

Although it was created only in May 1996 as a result of the merger between the CMA and the CEA (two very different organizations), the CME continued to have problems in accommodating Canada's linguistic diversity. Its national office was located in Mississauga, with a branch in Ottawa, and operated for the most part in English. Although some French services were available at the Ottawa office of the CME, with only one bilingual staff member at the national head office, it was limited in its ability to offer services in French. In contrast, the staff of the small Ottawa branch were largely bilingual. The location of the head office also reinforced a perception in Quebec that the national organization was more oriented to English Canada. With its English unilingualism, the national office was effectively unable to communicate directly with 25 percent of its members. The first president of the CME was a unilingual anglophone. His trips to Quebec were limited since he was unable to address francophone business persons in their mother tongue.[18] This pattern of unilingualism was an obvious potential source of frustration for francophone Quebec members. We noted above that the federal structure of the CME means that Quebec firms belong directly to both the national association and AMEQ.

Surprisingly, for a national association with a strong Quebec presence, its publications were also not fully bilingual. The main tool of communication of the CME at the time of the study was a magazine called *Alliance,* essentially an English publication. A couple of pages in *Alliance* were written in French, but these items typically pertained to issues originating in Quebec. They were not translations of the news items reported for the English Canadian membership. In place of a French version of its website, the CME's home page had a link to the AMEQ site, which provided completely separate information.[19] In addition, research items produced by the CME were normally translated into French only if they were to be used in official circles such as parliamentary committees. Consequently, if AMEQ wished to make such research studies available in French for its francophone members, it had to assume the costs of translation itself. Ironically, the CME also cited cost as the principal reason for not producing all documents in both official languages. Instead of perceiving bilingualism as a requisite of acting as a national-level association, the CME treated it as a cost of business to be considered relative to other costs.

Table 2.3 also shows that the relative representation of francophones on executive bodies was lower than their proportionate place in the country. Like the CCC and the CCCE, francophones were under-represented by about 10 percent on the Board of Directors and even more on the Executive Committee. For the most part, francophones did not partake in the annual general meeting either. Whether or not participation rates would have been higher if simultaneous translation was provided is difficult to say. Some of the other problems in communication and representation would also have needed to be addressed before patterns of attendance were likely to change.

These difficulties in bilingual communication and in representation of francophones put the association's Quebec division, AMEQ, in a rather unique position compared with other provincial divisions. Although all provincial divisions raised some of their own revenues, the Quebec association did so more energetically. It had a larger staff and a greater budget allocation, differences traceable only in part to the size and importance of the membership base in Quebec. The rather unilingual English character of the CME meant that AMEQ could not share resources with the national group in ways similar to provincial divisions of the association in other parts of Canada; it had to generate its own resources. These differences corresponded to other special features of AMEQ. The head of AMEQ was the only provincial division leader given the title of president. All provincial associations had autonomy in policy areas under provincial jurisdiction, such as education and labour relations. In addition, AMEQ occasionally had a role to play at the national level. Due to the lack of bilingualism of employees at head office, it was asked occasionally to intervene at the federal level to advance the cause of the CME. These various aspects of the CME's structure and approach to linguistic relations suggest that it had more difficulty accommodating linguistic duality than other comprehensive associations.

Turning Points in French-English Relations
We have argued that the relative harmony in French-English relations identified by Meisel and Lemieux in the 1960s in Canada's chamber of commerce system was sustained not only in these chamber organizations but also across the wider set of comprehensive business associations that populated the Canadian associational landscape at the turn of the millennium. We found that these associations had addressed the problems of the linguistic divide better than what had been found three decades before. Under these circumstances of relative continuity and gradual improvement, it is difficult to identify "turning points" in the relationships between the two official

Table 2.3

Linguistic representation

	Francophone representation on Board of Directors	Francophone representation on Executive Committee	Francophone participation at annual general meeting
Canadian Chamber of Commerce	8/49 (1998-99)	1/9 (1998-99)	Lower than normal due to scheduling conflicts with CCQ; location dependent
Chambre de commerce du Québec	65/69 (1997-98); 63/69 (1998-99)	11/12 (1997-98); 10/12 (1998-99)	Francophones dominate
Chambre de commerce du Montréal métropolitain/ Board of Trade of Metropolitan Montreal	19/28 (1998-99)	5/7 (1998-99)	Balanced participation by all language groups
Canadian Council of Chief Executives	4/31 (1998-99)	2/7 (1998-99)	Balanced participation by members
Canadian Federation of Independent Business	3/12 (1999)	1/5 (1998-99)	Francophones under-represented due to location
Fédération canadienne de l'entreprise indépendante – Bureau du Québec	Not applicable	Not applicable	Not applicable
Canadian Manufacturers and Exporters	5/34 (1998-99)	1/14 (1998-99)	Francophones under-represented due to language and location
Alliance des manufacturiers et exportateurs du Québec	36/39 (1998-99)	6/7 (1998-99)	Balanced participation by members
Conseil du patronat du Québec	27/29	7/7	Balanced participation by members

language communities. In reviewing the histories of these associations over the past thirty years, we wish to note instead two sets of events that have reinforced this pattern of relative harmony. The merger of the Montreal Board of Trade and the Chambre de commerce du District de Montréal in 1992 symbolized well the evolution of French-English relations within Quebec. The deft handling of constitutional issues by comprehensive business associations more generally illustrated well how these groups managed to maintain ethnic harmony despite some deep divisions in the wider Canadian and Quebec societies. We examine next each of these events.

The Montreal Merger

We noted earlier in this chapter that, since the end of the nineteenth century, Montreal was represented historically in the Canadian chamber of commerce system by two associations: the MBT, associated with the English-speaking business community since 1822, and the CCDM, founded in 1887 to represent the interests of the French-speaking business community. Such a situation was highly anomalous in the chamber of commerce system because normally only one chamber is permitted to represent a given community. The CCDM thus came into existence, in part, with the indulgence of the MBT. Its name featured the words *District of Montreal* as a legal bow to the idea of one chamber per locality, the word *district* implying a slightly different territory than the city proper.[20]

In 1992, the two organizations merged to form the Chambre de commerce du Montréal métropolitain/Board of Trade of Metropolitan Montreal. This event is important not only because it raised the level of organizational integration in the representation of business interests in the Montreal metropolitan area but also because it symbolized a new understanding of intercommunity relationships in the city that departed from the traditional "two solitudes" of the past. Historically, the CCDM focused on two principal objectives: the promotion and strengthening of the position of francophones in the business community in Quebec and in Canada, and the further development of Montreal as a place of business and trade. Pursuit of the first objective distinguished the francophone chamber from its anglophone counterpart, which operated principally as a pragmatic promoter of Montreal as a place of commerce. A century after the founding of the CCDM, many of the long-standing obstacles faced by francophones seeking influence in the world of business had been lowered considerably. In addition, the rise of a nationalist movement promoting the sovereignty of Quebec had lowered the attractiveness of Montreal as a place of investment and economic growth. The combination of these changes raised the second of the principal objectives of the CCDM to a position of primacy. With this change in orientation, the common interests between the CCDM and the MBT became self-evident if not overwhelming.

When viewed in historical perspective, the broader socioeconomic object-ives of the CCDM led it to develop an orientation and a role in Quebec society quite different from the MBT. Meisel and Lemieux observed that the legal status "board of trade" or "chambre de commerce" furnishes an organization with a mandate that permits it to look beyond the locality to the national and even the international scenes.[21] Thus, the MBT was known across English Canada as a promoter of Montreal and of the interests of the anglophone business elite in that city. In adopting the same legal form, the CCDM had similar ambitions but focused on improving the position of francophone businesses in Canada. In seeking to promote and develop a greater franco-phone presence in the Quebec business community, the chamber concen-trated in its early years on establishing a business school for francophones, eventually succeeding with the foundation of the École des hautes études commerciales (HEC) in 1910. After HEC became fully operational, the CCDM provided a forum in francophone Quebec society where broad social and political issues could be debated. Two professors from HEC, Esdras Minville and François-Albert Angers, worked closely with the association's secretariat in developing political positions in the 1940s and 1950s, with Minville be-coming its president in 1947.[22] Both were strong nationalists in the Lionel Groulx school and pushed the chamber to play a fairly central role in the struggle over taxation powers between the federal and provincial govern-ments during the Duplessis years.[23] Similarly, after the Parti libéral du Québec was elected in 1960, ushering in the Quiet Revolution, the CCDM con-tinued to supply key personnel in the public arena. The Conseil d'orientation économique, set up by the new Liberal government to develop a plan for strengthening francophone-controlled capitalism, was headed by René Paré, a former president of the CCDM, and included both Minville and Angers as members.[24]

This sociopolitical leadership role diminished as the nationalist debates intensified during the late 1960s and 1970s. The principal societal representa-tive for the nationalists became the Parti québécois, and as it pursued its political and linguistic objectives the CCDM feared increasingly that its second objective, building Montreal as a place of business and trade, was being placed in jeopardy. Accordingly, the chamber protested against Bill 101, the Charte de la langue française, introduced by the PQ in 1977.[25] It also began to develop a more coherent vision of Quebec as a pluralist society. Witnessing the flight of head offices that followed the PQ victory in 1976 and the introduction of Bill 101, it entered into a cooperative agreement with the MBT to form a new organization to defend and promote the city.

Establishment of the Comité de promotion économique de Montréal (COPEM) in 1979-80, jointly by the CCDM and the MBT, marked a new step in the reconciliation between the francophone and anglophone business communities. A few years earlier the MBT had rebuffed overtures by the

CCDM to merge. In the face of severe economic stress in the city in the late 1970s and early 1980s, however, the MBT became more predisposed to cooperate. The leadership role played by the CCDM in this initiative struck a very positive chord in the anglophone community. In fact, an anglophone, Philip O'Brien, was elected the chamber's president in 1984. Over the same period, the Board of Trade had a couple of francophone presidents. A further new element in the picture was the growing size of the allophone business sector, whose members tended to be bilingual and who felt at home operating in either the CCDM or the MBT environment. Their rise in importance coincided with the continuous decline of older, more traditional *anglophones de souche* in Montreal. Certainly, allophones were willing to raise questions about the relative financial efficiency and political clout that came with dividing the representation of the city's business community between two, potentially competing, organizations rather than unifying it in one organization. Perhaps it was no accident that the final steps to the merger began with a crucial phone call by Luigi Liberatore, then chairman of the MBT and an allophone, to his counterpart in the CCDM, Jean Guibault.[26]

The road to a merger was also paved by the careful thinking of the CCDM in the 1980s about how to balance the competing pressures of respecting French as the official language of the province and of creating an economic environment in the metropolitan area that would favour as much economic growth and development as possible. Working with the concept of a "pluralist society," the chamber emphasized that a strong English-speaking presence in Montreal was a decided asset in the developing global economy. In addition, the growing presence of other cultural communities active in business affairs when coupled with the increasingly strong francophone business sector that had developed in the postwar period helped to provide Montreal with important opportunities to expand as an economic centre. It was poised to recapture some of the initiative lost to Toronto, Calgary, and Vancouver. To fully realize this potential as a representative of business, the chamber adopted a policy of full bilingualism, all the while agreeing to operate within the constraints of Bill 101. This policy implied that all services would be offered in both French and English, both to members and to the general public. All of the infrastructure necessary for implementing bilingualism would be put in place, including efficient translation services.

When the merger did take place, this policy served as a template for the unified organization, as emphasized in Tables 2.2 and 2.3. An Implementation Committee oversaw the realization of the policy, focusing on the quality of written English, the relative availability of bilingual documents, and the further development of the language skills of the association's employees. The association also examined closely the degree of participation of anglophones in its various activities in 1993-94, a year after the merger. At the end of 1994, 74 percent of members were francophone, while 26 percent

were anglophone. The chamber noted that more anglophones failed to re-
new memberships than francophones. Further analysis indicated, however,
that this failure had much more to do with internal financial matters of
the firms than with dissatisfaction with the association per se. The study
showed anglophones participating at a level proportional to their representation in the association's business meetings (*rendez-vous d'affaires*).[27] Because
of the study, the association also changed its lineup of speakers at its mini-
conferences and increased the number of bilingual speakers at its luncheon
public affairs meetings to attract further interest among anglophones.

In our discussions with various interviewees, most of them believed that
the merger signalled that considerable reconciliation had taken place between
the various components of the Montreal business community over the 1980s
and 1990s. While cautious about attributing too much of a determining role
to the merger, informants did believe that it had helped to lower tensions
further. As one stated,

> I believe that there is more harmony than ever in the relationships between
> two groups ... The gesture that we made, a gesture that had a very, very im-
> portant symbolic force, contributed a great deal. Harmony is a constant
> preoccupation for us; we try to make members feel comfortable in their re-
> lationships with one another ... There is a tendency to put aside confronta-
> tion. These confrontations were much stronger twenty years ago but do not
> occur often anymore. Even in the broader society, when a person like Wil-
> liam Johnson [then president of Alliance Quebec] demonstrated in the centre
> of the city in favour of bilingual signs, the English-speaking community in
> Montreal did not really support him. The dynamic of confrontation is just
> no longer there. Harmony began to develop first in the business community
> but has since also advanced in the general population.[28]

As such, the merger was a crucial turning point in French-English relations
in Quebec's business community and perhaps added to a general climate of
reconciliation in the Montreal metropolitan area.

Business Interest Associations and the Constitutional Debate
The Royal Commission on Bilingualism and Biculturalism was initiated in
the 1960s to address long-standing grievances of francophone Canadians
regarding their place in Canada's national government and relating to protection of the distinct society and culture in Quebec. Since the initial Meisel
and Lemieux study completed for the royal commission, Canada has undergone several additional rounds of what Peter Russell has termed "mega
constitutional politics" in an effort to recognize Quebec's special status, or
distinctiveness, within Confederation.[29] Most important, a PQ government
has been elected on several occasions, the first time being in 1976, which

has resulted in the two referendums on independence of 1980 and 1995. During that time, the country also experienced two unsuccessful attempts to address Quebec's constitutional grievances. The Meech Lake (1987-90) and Charlottetown Accords (1992), Prime Minister Mulroney's attempts at negotiated compromise, were a direct response to the secessionist threat posed by the nationalists in Quebec.

Naturally, the business community in both Quebec and the country at large has been extremely concerned about the economic repercussions of the sovereigntist project. The overriding interest of this group has been to maintain a stable and prosperous climate for trade and investment. Despite the temptation and, more important, federalist overtures to get business to declare publicly a preference for maintaining national unity, the business interest associations examined in this study generally professed a desire to "avoid being pulled into the debate," to use the words of one informant. Nonetheless, different strategies and levels of involvement in these constitutional debates are clearly discernible, with some groups adopting a greater degree of neutrality in this process than others.

Meisel and Lemieux categorized these macropolitical concerns as the "external objectives" of the voluntary organizations. In their view, the most important external objectives of the voluntary organizations they examined were those that concerned the Canadian political regime, specifically Quebec's position in Confederation. "Nous verrons que ses objectifs à caractère politique ont été, dans plus d'un cas, source de tensions et de conflits entre anglophones et francophones."[30] In his follow-up study, Lemieux added, however, that external objectives did not cause problems for the chambers of commerce.[31] This conclusion appears to remain valid when we examine the specific responses of a number of these business interest associations to the constitutional debate.

The most objective intervention into the constitutional debate was undoubtedly that of the CFIB. It frames its positions on issues by conducting member surveys on a variety of issues so that a small-business perspective can be articulated for consideration in the policy-making process, be it at the federal or the provincial level. This approach was followed for both of the Quebec sovereignty referendums as well as for the referendum on the Charlottetown Accord. In each of the sovereignty referendums, CFIB members in Quebec were surveyed using the exact wording of the question being posed to the population at large, and the results were published without interpretation. For example, all 17,000 CFIB member firms were sent a survey prior to the 1995 referendum asking them to respond "Yes" or "No" to the following question: "Do you agree that Québec should become sovereign, after having made a formal offer to Canada for a new Economic and Political Partnership, within the scope of the Bill respecting the future of Québec and of the agreement signed on June 12, 1995?" The survey had a 38 percent response rate (4,440 firms). With 65 percent of the participants having voted "No" to the question, Quebec's small-business community unequivocally rejected the government's sovereignty proposal.[32] The CFIB constitutional survey on the Charlottetown Accord was somewhat more nuanced. In addition to asking members how they would vote in the national referendum, the federation asked a series of questions to ascertain how the business planning of its members had been affected by the constitutional discussions up to that point in time and how it might be affected in the event of a positive or negative vote.

Although the CCMM and the CCQ are both members of a federalist organization and openly supported the federalist position, neither group advocated the perpetuation of the status quo. Both argued that a significant decentralization of power was an absolute necessity, not just for Quebec but for all of the provinces. It is not surprising, therefore, that this position was formulated by the CCMM in conjunction with the boards of trade of Toronto and Vancouver. The CCQ shared the view that the Canadian political system needed to be radically restructured, but it was more outspoken in its condemnation of the existing arrangement. In a brief to the Bélanger-Campeau Commission, organized by the Quebec government in 1991 to provide recommendations on the political and constitutional future of Quebec, the CCQ stated that "Quebec's business people are convinced that Canadian federalism is an *economic failure*."[33] It did not, however, make any formal recommendation to accept or reject the Charlottetown Accord when that proposal materialized the following year. With respect to the 1995 sovereignty referendum, the CCQ was more reserved: its priority was to ensure that the government posed a clear question because ambiguity would only confuse the referendum result.

The involvement of the CCCE in the constitutional debate has been somewhat unique when compared with that of the other business interest associations. As a group of chief executive officers from the country's leading corporations with a mandate to provide a senior business perspective on public policy issues, the CCCE has been a key player in the process of constitutional renewal. It was, for example, visibly proud of the role that it played in fostering the round of constitutional discussions that ultimately led to adoption of the seven-point Calgary Declaration in September 1997.[34] After the narrow margin of victory in the 1995 sovereignty referendum, the CCCE decided that it wanted to assume a leadership role in advancing the constitutional agenda. The result was the Confederation 2000 Conferences held in March and May of 1996, whereby a group of academics, business leaders, and former politicians were brought together to explore ideas that could generate constitutional consensus across the country. One of the ideas to emerge from these meetings was that the provincial premiers needed to provide more leadership on this issue; it was seen to be a mistake to leave the resolution of the constitutional dilemma entirely in the hands of the federal government.[35]

Over the next several months, members of the CCCE worked quietly, fulfilling what was described as its "client-diplomacy role." In essence, these leading business executives met individually with the different premiers to convince them of the need to act. In the first half of 1997, Premier Ralph Klein approached the CCCE to create a memorandum outlining a set of principles that could serve as a starting point for discussions since the premiers were extremely reluctant to jeopardize their political futures by reopening the highly divisive constitutional debate. This memorandum was prepared and presented to Premier Frank McKenna, who was hosting the Council of Premiers meeting at the end of July in St. Andrews, New Brunswick. In that document, the council outlined its rationale for getting involved: "As business leaders, we are speaking now because we are concerned that strains and unresolved conflicts within the federation – most notably the threat of Québec secession – could derail Canada's otherwise very bright political and economic prospects and thereby alter the face of Canada in ways that we would all deeply regret."[36] A special meeting of the Council of Premiers was held in Calgary, and out of that initiative came the Calgary Declaration. Once the CCCE provided the impetus for getting the premiers together to discuss ways to build a better Canada, it was careful to remove itself from the subsequent public consultations. It did not want the progress that had been achieved to be summarily rejected by the people due to a perception that it was a "business-driven agenda."

Therefore, while the business interest associations have been cautious regarding the nature of their involvement in the ongoing constitutional saga, they have, in reality, been anything but passive observers. There may have been a general agreement that Quebec's constitutional future had to be decided by Quebecers themselves, but the voice of various business interests, both inside and outside Quebec, did not go unheard. That voice, however, was essentially one of caution. If Quebecers opted for sovereignty, most of the groups believed, then the population should be at least made aware that it would not be achieved without significant economic costs. Moreover, participation in the constitutional debate did not appear to be a source of tension between anglophones and francophones within these associations. A consensus on significant decentralization as a necessity for Canadian federalism was found in the chamber system. The CCCE acted forcefully after the narrow *"Non"* victory in 1995. The other associations did not spend a lot of time on constitutional issues, preferring to concentrate on what they considered the core economic questions of most concern to their members.

Conclusions

This study shows that comprehensive business interest associations in Canada at the turn of the millennium had accommodated themselves rather well to operating in a country with two principal *official* linguistic communities. Generally speaking, associations operating at the federal level provided a bilingual face to the broader public, communicated with their members in both official languages, and provided services to their members in the official language of choice. Their internal language of work was principally English. General business interest associations that worked at the provincial level in Quebec had a different approach. Consistent with provincial law, they offered a French face to the broader public, worked internally in French, communicated with their members in French, and offered their services in the language of Molière. Where members made the request, they were also prepared to communicate in English and offer their services in English. Association executives did note, however, that over time anglophone members were increasingly able and willing to function in French in the associational arena, as they must in the public arena.

The relative success of comprehensive business associations in managing French-English relations probably derived from several factors. First, we have emphasized that historically business leaders in Canada have found more interests in common as a class than they have with citizens of the same ethnic background but not class. This cohesion appears only to have strengthened under increased global integration and freer international trade rules.

Second, the institutional forms chosen by the various segments of the business community have permitted associations to accommodate Quebec's demands for autonomy while maintaining overall cohesion. We have emphasized the importance of the confederal structure of the chamber system, which permits the national and provincial chambers to operate autonomously from one another. The small-business constituency of the CFIB does not have time for a full associational life. Hence, the CFIB meets their needs by using a direct democracy approach to consultation on issues. The association also permits provincial offices to deal with more localized issues on their own. The federal structure of the CME is a more demanding one of members because it expects them to be active simultaneously in national and provincial associations. Such a structure fits a membership whose firms are larger, with operations in several provinces. It is also more likely to bring francophones and anglophones into systematic contact. Hence, language problems may have tended to surface more visibly in such an organization.

And third, individual leadership also explains some of the success that we found. Key business leaders in Montreal, particularly from the allophone community, helped to bridge the language divide. They were instrumental in the merger of the CCDM and the MBT in that city. Similarly, the initiative taken by the CCCE following the 1995 referendum illustrates the will of business leaders to put aside linguistic differences in a search for accommodating constitutional arrangements. The appointment of Perrin Beatty as president of the CME at the time of the study provided an additional test of the importance of leadership. Beatty's initial press releases were issued in both official languages, a first for the occupant of that office. His appointment may have signalled an attempt by the CME to confront directly some of the problems identified in this study.

The study also underlines one continuing problem faced by comprehensive associations at both levels. Most federal-level associations had difficulty filling their boards of directors and executive committees with a number of francophones commensurate with their relative share of the population. Part of this difficulty arises from a predilection in these groups to represent all provinces equally in their executive bodies, but this type of representational rule is not the sole source of the problem. All associations have "members at large" on their executive bodies with whom problems of linguistic representation might be addressed. Similarly, the comprehensive associations operating provincially in Quebec experienced some problems in attracting sufficient numbers of members of that province's minority communities.

These difficulties are important because the executive bodies are normally the "working" units of any interest association. They are charged with the task of defining what are the interests of the members of the group, how those interests might be best translated into policy options, and how best to pursue those policy ideas with bureaucratic officials and politicians. Accordingly, if the membership of these executive bodies does not provide sufficient opportunities for minority communities to "voice" their views on such matters, then the definition of interests and the choice of policy options might not address minority interests. If such an outcome were to occur consistently over a period of time, the given association would lose relevance for the respective minorities. Such an effect could then bring an unfortunate linguistic division into the associational landscape that not even the common interests of business as a class may be able to bridge.

3
Canada's English and French Farm Communities
Grace Skogstad

"'Good' or even 'excellent.'" These were the words John Meisel and Vincent Lemieux used to describe relations between Canada's French- and English-speaking farm communities in the mid-1960s. The authors concluded that relations between the Canadian Federation of Agriculture (CFA), the umbrella organization for farmers across Canada, and the Union catholique des cultivateurs (UCC), representing Quebec farmers, were "something of a model of a successful ethnic partnership."[1] Some thirty years later that characterization still holds. Through the vehicles of the CFA and the Union des producteurs agricole (UPA, the successor to the UCC), and a number of pan-Canadian commodity associations, Canada's English- and French-speaking farmers have developed amicable and cooperative organizational linkages to advance their mutual interests to government decision makers.

To the extent that pan-Canadian farm organizations constitute a model for transcending Canada's linguistic dualism, it is in their appreciable endeavours to function as bilingual national offices. Their practice of providing simultaneous interpretation at meetings of decision-making bodies and distributing materials and documents in both official languages provides useful instruction for other non-governmental organizations seeking to bridge the linguistic divide. However, other factors that promote linguistic harmony are more particular to agriculture and hence may not be so easily extrapolated elsewhere. First, the shared economic interests of farmers in Quebec and the rest of Canada undoubtedly facilitate their organizational cohesion and cooperation. Given their minority status in terms of both numbers and economic importance,[2] farmers everywhere recognize the need for collective action across the two language groups if they are to influence government policies and attain their socioeconomic goals. The fact that recent developments relating to government expenditure restraint and international trade liberalization pose significant and continuing threats to farmers' material well-being serves to reinforce the logic of pan-Canadian solidarity. The lessons that farm organizations provide of how to bridge linguistic cleavages may be less helpful for non-governmental organizations whose logic of collective action is not a shared material interest.

Second, and another reason for caution in generalizing from agriculture's experience, is that Quebec agriculture is a highly important component of Canadian agriculture as a whole[3] and thus merits considerable attention from any pan-Canadian farm organization seeking to speak for the sector. Provincial associational members are represented within national farm organizations – and pay fees – in proportion to the significance of their agricultural sector. As a consequence, Quebec tends to have more voices than many other provinces on decision-making bodies, even while it makes a larger financial contribution to national farm associations. In turn, the need for national organizations to have a bilingual capacity is reinforced. For those organizations in civil society where Quebec's presence is not so vital to the overall legitimacy and influence of the national sectoral group, the experience of Canada's farm organizations may be largely irrelevant.

Notwithstanding these caveats about the possible generalizability of Canada's farm communities' experience, a number of factors that affect the relationship between the two liguistic farm communities are not unique to agriculture but characteristic of the broader Quebec and Canadian societies within which agricultural relations unfold. Primary among these factors is the provincial reality of Quebec farmers' lives; their linkages to Canadian farmers and Canadian farm organizations are a far less significant part of their experience than their interactions with their provincial farm organization. Accordingly, the interaction between Canada's two linguistic farm communities does not penetrate very deeply and not much beyond the level of the senior leaders and permanent staff. Quebec farmers' perceptions of Canadian farm organizations are very much filtered by the experiences of their provincial farm leaders, as communicated by the latter. This intermediary role of Quebec farm leaders puts a heavy onus on the functioning of the executive bodies and secretariats of national farm organizations to act as effective liaisons between the two farm communities. It also renders the societal relationship vulnerable to tensions stemming from differences in the personal styles and tactics of Quebec and Canadian farm leaders. One would not expect either the intermediary role of Quebec farm leaders or the possibility of incompatible personal leadership styles to be unique to agriculture. Nor is the presence of cultural differences unique, relating to Quebec farmers' distinctive approaches to issues (in this case the role of governments and farm unions). But what is significant about farm organizations is that they have overcome these differences to a considerable degree. Such tensions as arise from time to time are almost never rooted in disputes over the use of language. Accordingly, their patterns of association merit detailed scrutiny.

Canadian and Quebec General Farm Associations

Canada's French- and English-speaking farm communities have been associated since 1940 under the mantle of the Canadian Federation of Agriculture, a federation of provincial farm organizations, commodity groups, and producer-owned and -controlled cooperatives.[4] The CFA is the only vehicle that brings together producers of all farm commodities from all provinces; the only other pan-Canadian farm body, the National Farmers Union (NFU), does not have any members in Quebec. The alliance of Quebec farmers with the CFA and not the NFU merits explanation, especially since the NFU's goals of collective marketing and state support, as well as its direct action tactics, put the UPA much closer philosophically to the NFU than to many of the provincial members of the CFA. Historical paths and the differing membership bases of the NFU and CFA figure prominently in why the NFU has been unable to make inroads into Quebec. The NFU's membership base is individual farmers – farm families, to be precise – and not organizations representing farmers – as is the CFA. Already directly represented in the UCC at the time of the birth of the NFU in 1969, Quebec farmers had little incentive, and their provincial UPA leaders even less, to join and pay membership dues in a second farm organization. The mediating role of the UCC/UPA in representing Quebec farmers in a national farm organization such as the CFA had already worked well for several decades, as Meisel and Lemieux noted. The chronic financial difficulties of the NFU and its inability to rival the CFA in terms of obtaining access to and influence with the federal government have given Quebec farmers little reason since then to reconsider their national affiliation.

Besides the CFA, Quebec farmers have always had institutional linkages with pan-Canadian organizations representing particular commodity sectors. Because they afford further opportunity to discern workable patterns of association, the pattern of relations between organizations representing Canadian and Quebec dairy and pork producers is also examined.

The Canadian Federation of Agriculture/La fédération canadienne de l'agriculture

From its inception, when it was named the Canadian Chamber of Agriculture (1935-40), the CFA has defined its mandate to be advancing the economic and social conditions and promoting the common interests of Canadian farmers. It does so by coordinating the efforts of member agricultural producer organizations and serving as the principal non-partisan channel of representation to governments. Its coordinating and representational capacities are importantly affected – and sometimes undermined – by both logic of membership and logic of influence factors.[5] With respect to logic of membership factors – the attributes of potential members that render them easier or more difficult to organize collectively – Canada's agricultural community is very diverse, composed of disparate provincial economies. Agriculture is of varying degrees of economic importance to various provinces,[6] and the significant commodities differ across provinces. In general, the prairie agricultural economy is based on Canada's major agricultural products – grains, oilseeds, and red meats[7] – all of which rely importantly on export markets. By contrast, some of the most significant commodities produced in the central Canadian provinces of Ontario and Quebec – including dairy, eggs, and poultry – are sold almost exclusively in the domestic market.[8] These divisions between domestic- and export-oriented commodity sectors and regions make it exceedingly difficult at times for producers to conceive of their interests – or at least the means to realize common economic goals – in mutually beneficial terms.

Logic of influence factors, consisting principally of state structures and state policies, also erect barriers to the organizational cohesion of agricultural producers, again especially at the national level. The fact that provincial governments are equally important jurisdictional players in agriculture alongside the Government of Canada gives provincial farm organizations strong incentives to organize at the provincial level. Besides this, provincial governments differ significantly in the extent to which they are prepared to respond to the interests of the farm community. Farm organizations clearly have stronger incentives to mobilize and direct their lobbying efforts to the provincial level when it is this level that appears to be most responsive to the community's needs. Since the 1970s, when Quebec provincial governments began to support their agricultural sector with appreciable expenditures and regulatory instruments, a gap has opened up between Quebec farmers and those in the rest of the country. The relatively greater significance of their provincial government to their economic well-being,[9] compared to their counterparts elsewhere in Canada, has not led Quebec farmers to disassociate with the CFA. But the more interventionist stance of Quebec governments in agriculture has created a wedge in the expectations of Quebec and English-speaking farmers elsewhere in Canada regarding the appropriate responsibilities of governments with respect to securing farmers' incomes. These differing expectations present one more bridging challenge for the CFA.

To an important degree, these logic of membership and logic of influence factors undermine the CFA's capacity to carry out its mandate to promote Canadian farmers' common goals. Realizing that goal is dependent on the existence of strong provincial federations of agriculture that have often been sorely lacking over the past decade and a half. In the wake of the highly divisive farm debate in the early 1980s over freight rate reform for export grains,[10] general farm federations on the Prairies either collapsed or were seriously weakened. After forty years of representing Saskatchewan farmers' interests, the Saskatchewan Federation of Agriculture disappeared in 1984. No other organization has yet emerged to pursue its mandate.[11] In Manitoba, the Manitoba Farm Bureau was replaced within two years by Keystone Agricultural Producers (KAP). In Alberta, although Unifarm survived the "Crow Debate," it subsequently dissolved and was replaced in 1996 by the organizationally weak Wild Rose Agricultural Producers Association (WRAP).[12] For a while in 1996, Alberta farmers were without representation at the CFA when WRAP was denied a seat on the CFA because of arrears with its membership fees. Its current associate status in the CFA allows it to participate as a non-voting member with a lower fee schedule.

In the late 1990s, the CFA was organizationally stronger than it had been for some time. It had twenty member associations and purported to represent 200,000 farm families.[13] Its members included the nine provincial farm federations; the two organizations representing the prairie wheat pools – Saskatchewan Wheat Pool and Agricore; the five organizations that represented producers of supply-managed commodities – Dairy Farmers of Canada, Chicken Farmers of Canada, Canadian Egg Marketing Agency, Canadian Turkey Marketing Agency, and Canadian Broiler Hatching Egg Marketing Agency; the Canadian Pork Council;[14] the Canadian Sugar Beet Producers Association; and the Canadian Aquaculture Industry Alliance. The only major commodity sector that is not currently a member of the CFA is the Canadian Cattlemen's Association, whose president and executive director are nonetheless in regular communication with the CFA. Nor do the extremely neoliberal oilseeds and grains organizations, such as the Western Canadian Wheat Growers Association and Western Barley Growers Association, belong to the CFA.

The Union catholique des cultivateurs and the Union des producteurs agricole

Created in 1924 to organize, promote, and defend Quebec farmers' (and woodcutters') political and professional interests, the Union catholique des cultivateurs was a member of the CFA from 1940 onward, as was the Coopérative fédérée de Québec (Coop fédérée), an organization representing the Quebec farm cooperative movement. In 1972, the UCC was renamed the Union des producteurs agricole when it lost its sectarian character and became the sole association recognized by the Quebec government to represent Quebec agricultural producers and to extract compulsory membership fees.[15]

Combined with its monopoly to represent Quebec's 50,000 producers, the UPA's internal structure allows it to function as a very strong and democratic associational system. The union is organized on territorial and commodity lines. The 178 local associations (*syndicats de base*)[16] are subsequently regrouped into sixteen regional federations. They coexist alongside 209 local specialist associations that are collapsed into twenty-one federations, each of which represents a distinct commodity (producers of milk, beef, pork, etc.). The general (territorial) bodies deal with those matters that affect all agricultural producers, while the specialist commodity groups are preoccupied with the production and marketing of their specific commodity.

Patterns of Association: 1940 to the mid-1960s

Along with the Coopérative fédérée du Québec, the UCC/UPA has been a continuous member of the CFA for almost fifty years. Membership in the CFA has afforded Quebec organizations[17] a vehicle through which to present the views of Quebec farmers to the federal government.[18] Quebec provincial organizations initially lacked the resources of time and money to press individually their farmers' interests on the national government.

As noted at the outset, Meisel and Lemieux's assessment of the pattern of association of the UCC and the CFA in the mid-1960s was highly positive. They observed that the UCC's senior officers and a selected few others participated actively in the CFA's annual and quarterly meetings and committees, as well as its presentations to the Government of Canada. Meisel and Lemieux concluded that there were "no lasting problems of unity threatening the effective functioning of the CFA."[19]

The successful UCC-CFA partnership that Meisel and Lemieux perceived rested, in their view, on a host of factors that included four formal and informal organizational and cultural procedures and practices of representation, communication, and coordination of the two linguistic farm communities:

(1) the CFA's "meticulous concern with fairness,"[20] as evidenced by its structural representation of producer and provincial members;
(2) the "loose" and decentralized structure of the CFA, which kept it out of "the hair of the Quebec farm unions"[21] and enabled the latter to pursue their own interests uninhibited by membership in the CFA;
(3) the CFA's practice of consulting UCC leaders on a Quebec issue and pursuing their recommended course of action;[22] and
(4) the long tenure of CFA staff, national leaders, and member organization leaders, which facilitated "mutual trust and easy and genuine consultation."[23]

In addition, Meisel and Lemieux pointed to a handful of other factors that they believed contributed to good relations:

(1) the two groups' shared goals, the principal one being the well-being of their farm members;

(2) the strong incentives for the CFA to avoid internal disharmony by diminishing differences among its members and highlighting their common interests; and

(3) above all, the personalities of the leaders of the Canadian and Quebec farm unions: their goodwill, talent, and "sensitivity to the problem of ethnic relations."[24]

A closer look reveals that the mechanisms of representation and coordination bore the brunt of the responsibility for facilitating the successful partnership.

Structures and Practices of Representation

The historical structures and practices of representation in the CFA continue intact today. Today, as at the time of the Meisel and Lemieux study, the CFA's constitution and by-laws provide for member associations to be roughly represented according to a formula based on the size of their province's farm population and gross farm receipts. The membership dues/financial contributions to the CFA are derived from this formula. It gives the Ontario and Quebec provincial federations, the prairie cooperatives, and the prairie farm federations greater representation within the CFA than provincial organizations representing smaller agricultural sectors (the Maritimes and British Columbia).[25] Quebec delegates and UPA leaders are thereby well represented on CFA decision-making bodies: at the annual meeting of delegates,[26] selected by member associations, where CFA policy is set and executive officers elected; on the National Council,[27] authorized to set CFA policy and direct its affairs between annual meetings; and on the Board of Directors,[28] comprised of representatives of the provincial members, normally their presidents, selected by and from the National Council. The Board of Directors exercises decision-making powers between meetings of the National Council. By convention (but not as a matter of its by-laws), Quebec has two seats on the Board of Directors, one each for the UPA and Coop fédérée presidents. By comparison, all other members have one seat. Quebec is also represented on the Executive Committee,[29] where the president of the UPA is the first vice-president.

The broad similarity between the CFA's decision-making apparatus and that of the UPA helps to legitimize the outputs of CFA procedures – that is, CFA policies – within the francophone community. The line of authority in both organizations runs from farm delegates up to the executive officers. Thus, the UPA's annual general congress, composed of delegates representing the regional and specialized unions, decides official policy of the UPA and biannually elects the directors of the union. The elected General Council, which exercises power between the annual congress and approves the UPA budget, consists of the UPA president, its two vice-presidents, and the thirty-seven presidents of the regional and specialist federations. The seven-member Executive Council, consisting of the president, two vice-presidents, and four other members chosen from the federation presidents, meets monthly to manage the current affairs of the UPA and oversee its general direction.

One important organizational distinction between the CFA and UPA concerns the policy-making role of annual/biannual meetings of member delegates. Delegates to CFA meetings are likely to be presented with proposals for which a consensus has already been built. By contrast, the annual December congress of UPA delegates functions very much as a deliberative and consensus-building forum, with policy being argued out on the floor of the congress. The two different traditions are undoubtedly related to the broader diversity of interests that must be brokered in the CFA as compared to the UPA (where divisions across commodity lines are tempered by a shared language and esprit of solidarity). Building a consensus that brokers the distinctive interests and perspectives of export- and domestic-oriented producers, of laissez-faire proponents and advocates of orderly marketing, requires considerable experience and skill, and apparently CFA executives are not comfortable leaving this task in the hands of member delegates.

While organizational procedures and practices provide Quebec farm unions with proportionate and even preferential representation on CFA decision-making bodies,[30] the majoritarian formal decision-making rule means there is no special treatment for Quebec – or any other member. UPA delegates, for example, have no veto, nor are they guaranteed representation on CFA committees. As with that of other CFA members, Quebec's representation on committees derives from the importance of the issue to its farmers rather than from any perceived need to represent the two language groups. The effort to proceed by consensus, and respect for the moral authority that any provincial member enjoys by virtue of the importance of the issue to its own constituency, contribute to Quebec's satisfaction with policy-making procedures at the CFA.

Coordination Mechanisms

Meisel and Lemieux identified three main mechanisms of coordination across the CFA and UCC: the annual meetings of delegates, the annual regional conference of eastern agricultural producers, and the more frequent meetings and activities of the CFA directors and executive. The first, they believed, promoted the exchange of ideas and mutual understanding among delegates from different regions and sectors of the agricultural industry, as delegates showed themselves willing to adjust resolutions "to the particular needs and viewpoints of one of the constituent groups of the CFA."[31] The second, the eastern regional conference, also served "to underline the common interests of eastern farmers, regardless of their ethnic origin."[32] Clearly, a major responsibility for coordinating the activities of and forging a consensus among the constituent members of the CFA, including those of the UCC, fell to the Board of Directors and the executive. It was Meisel and Lemieux's judgment that these CFA bodies were successful in this regard despite the handicap posed by difficulties of communication.

Communication Practices
The CFA in the mid-1960s was "basically an Anglophone organization," in terms of its oral and written communications.[33] Meetings of the executive, the general council, and committees were all in English only. The sole recent exception was the introduction of simultaneous translation at the annual meeting. The lack of translation, owing to its costliness, prevented francophone members from participating fully in the activities of the annual meetings. The unilingual character of the CFA handicapped the UCC's effective participation in the CFA more generally because the union was forced to send delegates who could speak English rather than individuals who were experts on the issues. Meisel and Lemieux nonetheless described this situation as creating "relatively minor difficulties."[34] However, the unilingual character of written communications – with practically none published in French – was deemed more problematic and a serious obstacle to coordination of relations between the UCC and CFA.[35]

Current Patterns of CFA-UPA Association
Today relations between Quebec's farm community and its anglophone counterpart in the rest of Canada, as conducted under the rubric of the Canadian Federation of Agriculture, are invariably described as "harmonious," "cooperative," and even "superb."[36] The CFA enjoys a good reputation in Quebec. This happy situation is the result of a combination of structural and non-structural factors that has traditionally produced an amicable and effective partnership between Canada's two linguistic farm communities. The mechanisms of representation and coordination remain those described earlier; however, the communication practices of the CFA have changed significantly.

In sharp contrast to the unilingual character of the CFA through to the 1970s, the CFA now functions as a bilingual organization. This bilingual capacity has been put in place over time and was solidified during the CFA vice presidency of Jacques Proulx (1981-93), the unilingual francophone UPA president. Able and willing to speak only in French and working alongside anglophones of whom very few could speak French, Proulx insisted upon and received translation services for all CFA events in which he participated.[37]

Instantaneous translation is provided at all meetings and teleconference calls of the CFA decision-making bodies: the annual meeting of delegates and those of the Board of Directors, National Council, executive, and executive committees. In addition, the secretariat of the CFA,[38] including its executive director, functions in both official languages. French-speaking staff normally give presentations in French at meetings of the Board of Directors. All documents are translated into French.[39] Beyond this central office staff, various members of the Board of Directors from provinces with a francophone community, such as Ontario, Nova Scotia, and New Brunswick, are often able to converse in French with their Quebec francophone colleagues.[40] The ability of the senior leadership levels of the UPA and CFA to communicate easily with one another has been aided appreciably in recent years by the English fluency of the current CFA vice-president and UPA president, Laurent Pellerin (1984-).

Pellerin's bilingualism is unprecedented among UPA leaders. The UPA itself remains a decidedly unilingual francophone organization. Increasingly, however, a number of its younger federation presidents and several of its staff are able to function in English.[41]

UPA officials have nothing but praise for the CFA's efforts to provide translation services, seeing them as an important example of accommodation by the CFA, particularly given the cost of translation (approximately $120,000 per annum).[42] And UPA spokespeople are quick to declare that there are no major problems of communication within the federation. The greatest challenge to overcoming the language gap occurs with informal oral communications at annual meetings, which are overwhelmingly dominated by unilingual English delegates. On these occasions, the professional translators, some of whom have worked for the CFA for a sufficiently long time that they know the personalities and their modes of expression well,[43] are ever present to assist with small-group conversations. Bilingual CFA and UPA staff play a significant role here as well, acting as intermediaries for unilingual farmers. Meetings of technical officials are sometimes in English as well, especially when the Quebec delegates are able to function in English. Some of these officials find translation to be impractical and unhelpful when highly technical matters are being discussed and prefer to speak in English to make themselves understood clearly. At these times, translation is provided by other, bilingual committee members. Thus, the overwhelming sentiment is that linguistic relations within the CFA are unproblematic, owing to a combination of high-quality translation services and a sufficiency of francophones who are able and willing to revert to English when it is prudent to do so.

The current relationship between the Union des producteurs agricole and the Canadian Federation of Agriculture appears to be shaped by many of the same structural and non-structural factors identified by Meisel and Lemieux some thirty years ago. An important non-structural factor continues to be the personalities of the CFA and UPA leaders. CFA and UPA officials concur that personality makes a "phenomenal" difference to relations between francophone and anglophone farm communities. Quebec farmers appreciated CFA President Jack Wilkinson's (1993-98) rabble-rousing style and "fighter" stance, which mirrored the styles of their own UPA presidents, despite his inability to converse with them in their own language. When personalities clash, as they did during the final years of Jacques Proulx's vice-presidency (and presidency of the UPA), interorganizational relations within the CFA risk deterioration.

In addition to the sharp contrast in current CFA communication patterns compared with thirty years ago, another notable difference pertains to the tenures of CFA elected and appointed officials. Meisel and Lemieux surmised that the longevity of CFA officials contributed to the excellent relations with Quebec's farm community. Long presidential terms are no longer a feature of the CFA. The nine-year presidency of Charles Munro (1969-78) was clearly the exception; subsequent CFA presidents have served from two to six years.[44] Indeed, the CFA constitution provides for a two-year term, with a limit of three consecutive terms. UPA presidents have served considerably longer terms recently, Jacques Proulx's tenure being twelve years (1981-93).[45] The experience that member leaders bring with them to the Board of Directors and executive is deemed highly important in enabling the CFA to function "as an adult organization." Given the diversity of most of their own provincial agricultural sectors, provincial farm leaders serving on the CFA have had extensive experience with seeking compromise solutions and working to resolve problems in a timely fashion. Their experience and pragmatism contribute importantly to the effective functioning of the CFA.

The skills, personalities, and experiences of individuals clearly make a difference to intercommunity relations. The productive coexistence of francophone and anglophone farm organizations is also the result of sound organizational foundations and mutual economic interests. An examination of the pattern of relations in other pan-Canadian farm organizations reinforces this assessment.

English and French Specialist Farm Organizations
Francophone and anglophone farmers in Canada interact with one another in organizations that represent their interests as producers of specific commodities. The experiences of organizations representing Quebec's two largest commodity sectors – dairy and pork – are instructive in elaborating on the picture of francophone-anglophone agrarian relations.

The Dairy Farmers of Canada/Les producteurs laitiers du Canada and la Fédération des producteurs de lait du Québec
In the mid-1960s, Meisel and Lemieux noted the poor relations between Quebec dairy producers and the Dairy Farmers of Canada (DFC), which they viewed as stemming from the English-only communication practice of the

DFC, as well as its lack of coordination with the association representing Quebec milk producers, the Fédération des producteurs de lait du Québec (FPLQ). The disenchantment of the FPLQ with the DFC had led some UCC directors to call for the DFC to be dissolved on the grounds that it was costly and overlapped with the CFA.

Since then, the relations between dairy farmers in the two linguistic communities, as reflected in relations between the DFC and the FPLQ, have improved dramatically. Today spokespersons in both communities describe them as harmonious and cooperative and say that "language is not an issue." Formal and informal procedures and practices with respect to communication and representation, alongside other non-structural factors, appear to account for this improved relationship.

Patterns of Representation

Like the CFA, representation on DFC decision-making bodies is according to a weighted formula, based on (but not directly proportional to) a province's share of overall Canadian milk production and its consequent membership fees to the DFC. This weighted formula ensures Quebec and Ontario (with 47 and 31 percent of Canadian production) greater numerical representation than other provincial members on DFC governing bodies and requires these provinces to pay the largest share of member fees.[46] By practice but not by-law, Ontario and Quebec each enjoy a seat on the Executive Committee, while western Canada and eastern Canada must share the two executive positions assigned to these regions.[47] Four DFC presidents in the past twenty-five years have come from Quebec; two were bilingual, and two were unilingual French.

The policy-making procedures of the DFC, as practised at the annual policy meeting, echo with those of the UPA in two senses: they are highly democratic, and policy is developed on the floor of the conference. In contrast to the CFA, DFC policies are talked out until a consensus prevails. In the absence of a consensus, it falls to the executive director to draft a compromise position or two policy statements reflecting the two positions. The pattern is for producer delegates themselves to discuss the issue through informal exchanges and to hammer out a position that all can live with. There is an unwritten understanding among milk producer delegates that, if an issue is crucial to the industry, no decision will be forced to a vote. This normative context – a desire to work by consensus, to learn and listen, to demonstrate goodwill, and to respect others' points of view – is seen as important in promoting harmonious relations within the DFC.

Patterns of Communication

In the late 1960s, the Dairy Farmers of Canada began to translate documents into French, and by the mid-1970s it was functioning as a bilingual association. Its executive director of twenty-two years and a francophone, Richard Doyle, is fully bilingual, and seventeen of the twenty-one current staff in the DFC Ottawa office are fluently bilingual, while another two can function in French.[48] All internal and external communications are also in both French and English, with a strong effort made to send out both linguistic versions in the same mailing.[49]

All meetings of decision-making bodies are now conducted in both official languages with simultaneous interpretation, credited with being "reliable." Until the mid-1970s, most DFC directors from Quebec were bilingual by necessity; whether this constraint detracted from the quality of Quebec's representation in the DFC and the latter's policy expertise is impossible to determine. Since then, owing to the translation services, most Quebec directors have been unilingually French. Communication among directors is also facilitated by the likelihood that at least one of the directors from New Brunswick, Manitoba, and Ontario[50] will be bilingual. Quebec's FPLQ is also able to function as a bilingual organization: its secretary is bilingual, and the four staff officials who liaise with the DFC office are comfortable in English. This bilingual capacity in the provincial members of the DFC enables communication directly with one another rather than always through the offices of the DFC. The annual policy conference and summer meeting rotate among provinces, with the DFC bearing the translation costs associated with making documents available in both official languages.

These formal and informal practices of communication and representation contribute to the strong associational linkages between English- and French-speaking dairy producers within the umbrella framework of the DFC. The bilingual and consensus-building skills of senior administrative officers, in particular Doyle, are cited as key. A past DFC president, Louis Balcaen from Manitoba, is fully bilingual. Undoubtedly, the skills of these leaders facilitate good relations across the two linguistic communities. So too does the experience and expertise of the DFC Board of Directors and executive, whose members have often previously served for some time at the provincial level. No less significant is directors' commitment to the common goal of collective marketing, an objective that surmounts all other differences.

The Canadian Pork Council and the Fédération des producteurs de porc du Québec

Since 1966, when it was called the Canadian Swine Council, the Canadian Pork Council (CPC) has existed to promote the interests of Canada's pork and hog industries. The council has a strong export marketing focus alongside its research and quality improvement activities. Its members include eight provincial marketing boards and commissions, including the Fédération des producteurs de porc du Québec (FPPQ), created in 1966.[51] The CPC is a sparse organization, with fewer staff and a much smaller budget than many of its provincial members, including the FPPQ. Accordingly, it is dependent on its provincial marketing board/commission members for policy capacity.

Patterns of Representation

The primary decision-making body of the CPC is its eighteen-member Board of Directors, appointed from provincial membership according to a formula based upon shares of national production and adjusted as production shares shift. Quebec, with about 35 percent of national production, and Ontario, with approximately 25 percent, are each represented on the board by four directors, while other provinces have one to three directors depending on their share of national production. Decisions are talked through to consensus, and although voting is by a simple majority the practice is to proceed cautiously and take a second look if any province strongly opposes the majority. The six-member Executive Committee, which oversees CPC matters between board meetings and appoints committees, provides representation for each region. Thus, Quebec always has a representative on the board. Edouard Asnong, from Quebec's FPPQ, has served as both CPC president and vice-president.

Patterns of Communication

As recently as the late 1980s, the CPC was a purely English organization, particularly in terms of its staff. The introduction of bilingual capacity came in response to the insistence of Quebec's FPPQ. Although a member of the CPC, the FPPQ had not been paying its full dues, owing to its financial precariousness. In 1987, the FPPQ obtained the right to levy an automatic "check off" fee on all hogs sold and, equipped with this new financial bargaining leverage, served notice to the CPC that it needed French service as a condition of its paying membership dues. Since then, the CPC has acquired considerable bilingual capacity. Although its executive director is not fully bilingual,[52] the CPC office staff are. All documents for meetings of the Board of Directors are translated into the two official languages, and meetings proceed with interpretation. However, the same practice does not apply with respect to Executive Committee meetings, whose written materials and oral transactions are not translated. Most committee meetings where Quebec representatives are present are provided with simultaneous translation. The consequence is that Quebec Executive Committee members have usually been people who speak English. As with the Dairy Farmers of Canada, communication is considerably facilitated by the frequent presence of francophone directors from outside Quebec.

The practice with respect to notices and materials sent to provincial member federations varies. If the (Quebec) individual is at ease in English, then only English materials are sent. However, if the document relates to a policy matter, and one likely to require the approval of other provincial officials/

producers, then there is an effort to have the document available in French.

When the experience of the Canadian Pork Council is put alongside that of Dairy Farmers of Canada and the Canadian Federation of Agriculture, it becomes clear that Canada's pan-Canadian farm organizations have organized themselves internally to be vehicles through which both anglophone and francophone farmers can pursue their socioeconomic interests. The pan-Canadian general farm and specialist commodity organizations examined here share similar mandates with their Quebec member associations: to represent the professional interests of their farm constituencies in a non-partisan fashion. This shared goal among a constituency whose members, whatever their language, think of themselves primarily as business persons obviously facilitates cooperation. The essentially harmonious character of the relationship is also furthered by the reality that membership in national farm organizations entails few costs and potentially considerable benefits for Quebec farmers. Given the opportunities that the CFA affords for collective national and even international action, membership in it is considered good value for the money. Quebec farm organizations are considerably better resourced and organized than their Canadian counterparts. The CFA's annual budget is about $850,000, while that of the UPA (including that of its federations) is $100 million.[53] The CFA's central office staff number fewer than 10; by contrast, the UPA has 400 staff alone in its provincial office in Longueuil and 800 in total when the staff in regional and specialized federation offices are included.[54] In short, membership in the CFA (and the DFC and CPC) does not cut deeply into the UPA (FPLQ, FPPQ) budget.

Nor does membership in national organizations jeopardize the autonomy of Quebec farm organizations. Member associations of the CFA, DFC, and CPC can count on not being swamped in these national organizations or over-ridden by large, central bureaucracies. Such bureaucracies simply don't exist, particularly at the Canadian Federation of Agriculture and at the Canadian Pork Council. While the CFA does take the leadership on several policy issues, on many others it works in close cooperation with the larger provincial farm federations, including those in Ontario[55] and Quebec, drawing on their policy expertise and avoiding duplication of their activities. This sharing of responsibilities extends to the international arena, where the UPA sits alongside the CFA on the International Federation of Agricultural Producers (IFAP). The UPA is the only provincial federation to do so.

Far from dictating policy from the centre, the CFA conceives of itself as performing a coordinating function among its provincial members: as a forum within which to develop a consensus on policies where the jurisdictional authority is national or crosses national and provincial boundaries. The DFC defines its role in similar terms: as an intermediary to facilitate understanding among producers in different provinces. A division of responsibilities occurs between the CFA and all provincial federations, with the CFA handling national issues and provincial federations dealing with provincial matters. Additionally, the UPA often performs the role in Quebec that the CFA exercises elsewhere in Canada.[56] As Meisel and Lemieux observed of the UCC-CFA, such a delineation of responsibilities keeps the CFA out of the UPA's hair and promotes harmony.

The Impact of Non-Organizational Factors on Anglophone-Francophone Farm Relations

Even while the CFA-UPA relationship is described as "an old one that is getting better and better," it remains the case that there are ebbs and flows in the degree of harmony and cooperation. Observers are in accord that such tensions as arise from time to time are not rooted in linguistic differences. Like those that crop up in the Dairy Farmers of Canada and the Canadian Pork Council, disagreements are more likely to stem from cultural and philosophical differences between Quebec and anglophone farmers regarding the agricultural and non-agricultural policies of governments.

Two Cultures, Two Philosophies

Quebec farm organizations are distinguished from their English Canadian counterparts in pan-Canadian bodies by a set of shared beliefs reflected in their organizational logic and tactics. The UPA, like the UCC before it, is a union of farm producers alone. By contrast, the CFA's membership has always included commercial and quasi-commercial enterprises, such as the prairie wheat pools.[57] (Such cooperative commercial enterprises are organized and represented separately in Quebec by the Coopérative fédérée du Québec.) Quebec organizations, as provincial members of the DFC and CPC, are alone in being unions of producers (dairy and hogs respectively) and not provincial marketing boards, mandated to perform commercial functions. The membership bases of these federations and the UPA reflect the distinctive syndicalist mentality of Quebec producers.[58]

Two further cultural and philosophical beliefs separate the two linguistic communities. Quebec farmers perceive themselves to adhere more strongly to a collectivist tradition compared with their English Canadian counterparts' individualist inclinations. Cohesive in their belief in the efficacy of collective action to overcome problems and effect change, Quebec farmers are often aggressive and militant in pressing their claims on governments. Backed by the organizational strength of the UPA, federations representing Quebec milk and hog producers, for example, are able to rally producers quickly and effectively and mount massive traffic-disrupting and media-grabbing demonstrations. Their outlook and behaviour have often distinguished them from English Canadian farmers, whom francophone farmers characterize as more likely to blame themselves for socioeconomic problems, to believe that the solution is only to work harder as individuals, to be more compromising, and to take to the streets only as a last resort. (In any event, with the exception of Ontario's Federation of Agriculture, the weakness of many provincial federations tends to rule out equally effective mass protest.) These cultural differences are accompanied by quite different views regarding the appropriate roles and responsibilities of governments with respect to the agricultural sector. While Quebec producers perceive English Canadian farmers to have shifted in recent decades away from espousing government support for agriculture, they themselves continue to adhere to the view that government support for farmers' incomes is a societal obligation.

Such differences of identity and philosophy often lead the UPA to be more aggressive and confrontationalist vis-à-vis governments than are its English Canadian counterparts, including the CFA. Within national organizations, such as the Dairy Farmers of Canada and the CFA, periodic divisions arise between Quebec farmers and their English Canadian counterparts over the appropriate tactics – resistance versus compromise, activist versus spectator – when farmers' interests are in jeopardy. The debates over trade policy in the late 1980s and early 1990s illustrate this difference of perspective. These debates also reveal the earlier cleavage lines of supply-managed producers in every Canadian province versus export-oriented producers, principally, but not exclusively, situated in western Canada.

Government Policies

Government policies are an ongoing feature of the landscape, affecting the incentives for collective action across the two agrarian communities, rendering the building of coalitions more or less easy, and constraining or enhancing the capacity for distinctive preferences to be mutually accommodated. A decade ago Canada's farm community struggled to achieve a coherent, united trade policy in response to bilateral and multilateral trade developments. More recently, trade developments have been a rallying call for policy coordination and unity. In the early 1990s, provincial sovereignist goals drove a wedge between the two farm communities; no similar chasm opened up in the 1995 referendum. These differing experiences illustrate that, while government policies can render easier or more difficult harmony and cooperation between Quebec and Canadian farmers, it is ultimately the organizational development[59] of national farm organizations and the styles and skills of farm leaders and officials that determine the salutary or deleterious impacts of government policies on francophone-anglophone agrarian relations.

Trade Policy

The Canadian government's decision to pursue the liberalization of trade, first with the United States and then multilaterally during the Uruguay

Round of GATT negotiations (1986-93), presented a major challenge for the Canadian Federation of Agriculture. The CFA was faced with the enormous task of reconciling the interests of its western Canadian members promoting more open markets for their export grain producers with those of its members representing the domestically protected supply management sectors (dairy, poultry, and eggs). While the UPA sided unequivocally with the latter, the CFA sought to "balance" the interests of the two groups. Its capacity to do so was handicapped by the fact that it was then a weak associational system; a number of specialist commodity sectors representing the grains, oilseeds, cattle, and pork sectors were not members of the federation. The CFA managed to avoid taking sides during the Free Trade Agreement, as the Canadian government refused to negotiate supply management. It attempted the same stance during the multilateral Uruguay Round negotiations, supporting (like the Government of Canada) a "balanced position" that simultaneously called for the opening of markets for western Canada's export commodities and continuing domestic protection for the supply-managed sectors. The stance drew criticism from UPA President Jacques Proulx, who suspected that the CFA would eventually bow to the interests of its western grain and oilseed sectors. Tensions grew between the Quebec and Canadian farm organizations, with Proulx denouncing what he perceived to be an inadequate CFA lobbying campaign and threatening to withdraw the UPA from the CFA.[60] When a significant degree of tariff protection was retained for supply-managed commodities in the WTO Agreement on Agriculture, Proulx took full credit for it, arguing that this outcome would not have resulted but for the UPA's unrelenting lobby in Canada and Europe.[61]

The tensions that surfaced between francophone and anglophone farmers and the UPA and CFA during the Uruguay Round negotiations undoubtedly derived in some significant measure from the differing approaches of English- and French-speaking farm leaders.[62] While at least one of the CFA presidents whom Proulx worked alongside as CFA vice president was more comfortable with a low-keyed, behind-the-scenes lobbying approach, Proulx's strong personality and perception of the role of a farm leader led him naturally to an overtly aggressive, *demandeur* style before the Canadian government. In this sense, then, the tensions between the UPA and CFA during the Uruguay Round negotiations were rooted in differences over appropriate tactics and strategies on how to achieve the farm community's goals rather than over the goals themselves.

Some six years later the internal tensions over trade policy disappeared, and in the run-up to the commencement of multilateral agricultural negotiations in late 1999 Canadian farm unions, under the mantle of the CFA, succeeded in devising a united trade policy. Signed by twenty farm organizations representing both supply management and export-oriented sectors, and the first ever common trade position among Canadian farm groups, the trade policy statement was drafted by CFA, provincial, and commodity group leaders and representatives working in both languages, with ideas injected by all provinces. It was hailed by Quebec and Canadian farm officials as evidence of the ability of all Canadian farmers to work together to realize common economic interests.

The experiences of the CFA during the Uruguay Round of GATT talks and more recently illustrate the CFA's consensus-building capacity. The coalition it forged between the export-oriented and supply management sectors during the Uruguay Round was certainly fragile. But it held for the duration of the multilateral negotiations, with both factions inside the CFA participating, alongside Quebec farmers, in large rallies on Parliament Hill in 1992 and in lobbying campaigns in Brussels. No member organizations left the CFA as a result of its trade position during the Uruguay Round, and the organization was not paralyzed in anything like the manner it was during the Crow Reform debate over termination of export grain freight subsidies.

The current coalescing of farm organizations on trade policy does, however, indicate a greater degree of internal CFA policy coherence than marked the Uruguay Round. It can be explained by recognition among all farmers of the heightened importance of farmer solidarity in the current context of globalizing markets. As Quebec farmers have always appreciated, farmers' ability to shape the direction and magnitude of change is likely to be much greater if they are united behind carefully thought-out policy positions. At the same time, a CFA president whose aggressive style and ardent defence of agriculture strike a familiar and highly acclaimed chord in Quebec, a bilingual UPA president noted for his pragmatism, and a more organizationally developed CFA have all contributed to the current unity of Canadian farmers around one trade policy.

The National Unity Debate

Quebec's farm union is officially non-partisan and has traditionally avoided taking a position on debates about the future of Quebec in (or out of) Canada. Meisel and Lemieux[63] noted that the Union catholique des cultivateurs did not present a brief to the Laurendeau-Dunton Bilingualism and Biculturalism Commission, having consulted its federations and concluded that the state of relations between the French- and English-speaking communities and the problems of francophone farmers did not justify such a brief. The UPA remained neutral during the 1980 referendum campaign. However, Quebec's farm community was caught up in the broad debate about Quebec's place in Canada as relations between the Canadian and Quebec governments and societies deteriorated in the aftermath of the defeat of the Meech Lake Accord in 1990. Led by Jacques Proulx, a strong nationalist with close ties to the sovereignist Parti québécois, the UPA endorsed Quebec's economic and political independence at its annual convention in 1990.[64] Two years later it returned to its position of official neutrality, which it maintained throughout the 1995 referendum campaign.

During that campaign, and under the presidency of Laurent Pellerin, the UPA indicated its desire and intention to continue to work with English Canadian farmers, whatever the outcome of the referendum vote. Pellerin argued that broader political debates about Quebec-Canada relations should not colour the successful working partnerships Quebec farmers had with producers in other Canadian provinces.

The UPA leader's call for "business as usual" even with a "yes" vote went to the heart of francophone farmers' objectives in forging organizational linkages with Canada's farm community. These networks are designed to expedite common economic interests through collective action. Built on mutual self-interest and the respect and trust that have accumulated over decades, these ties are not sentimental. Nor do they possess the glue that binds Quebec farmers to one another and to their own provincial government and province. They persist because – and to the extent that – they work.[65] English Canadian farmers, equally pragmatic, would not disagree.

Decentralist Initiatives and Other Policies
While trade and national unity issues are highly visible in their effects on the unity and harmony in the farm community, other policy endeavours have had less obvious but nonetheless salutary effects on relations between the two linguistic communities. Since the mid-1990s, the Government of Canada has endeavoured to design agri-food policies in concert with producers and provinces, to devolve responsibility for their direct delivery to producers, and to minimize intergovernmental duplication of programs. These decentralist initiatives tend to facilitate harmony across the francophone and anglophone communities. They bring anglophone and francophone farmers closer together in formulating policies alongside governments. At the same time, decentralization leaves considerable leeway for Quebec farmers to administer these programs within their own province.[66] While such decentralization tends to reinforce the importance of strong provincial farm unions, other items on the policy agenda, such as food safety, biotechnology, and the heightened salience of trade issues, continue to create incentives for national and international collective action. The CFA fulfills this function, so much so that more than one UPA official has suggested that, "if the CFA did not exist, it would be necessary to invent it."

Conclusion
The Quebec farm union's membership in the Canadian Federation of Agriculture is a long-standing one. It now spans almost fifty uninterrupted years. While other farm groups in English Canada have come and gone among the CFA's ranks, the UPA has remained a stalwart. Clearly, the UPA has the

policy capacity and financial resources to operate independently of the CFA if it believes that it is not getting "good value for its money." The UPA continues as a member of the CFA because Quebec farmers find it an efficacious tool through which to pursue their economic and social objectives. On the whole, the CFA works – and works well – as a forum for promoting the collective interests of English- and French-speaking Canadian farmers. The same can be said of the two national commodity organizations examined here, especially the Dairy Farmers of Canada. As bilingual pan-Canadian organizations with democratic structures, consensual decision-making practices, and representation proportionate to member bodies' financial contributions, these farm groups build bridges across Canada's two official language communities and further the possibility for individuals in each to realize their shared goals.

The linguistic pattern of association in Canada's farm community presents a model of essentially elite accommodation based on an organizational culture of respect for linguistic equality that is entrenched in practices of bilingualism. This model is grounded in shared material interests, is made both possible and necessary by the weight of Quebec in the Canadian agricultural sector, and is sufficiently strong to overcome cultural divisions between the anglophone and francophone farm communities.

The linguistic model of Canada's farm community minimizes the likelihood that linguistic barriers will impede the two farm communities from realizing their mutual interests. The Canadian Federation of Agriculture and pan-Canadian specialist organizations are certainly stronger organizations in terms of financial resources, policy capacity, and political influence because of their Quebec members. Quebec farm leaders and delegates have provided leadership on many issues inside all three farm bodies examined here. The tensions that any national farm organization faces in seeking to reconcile the different interests of export-oriented and domestic market sectors would not disappear were Quebec to leave the federation. They are fully visible in several provinces, including Ontario, and would still need to be bridged by any national federation.

To say that the farm organizations are good examples of how to overcome language barriers in advancing common goals among groups in civil society is not to say that more could not be done. Even while language is not a barrier to understanding and does not stand in the way of a good working partnership between francophone and anglophone farmers, bilingual fluency does not penetrate very deeply into the farm community. This reality is lamentable. Were more English- and French-speaking farmers able to communicate directly with one another – to trade stories about their farming experiences and swap tales about their families – they would, like their leaders, recognize how much they have in common. Face-to-face communication would only strengthen their mutual respect and their capacity to act collectively in pursuit of goals that transcend the interests of unilingual communities.

Such a bilingual world would be an ideal one. Canadian farmers and the Canadian Federation of Agriculture do not live in it. Rather, they cope with the reality of language differences. And they cope well – arguably much better than the significantly better resourced officials in Agriculture and Agri-Food Canada who have been known to address Canadian farm meetings entirely in English.

4

Municipal Associations

Don Stevenson and Richard Gilbert

Municipalities are an order of government in Canada, but their associations possess many of the characteristics of the other groups analyzed elsewhere in this book. The Canada-wide and Quebec municipal associations were among the case studies undertaken by John Meisel and Vincent Lemieux for the Royal Commission on Bilingualism and Biculturalism in the late 1960s.[1] Since then, these and other municipal associations have had to adapt their objectives and their methods of operation to reflect both the changing political context of Canadian federalism and changes in the linguistic reality of the country. This chapter analyzes the success of these adaptations and their wider implications for Canadian society.

The Changing Municipal Context

Municipal associations are becoming more important in Canada because local governments are assuming greater importance in the governance of the country. Since the 1960s, there has been a decentralization of power in Canada, chiefly from the federal government to the provinces and more modestly from both federal and provincial governments to local governments and the private and non-governmental sectors. This decentralization has been accompanied by further urbanization of Canada's population.[2] Neither federal nor provincial governments are well organized to deal with many of the resulting issues. Local governments, particularly in the more populous areas, have been gradually transforming themselves from their 1960s role of delivering services to assuming responsibility for the economic, social, cultural, and environmental health of their communities.

At the end of the 1990s, there were some 3,700 municipal governments in Canada. Their structure and average size varied widely from province to province, both because of historic and geographic characteristics and because provincial governments exercised their control of local governments in different ways.

The first national association of municipalities was created in 1901, and one or more associations of municipalities were active in each province for most of the twentieth century. In 1999, there were seventeen provincial-municipal and territorial-municipal associations. Some provinces had more than one, often reflecting the divergent interests of large urban areas and smaller municipalities. Most municipal associations worried about the largest cities bypassing the associations and taking all of their concerns directly to the federal or provincial governments.

In recent years, linguistic issues have given rise to separate associations for primarily francophone municipalities in New Brunswick, Ontario, and Manitoba. At the end of the 1990s, close to 700 municipalities belonged both to a provincial association of municipalities and to the national body, the Federation of Canadian Municipalities (FCM). The FCM's predecessors were the Canadian Federations of Mayors and Municipalities (CFMM) from 1937 to 1976 and the Dominion Conference of Mayors from 1901 to 1937.[3]

The B and B Commission on Municipal Associations

In their study, Meisel and Lemieux concentrated on relationships between anglophones and francophones within the Canadian Federation of Mayors and Municipalities and between the CFMM and l'Union des municipalités de la province du Québec (UMPQ). The study showed that until the 1960s there were few tensions between the pan-Canadian association and the Quebec association. Municipalities in Quebec often joined both associations. But tensions increased in the 1960s as a result of the rise of Quebec nationalism and ensuing tensions within the Canadian federal system. Quebec municipal leaders were caught in a debate about the relationships between Quebec municipalities, their provincial associations, and the federal and provincial governments.

With respect to the CFMM, Meisel and Lemieux concluded the following:

- The crisis in the CFMM and the loss of some of its Quebec membership in the 1960s was primarily produced by the changing political climate in Canada rather than by internal causes.
- The CFMM's internal vision and method of operating were too rigid to adjust successfully to the changing circumstances in Canada.
- One of the reasons for this rigidity was the centralist outlook of the CFMM's long-term executive director, who was sensitive to the bilingual nature of the country but not to the differing objectives of many francophone Quebecers.
- Many of Quebec's active participants in the CFMM were older, small-town mayors who were unrepresentative of the changes taking place in Quebec in the 1960s.

- Some of the more nationalistic younger mayors of Quebec were much more attuned to the decentralist views of the Quebec government than to the outlook of the CFMM.
- As a result, when faced with a choice between some of the advantages of CFMM membership and the political "penalty" of supporting a seemingly centralist organization, many Quebec municipalities withdrew from the CFMM.

The Meisel-Lemieux report concluded that the CFMM was not adapting well to Quebec's Quiet Revolution. Several factors contributed to this lack of adaptation. Perhaps the most important was the personality of the executive director. George Mooney was described in the report as "a person of exemplary goodwill insofar as [English-French] relations were concerned." He "spoke both languages, assured the publication in both languages of the association's literature, and saw to it that the Federation was one of the earliest pan-Canadian organizations to translate the speeches of its members at conventions. But while he was linguistically aware, he was insensitive to the different objectives sought by members belonging respectively to the two ethnic groups and he therefore failed to perceive the need to alter his own centralist outlook and that of his Federation."[4]

The result was insensitivity within the CFMM to the emerging quest for more provincial autonomy in Quebec and the consequent declining interest among its Quebec members in securing better federal treatment of local government across Canada. Meanwhile, the UMPQ embraced the Quiet Revolution. It became more unilingual and more supportive of provincial positions.

CFMM-FCM: Seventeen Years of Decline, Then Seventeen Years of Growth

Mooney died in 1965 after twenty-seven years as executive director of the CFMM. The following three and a half decades could be loosely characterized as seventeen years of turbulence followed by seventeen years of relative tranquility. The pivotal event may have been the appointment in 1982 of James W. Knight as executive director, a position he continued to hold – later named chief executive officer – into the twenty-first century. There were several executive directors between Mooney and Knight. None was able to inspire the board of the day to address effectively the waning size and influence of the organization. A vicious circle involving loss of membership and loss of influence had begun with the withdrawal of Montreal from the CFMM in 1961. Membership loss became particularly pronounced during the 1970s.[5] At the lowest point, in 1981-82, fewer than 200 municipalities belonged to the FCM, compared with more than 300 belonging to the CFMM in the 1960s and more than 700 in the 1990s.[6]

The 1970s saw a greater reaching out to francophones within the CFMM-FCM than ever before. Federal grants made possible simultaneous interpretation at annual conferences and other meetings as well as translation of most documents. The Official Languages Act of 1969 had presaged growing acceptance of bilingualism in English Canada, which had influenced the CFMM-FCM and made the grants possible. The CFMM also received research support and backing from the ill-fated federal Ministry of State for Urban Affairs for a series of national tri-level conferences in the 1970s. These conferences caused problems for the CFMM with most provincial governments and especially that of Quebec.

Quebec, meanwhile, was becoming more unilingual. In 1973, the provincial government decreed that French was to be the sole official language (except where the Constitution provides otherwise). Language rules were strengthened following the election of the first separatist government in 1976. What was now the Union des municipalités du Quebec (UMQ) became almost entirely unilingual.

The Pivotal Year

The pivotal year for the CFMM-FCM was 1982: after seventeen years of continuous decline, there would by 1999 be seventeen years of growth. In retrospect, Knight's appointment was an obvious turning point, but several other factors may well have contributed to the change in trajectory.

The annual conference in Halifax in 1980 set a record for attendance, with three-quarters of the membership present and a delegate count 24 percent above that for the previous year. The FCM was finding its *raison d'être*, focused now on delivering value to members rather than on fruitless and divisive quests for constitutional recognition or on the arcane and unsuccessful re-arrangements of the membership structure that had been a feature of the 1970s.

Another factor was the enthusiasm and skill of members of the FCM's board. It was especially well led by the mayor of Quebec City, who was president during the critical year between the annual conferences of June 1982 and June 1983. An aggressive and effective membership campaign reached into every part of the country, set clear targets, and made good use of existing members. Several larger municipalities helped the campaign by contributing funds beyond their membership fees. The president was able to report to the 1983 conference that the FCM had experienced its first net gain in members since 1975: twenty-five new or returning members, but still fifteen withdrawals.

A 1984 assessment of the membership indicated that in simple numbers Quebec was holding its own with other populous provinces; for example, Quebec and Ontario each had 41 of a total of 254 FCM members in that year. However, Ontario's members were much larger: its 41 members embraced

4.5 million or 52 percent of Ontario's 8.6 million population; Quebec's 41 members embraced only 1.4 million or 22 percent of that province's 6.4 million population. The continued absence of the City of Montreal was a particularly strong factor in this discrepancy.

But that was soon to change. The long-serving Montreal mayor, Jean Drapeau, retired in 1986. Among the first acts of his successor, Jean Doré, was to lead the new council to rejoin the FCM. This was no federalist gesture – Doré had been Réné Lévesque's press secretary – but a practical move that acknowledged the continuing importance of the Government of Canada for Montreal and the advantages of dealing with that government through a strong Canada-wide municipal organization as well as through the Government of Quebec.

Part of the attraction of the FCM for the City of Montreal was the emergence of the Big-City Mayors Caucus. It met the need of the mayors of Canada's dozen or so largest cities to meet regularly, share common problems and approaches, and apply collective pressure on matters such as gun control and homelessness. Although the Big-City Mayors Caucus has served both the mayors and the organization well, it has also brought some problems. For example, pressure for federal action on social policy can run counter to Quebec's insistence that such matters are entirely a provincial prerogative and, as a consequence, put the mayor of Montreal in a difficult position.

By 1990, the FCM had almost tripled its numbers compared with the nadir of 1982. The proportion of Quebec members had declined, although the absolute number had increased to its highest level ever. Now, with Montreal and the rest of the Montreal Urban Community (a regional governance body) on board, well over half of Quebec's population was represented compared with 22 percent in 1984.

Meisel and Lemieux had compared resolutions moved at annual conferences by Ontario and Quebec members as a measure of involvement in the organization. They noted that "the Quebec delegations were considerably less active than their Ontario colleagues and that their participation in recent years had declined."[7]

We were able to examine resolutions moved at eleven annual conferences distributed across the period since the mid-1960s. Of the total of 725 resolutions presented to the eleven conferences, only 17 (2 percent) were proposed by Quebec municipalities. In this respect, Quebec participation remained at a low level. (We have been told that we should not be surprised by the lack of resolutions from Quebec municipalities. It is not the way things are done in Quebec. Relatively few resolutions are presented for consideration at UMQ conventions.)

In other respects, the level of Quebec participation and support was high. FCM delegations and presentations to federal ministers and parliamentary committees usually included representation from Quebec, often with great effect. In particular, the participation of Quebec mayors and councillors was critical to achieving favourable arrangements with respect to the GST rebate.

The FCM and Official Languages
At its 1984 annual conference, the FCM reaffirmed its commitment to protect and promote official language rights. By the end of the 1990s, the two official languages had become essentially equivalent within the administration of the FCM. French is now heard at the FCM offices almost as often as English; no official documents are in one language only. At conferences, workshops, and board and committee meetings, the predominant language is English, reflecting the balance of numbers within Canada, but simultaneous interpretation is almost always available, and French is used readily.

The acid test for the FCM was the existence of a unilingual francophone on the national Board of Directors for four years in the 1990s. This councillor participated fully at the board level and on committees. She said she felt a high level of comfort when participating and became a firm believer in the effectiveness of the FCM as a vehicle for securing municipal objectives. She also praised the FCM for its promotion of understanding between francophones and anglophones and between Quebecers and people from other provinces.

A unilingual francophone councillor would have been unlikely to have sought membership of the FCM board before the mid-1990s. Had it happened, it is doubtful the comfort level would have been as high. There is still reluctance among Quebec mayors and councillors to put themselves forward for board membership, but the reluctance manifestly lessens with the passing years.

Part of the comfort level of Quebecers with the FCM arises from the structure of the organization. One of its five table officers is always from Quebec. In one year, a Quebecer will be third vice-president, in the next year second vice president, and so on through first vice-president, president, and past president. It is usually but by no means always the same person who goes through this cycle. Representatives of the other four regions – Atlantic; Ontario; British Columbia and Yukon; and Prairies, Northwest Territories, and Nunavut – go through the same cycle. Nominating committees over the years have been especially sensitive to requests to avoid Quebec's occupancy of the presidency at times of heightened tension over sovereignty issues, such as the periods around the referendums.

The relative regularity of accession of Quebecers to the FCM presidency – Quebec presidents, all francophones, were elected in 1978, 1982, 1987, 1992, and 1998 – is in sharp contrast to the previous decades, when Quebec presidents of the CFMM were elected only in 1953, 1962, and 1971.

Questions of Quebec's distinctiveness have not become major issues in the FCM's discussions in recent years. The leadership of the FCM has become skilled at focusing the attention of the organization on matters of concern to municipalities throughout Canada. The everyday predicaments of Quebec municipalities differ little from those of their counterparts in Nova Scotia or Saskatchewan. Once the mission of the FCM had been clarified in the early 1980s, it became much easier to steer activity away from matters that evoke the differences between Quebec and the rest of Canada and toward areas in which Canadian communities face similar challenges.

What Caused the Turnaround
Meisel and Lemieux attributed many of the difficulties experienced by the CFMM in relation to Quebec municipalities to the insensitivities of George Mooney, who served as executive director from the CFMM's founding in 1937 until his death in 1965. The CFMM declined further during the next seventeen years. James Knight became the executive director in 1982, and the organization has prospered since then. The personality and skill of the executive director of an organization such as the CFMM-FCM are profoundly important, but there are other factors at play too.

Knight soon proved himself to be a master organization builder with unusually well-developed sensitivities to the nuances of both Canadian federalism and the aspirations of municipal governments. As an organization builder, he saw the need for members, members, and more members. They would come, above all, through visits by representatives of member councils to non-member councils at which the many advantages of membership could be explained. This meant having a strong case and strong staff support, both of which Knight supplied. He also saw the need for symbols of permanence, hence the move to purchase a landmark headquarters building. He saw the need too for a major expansion of activities, such as a dynamic International Office, which often dealt in French with the Canadian International Development Agency (CIDA) and with francophone countries. His handling of Quebec issues was especially deft. He understood well that Quebec was not like the other provinces, and he understood equally well just how far this view was shared in the rest of Canada. The strength of the opposition in Quebec to establishing the FCM's International Office provided a powerful lesson, if one was needed, as to how matters concerning Quebec had to be handled.

Having said this, we should also add that much of the organization's growth during the 1980s may have happened with just about whoever was the executive director. The FCM was ready for growth, and other organizations – for example, the UMQ – grew at this time. The growth may have been greater with Knight than it might have been with another executive director, but the FCM would surely have grown or died.

Knight's particular value to the FCM may have been during the 1990s, when the fierce storms that buffeted municipalities were weathered. The strength and effectiveness of the administration Knight had built during the 1980s were invaluable to the FCM. The combination has enabled the organization to thrive in difficult times, although it has attracted some criticism that the organization has become overly prudent and cautious. The robust survival of the FCM during the difficult 1990s has made it possible to think about new roles for the organization, one being the development of a stronger research capacity with respect to current and emerging issues of local government.

The Dynamics of Affiliation of Quebec Municipalities with the CFMM-FCM

Despite some positive developments, there is no avoiding the fact that the weight of Quebec members within the FCM has fallen slowly and steadily over the past four decades, from being over-represented in relation to Canada's population in the 1950s to being under-represented today. Now, about 15 percent of FCM members are Quebec municipalities. A weighting by municipal size would bring this share to nearly 20 percent – largely on account of the City of Montreal – slightly below Quebec's proportion of Canada's population. We should stress again that the decline has been *relative*. As the CFMM-FCM's overall membership weight has fallen and then risen, so has the membership from Quebec. Indeed, the current level of membership from Quebec, while being relatively the lowest for decades, is also absolutely the highest, at close to 100 municipalities.[8]

Meisel and Lemieux emphasized the impact of events in Quebec on the participation of Quebec municipalities in the CFMM. A more complete view should also give weight to the extent to which the organization is seen to be useful to its members, whether in Quebec or in the rest of Canada.

The basic dynamic of affiliation of Quebec municipalities with the CFMM-FCM during the period studies is thus as follows. The overwhelming feature is that Quebec was like any other province in that the number of its municipal members rose and fell in parallel with the rise and fall of the overall membership of the organization. A second and much weaker feature is that over time there has been a very gradual disengagement of Quebec municipalities. The third fact has been the departure and rejoining of the City of Montreal, which, in the years it happened, overshadowed everything else.

Provincial Associations of Municipalities

During the 1970s, the municipal associations in the provinces were less dramatically affected by the events that were so traumatic for the CFMM-FCM. Their focus was largely on their day-to-day relationships with their provincial governments. In Ontario and Quebec, they had to cope with the creation of regional governments and urban communities, which added a new type of upper-tier municipal government. Quebec also transformed the system of counties by creating ninety-six new regional county municipalities. Municipalities and their associations also had to cope with a harsher fiscal environment and resulting constraints on provincial-municipal transfers than had been the case in the free-spending 1960s.

Quebec

The Quebec government, especially after the election of the Parti québécois in 1976, was resolutely opposed to the concept of tri-level conferences and to most of the aspirations of the federal Ministry of State for Urban Affairs. The UMQ was careful to steer clear of any formal involvement in the national tri-level experiment. Quebec's minister of municipal affairs, a former mayor, nevertheless, gave a laudatory impromptu statement at the first tri-level conference in 1972, but his sentiments were quickly disavowed by the provincial government.

During the early 1970s, the federal government tried through various means to establish a more direct presence in local communities, partly in an effort to appear more relevant to voters (especially in Quebec and in urban areas) and partly to overcome regional disparities within Canada. These efforts produced a strong reaction from the provincial ministers of municipal affairs, who issued a declaration protesting federal interference in municipal activities.

During the first term of the Parti québécois government after 1976, Minister of Municipal Affairs for Quebec Jacques Léonard introduced legislation to prevent Quebec municipalities from dealing with the federal government without going through the provincial government. The legislation also provided that any direct transfer of funds to a municipality by the federal government would be deducted from provincial transfers to that municipality. Léonard had wanted even tougher legislation to counter what he saw as federal interference through direct aid for municipal infrastructure under winter works and regional economic development programs.

The UMQ, led by Francis Dufour, the separatist mayor of Jonquière, led a fight against the more extreme elements of Léonard's proposed legislation. Eventually, an agreement was negotiated between the UMQ and the Quebec government. In this agreement, the municipalities accepted the general principle that the federal government should not be involved in municipal activities and that municipalities would not seek federal money (though common-sense exceptions would be permitted).

Although the law is still on the books, it is no longer a major source of tension. The need for day-to-day practical communications between some municipalities and federal agencies (e.g., some 40 percent of the Quebec

City downtown is federally owned property) on matters such as ports and canals has been recognized informally.

Closer relations developed between the UMQ and the FCM in the 1980s and 1990s. The executive directors of the UMQ from 1978 on, Luc Lacharité (1978-86) and his successor, Raymond L'Italien, both developed good working relationships and a mutually agreed scope of activity with their counterpart at the FCM, James Knight. This relationship was strengthened with the return of the City of Montreal to the FCM. Two Quebec mayors (Jean Pelletier and Jean Corbeil) served as presidents of both the UMQ and the FCM during this period.

The "no" results of the Quebec referendums of 1980 and 1995 led to a more relaxed atmosphere for Quebec municipalities and their associations in their dealings with the FCM. The message of the referendum results even to supporters of Quebec independence was that Quebecers should work constructively within the existing constitutional framework at least "until next time."

The UMQ has developed a mutually beneficial relationship with the FCM. The Quebec association believes that the FCM has been useful to Quebec municipalities because it has been effective in dealing with some difficult issues with the federal government, such as the GST and payments in lieu of taxation on federal property. The FCM has also been useful in providing benchmarking information from experiences in other Canadian municipalities.

At one point, the government of Quebec attempted to impose a provincial coordinating committee to review the international activities of Quebec municipalities, particularly those organized through the FCM. The committee, to have been made up of provincial civil servants and staff of the UMQ and the UMRCQ (l'Union des municipalités régionales de comté et des municipalités locales), was to approve any CIDA funding that might have gone to Quebec municipalities. The UMQ boycotted this technocratic approach and tried to persuade the provincial government to permit municipalities to take part freely in international programs. (Montreal and Quebec City had engaged in international activities well before the CIDA-supported FCM international municipal cooperation program.)

Because the Quebec government did not provide funding for an alternative Quebec-based international municipal cooperation program, Quebec municipalities continued to participate in the FCM program. In the 1990s, the UMQ itself was operating one FCM-managed, CIDA-supported, international cooperation program involving collaboration on staff training with the Association of Municipalities of Chile. Staff from the FCM and UMQ worked together in a program to strengthen the municipal association of Vietnam. The FCM has also dealt directly with l'Association des directeurs-généraux municipaux du Québec. In some of these FCM programs, senior municipal staff in Quebec have taken leave – sometimes paid, sometimes unpaid – to organize and participate in international missions funded by CIDA.

Overall, the successful cooperation between the FCM and provincial associations in Quebec on international programs demonstrates that it is possible to accommodate conflicting views and achieve positive results through sensitive management. These events suggest that the issues of the 1960s that bedevilled relationships among Quebec municipalities, their associations, and the federal and provincial governments have been overcome and that a new equilibrium has emerged in which the federal government is essentially absent.

Ontario

Since 1982, when it absorbed the rural and upper-tier associations, the Association of Municipalities of Ontario (AMO) has been the acknowledged representative and voice of Ontario municipalities. It has been a traditional and effective association focused on service to the membership. In the 1990s, AMO went through several ups and downs, several executive directors, and a fluctuating number of staff, particularly those devoted to policy and research. It has always had a somewhat smaller staff than the UMQ, even though in 1999 its membership covered almost all Ontario municipalities.

AMO presented a series of position papers in the early 1990s to the provincial government on the future of the municipal sector, culminating in a proposed bill of rights for local governments, the Ontario Charter. It called for a disentanglement of provincial and municipal responsibilities and a new municipal act that would treat municipalities as an order of government.

In 1997, the Ontario government, as part of its policy of deregulating, simplifying, and downsizing government, reshaped the entire framework of provincial-municipal relations. It responded to AMO's position on disentanglement in a provincial-municipal "who does what" exercise by abolishing almost all conditional grants to municipalities, assuming more provincial control over education, but giving municipalities unfettered responsibility for most local services. It brought forward a draft municipal act along the lines of AMO's proposal and reduced the number of municipalities in the province from 820 to fewer than 590. Among the dramatic actions it took was the amalgamation of Metropolitan Toronto and its six local municipalities in January 1998 to create a single city of 2.4 million people.

These changes will have an impact on AMO and the FCM. The increased size and strength of municipalities provide a potential base for stronger municipal associations. On the other hand, creation of a city the size of Toronto (more populous than six of the ten provinces) opens the potential of an increase in the direct relationships of the city with the provincial and federal governments, bypassing the associations.

National linguistic issues have had an impact on AMO. In 1986, linguistic tensions were raised by the passage of Ontario's French Language Services Act and the reaction to it by groups such as the Alliance for the Preservation of English in Canada. The French Language Services Act, which came into full effect in 1989, gave Ontario francophones the right to receive provincial government services in French in municipalities with at least 5,000 franco-phones or where at least 10 percent of the population had French as their mother tongue. The act does not provide for an absolute right to French-language *municipal* services in the designated areas, but it allows municipal-ities to opt in to the act's coverage.

A linguistic "crisis" was provoked in January 1990 by Mayor Joe Fratesi of Sault Ste. Marie – among the largest designated centres – who persuaded his council to adopt a resolution declaring the city to be unilingually English (eventually rescinded in August 1999). After a campaign by the Alliance for the Preservation of English in Canada, sixty-six other municipalities followed Sault Ste. Marie in adopting English-only resolutions. These municipal ac-tions were covered extensively in the Quebec media and in the French-language media in Ontario and were probably one of the causes of the loss of support in the public of both provinces for the Meech Lake Accord. They also gave rise to resolutions in seventy-five other Ontario municipalities supporting the principle of the French Language Services Act and opposing the position of the "unilingual" municipalities.

One result of these controversies was the establishment of l'Association française des municipalités de l'Ontario (AFMO), which grew to some twenty-eight members. Its basic objective is to promote the use of French within municipal governments and in the delivery of services and to protect the rights of francophones to municipal services in French. It provides a forum for francophone municipal councillors and administrators and advises On-tario government ministries and agencies on French language service needs. Its operating language is French.

AFMO became an associate member of AMO. Almost all of its members who had left AMO in 1990 rejoined it. AFMO also intended to seek affiliate membership in the FCM and the right to appoint a member to the FCM board, as is the case with the francophone municipal association in New Brunswick, noted below. Following the creation of AFMO, linguistic issues virtually disappeared from the AMO agenda. AFMO claims that AMO oper-ates unilingually in English. AMO claims to have some bilingual capacity but that financial constraints have prevented it from becoming a bilingual association. It has rarely adopted a bilingual format for its events.

AFMO has neither the strength nor the recognition its New Brunswick francophone counterpart enjoys. Nevertheless, it has added an important element to the preservation of the francophone society in Ontario. Its mem-bers are drawn primarily from eastern and northern Ontario, but its heart is in the Ottawa area, with leadership from Vanier and Gloucester. It maintains close links with other francophone organizations in Ontario and with its sister municipal organizations in New Brunswick and Manitoba. A representative of the UMQ is always invited to its annual meetings.

New Brunswick
There are now three associations of municipalities in New Brunswick, the Union of Municipalities of New Brunswick (UMNB), l'Association francophone des municipalités du Nouveau-Brunswick (AFMNB), and the Cities Association. This structure reflects the dual nature of New Brunswick society, where the Acadians have established over the past generation francophone educational, social, and economic institutions. The UMNB and AFMNB by and large reflect the towns and villages of the anglophone south and the francophone north of the province respectively. The Cities Association, with its seven members, represents larger centres, where the two language groups meet.

Before 1989, there had been no linguistic split in the structure of municipal associations in New Brunswick. The provincial government in the late 1980s had been against the establishment of a francophone association. But after the election of 1992, Premier McKenna appointed a francophone minister and deputy minister of municipal affairs, and soon after the provincial government formally recognized the AFMNB.

Linguistic tensions lessened in New Brunswick toward the end of the 1980s. By the 1990s, the provincial government and its services were bilingual; the Confederation of Regions Party, which opposed bilingualism, had virtually disappeared; and there was general acceptance of a dual society. Latterly, studies and actions relating to municipal amalgamations raised some linguistic issues. A proposed amalgamation of the greater Moncton area fell through because of the opposition of francophone Dieppe and anglophone Riverview.

There is a harmonious relationship between the FCM and the three New Brunswick municipal associations, each of which is represented on the FCM board. The provincial-municipal associations appreciate the FCM's support on networking, advice, and information on what is happening elsewhere, and on issues where federal government programs apply.

Analysis and Conclusions

A Relative Success
Our most important finding is that municipal associations in Canada, particularly the Federation of Canadian Municipalities, have helped Canadians to connect with and understand each other. Unlike many other national

organizations, the FCM has not only held together but has strengthened since the 1960s. The FCM has changed from an organization within which English was the rule, with some bilingual services, to an almost completely bilingual organization in which a unilingual francophone is nearly as comfortable as a unilingual anglophone. The federation made significant gains in respect and influence between 1982 and 1999 as the Canada-wide voice of municipalities. When it counts, Quebec members have been at the forefront of FCM initiatives and approaches to the federal government. Unlike the 1960s and 1970s, there has been almost no conflict between the FCM and the provincial associations of municipalities. The FCM stays close to federal issues and *never* deals with a provincial government or issue without dealing through the respective provincial-municipal association. Also unlike the 1960s and 1970s, there has been virtually no questioning of the value of the FCM among its members or other municipalities.

If there are caveats about the success of the FCM, they relate more to what could be done rather than to what has been done. There are nagging concerns that the FCM could be doing more to be an activist bridge between French-speaking Quebec municipalities and municipalities in the rest of the country and thereby increase its Quebec membership, which appears to have been declining slightly in relative terms. There is also a concern that the FCM may not be taking full advantage of its potential to be the only major national centre of municipal and urban expertise at a time when municipal and urban issues are becoming more pivotal to public policy, both in Canada and elsewhere in the world.

The Futility of Engaging in "High Policy"
In an essay entitled "How Canadians Connect," Harvey Lazar and Tom McIntosh concluded that solutions to Canadian issues are more likely to be achieved through "low politics" rather than the "high politics" of national constitutional or tax-sharing negotiations.[9] The FCM has learned to accept this truth, switching from the high politics of the 1970s to the pragmatism of the 1980s and 1990s.

The FCM in the 1970s tried to negotiate with the federal and provincial governments on the macrolevel on the highly symbolic issues of the Constitution and overall revenue sharing. These negotiations led to much symbolic posturing with few positive results for the municipal sector. The FCM became caught up in the constitutional exercise with a position contrary to that of Quebec and, to a lesser extent, those of other provinces. The attempt by the FCM to involve itself and the municipalities – when the federal government and the provinces were focused on trying to find an accommodation between Quebec and the rest of Canada – was doomed to failure.

The eleven governments were at the same time trying to fend off demands by other groups, such as Aboriginal and women's organizations, to play a direct role in the constitutional process. To have allowed these groups or the municipalities into the constitutional process would only have magnified the difficulties of trying to find an accommodation with Quebec. Thus, the constitutional venture by the FCM was essentially undertaken without allies among federal and provincial governments. Although the venture may have had the marginally beneficial impact of raising the profile of the FCM, it undermined the FCM's position with the provincial governments, the municipal associations in Quebec, and many of its own members, especially in Quebec.

Much the same result came from the FCM's emphasis through the tri-level negotiations on federal-provincial-municipal revenue sharing. The FCM had no allies among the federal and provincial governments – not even, on this issue, the federal Ministry of State for Urban Affairs – and no beneficial outcomes resulted for the municipal sector.

The Benefits of Engaging in "Low Policy" Negotiations

When municipal associations began to switch their policy priorities in the 1980s to a lower level, by negotiating on sectoral issues, and began to concentrate their lobbying efforts on provincial governments, they started to get better results. As for the FCM, it became more adroit in its relations with the federal government. By focusing on issues where that government had direct responsibility and could act pragmatically, as in the case of the GST or payments in lieu of federal taxes, the FCM succeeded in negotiating direct benefits for its members and for the entire municipal sector. In the case of the municipal infrastructure program in 1994, the FCM was able to assist the federal government with the implementation of a campaign promise in a manner that avoided the opposition of the provinces yet was of great benefit to its members. In the case of municipal international cooperation, the FCM has been able to use its expertise and legitimacy to assist in delivering a program that the federal government would be unable to undertake directly without opposition from Quebec and other provinces.

By declining to become involved in matters within provincial jurisdiction, the FCM has adapted itself to the changing political context in Canada. It has assisted in reaping the benefits of a disaggregation of the state and a new form of governance where more public policy decisions are made at the local level, sometimes with the public sector being only one actor among several.

Municipal Associations and Language

The FCM

What has happened on the language front reflects the gradual adaptation of Canadian society to a linguistic equilibrium. The FCM has improved both its formal and its informal linguistic capacity so that it now operates both externally and internally in both languages (which would be much more difficult if the head office were not in Montreal or Ottawa). Its permanent staff are almost all functionally bilingual, and most of its official external communications are in both English and French. Because of a predominance of unilingual anglophones among its members, its activities (except for the international office) are carried out more in English than in French. Nevertheless, it has reached a point where a unilingual francophone member of the Executive Committee can be both comfortable and effective. This is a major difference from the situation described in the research for the Meisel-Lemieux report, wherein the CFMM was an organization that provided some bilingual services but within which English was the rule. This transformation is not unlike that which took place within the federal government in Ottawa from the late 1960s to the late 1990s.

Quebec
L'Union des municipalités du Québec has not experienced linguistic crises over the past thirty years. It was never a formally bilingual organization and has not had formal policies requiring simultaneous interpretation or publication in both languages. Its key staff have always been bilingual and able to communicate in English with the declining anglophone proportion of the membership. The UMQ (and its sister organization representing regional county and rural municipalities) has followed overall trends toward a more unilingual "official" Quebec. At the 1999 annual conference of the UMQ in Montreal, French was virtually the universal language of the formal sessions and in the corridors.

In 1997, a group of suburban municipalities in the Montreal area broke away from the UMQ. Because many of these municipalities were primarily anglophone, the newly formed organization operates in both languages. What may be of interest here is that the breakaway took place because of financial, not linguistic, issues.

New Brunswick
Municipal associations in New Brunswick have followed the path of language practice in the province. From an essentially unilingual English-language framework for municipalities and their associations in the 1960s, there are now parallel francophone and anglophone municipal associations for the smaller local governments. The third association (of the seven largest cities) is more informal, and even though the membership includes both primarily francophone and primarily anglophone cities it operates mainly in English.

Ontario

As in New Brunswick, an association of francophone municipalities was created in Ontario at the beginning of the 1990s, largely because of a perceived lack of sensitivity to the French factor in the province's major municipal association. Unlike the situation in New Brunswick, however, the francophone association is not a parallel organization and does not replace the need for francophone municipalities to join AMO. The francophone association in Ontario has essentially restricted itself to lobbying and information activities specifically related to language issues. In this respect, the municipal association structure is closer to the institutional arrangements for Ontario's language policy, where French-language provincial services are concentrated in areas with francophone populations.

Summary

The four situations – in three provinces and at the national level – reflect the linguistic regimes and structures of the respective governments to a remarkable extent.

- In Ottawa, there is a formally bilingual national association.
- In Quebec, the main association essentially operates in French but with an informal capacity in English.
- In New Brunswick, there are parallel francophone and anglophone associations for towns and villages.
- In Ontario, the main association essentially operates in English, but a small francophone association operates in French for specific purposes.

Prospects for the Future

The Government of Canada is becoming less involved in the day-to-day aspects of running the country and more occupied with the crucial task of trying to reconcile domestic needs with increasing international pressures. In this context, municipalities and particularly the major metropolitan centres are becoming more important players in determining what happens in the country. Their associations will continue to have important roles in building linkages among them and in acting as the municipal voice for the province or the country.

The structure of municipalities in Canada is undergoing changes that will have an impact on their associations. Most of the provinces have come to the conclusion that, if municipalities are to undertake more responsibilities effectively, they need to be large enough and sophisticated enough to plan and implement a greater range of programs than many now carry out. Consolidation of municipalities is taking place in several provinces, particularly in urban and urbanizing areas. Between 1995 and 1999, for example, the number of municipalities in Ontario was reduced from 820 to fewer than 590. A study commissioned by the Quebec government on municipal finance released in the spring of 1999 recommended a sharp reduction in the total number of municipalities and the creation of strong regional governments around the major metropolitan areas.[10] The number of municipalities in Nova Scotia and New Brunswick has recently been sharply reduced.

Differences between rural areas and smaller centres, on the one hand, and larger urban centres, on the other, are increasing around the world. Whereas Canada was less than 70 percent urban at the beginning of the 1960s, it was almost 80 percent urban by the end of the 1990s. Some two-thirds of immigrants to Canada settle in three or four metropolitan areas. Toronto, Montreal, and Vancouver are becoming more like each other and less like the rest of their provinces. In these large multicultural metropolitan centres, old loyalties and old communities are no longer the sources of identity of the vast majority of their residents. In the debate over amalgamation of the City of Toronto, for example, the opposition was led by people whose roots in local communities were deep and long-standing. On the other hand, there was little apparent concern about the abolition of the former local municipalities among the hundreds of thousands of recent immigrants to Toronto whose new loyalties were to the metropolitan area and the country. In the large metropolitan centres, particularly among the young, French/English differences and the traditional themes of past constitutional debates are becoming less relevant. Change is the norm as people adapt to a more international and less parochial context.

The municipal governments of the large urban areas are facing similar issues:

- how to cope with new or downloaded responsibilities without new sources of revenue;
- how to deliver services sensitively to increasingly diverse populations;
- how to cope with urban sprawl, increased road traffic, and related matters;
- how to make urban transit systems viable;
- how to deal with an increasing polarization of incomes and an increasing incidence of poverty and homelessness;
- how to involve the private sector in the provision of infrastructure or the delivery of programs that were previously the sole responsibility of government;
- how to assist local employers to cope with the pressures of international competition; and
- how to restructure their local government system to manage the economic, social, and environmental challenges of their urban region.

Increasingly, local governments are having to face these issues without the kind of federal or provincial government assistance that was often important in the past (e.g., the abandoning by the federal and most provincial governments in the 1990s of support for subsidized housing). Cities are increasingly looking to the experiences of other local governments faced with similar challenges rather than seeking assistance from the federal or provincial governments.

The *de facto* decentralization of government means that in the future there will probably be even less direct federal-municipal program activity and less detailed provincial-municipal program relationships. For most issues, the Federation of Canadian Municipalities will be less relevant to the day-to-day concerns of local governments than was the CFMM in the early 1960s. No matter how sensitively and effectively it may operate, the federal government will not likely be a day-to-day presence in municipal operations.

Traditional Canadian debates about dualism, on language or on relations between Quebec and the rest of Canada, are more easily resolved within provinces than in the federal-provincial or tri-level arenas. The necessary accommodations have already been arrived at within the FCM and in its relations within the UMQ. The pragmatic problem-solving relationship is much less likely to break down on questions of principle.

The municipal associations and their large urban caucuses in particular are beginning to meet the growing need for forums where major centres can exchange experiences and develop common positions on the challenges that most of them face. Thus, the municipal associations have been building the agendas of their annual meetings and the caucuses of their large urban centres around issues such as transit, homelessness, regional restructuring, and public-private partnerships.

The federal and provincial governments are by and large not well structured to deal adequately with these urban issues. The federal government has no centre of expertise or responsibility in urban affairs and has dismantled the urban programs it once had. Most provincial governments are organized around traditional responsibilities reflecting their more rural and resource-oriented past. Their ministries of municipal affairs tend to focus on the concerns of smaller and more rural municipalities, which have required more provincial technical assistance than have the urban centres. Provincial governments in the 1990s began to realize that their future economic competitiveness will increasingly depend on the health and transformation of their major urban centres. This realization, however, coincided with their abdication of responsibility from urban issues through programs of deregulation, downsizing, and downloading.

When the Ministry of State for Urban Affairs was abolished in 1979, the most important source of funding and ideas in urban research in Canada was lost. Although there are several institutions in the country carrying out urban research, they are almost all in precarious financial situations. Many organizations that used to concentrate on Canadian urban issues have become increasingly dependent on funding by agencies concerned with international cooperation and have shifted their focus to urban issues in the developing world. The FCM has never been heavily research-oriented, but there is a gap that it is perhaps in the best position to fill.

Current issues in provincial-municipal relations, as well as internal urban issues, are similar in Quebec and in the other, especially more urban, Canadian provinces. As with many other issues in Canada, the debate is taking place in Quebec in French and elsewhere in mostly in English, albeit with insufficient cross-pollination. By and large, Quebec francophones are unaware that Canadians in the rest of Canada are dealing with the same issues. Anglophones outside Quebec who are much less bilingual are even less aware of the striking similarities among current challenges. The intense interest in Montreal in 1999 in the amalgamation debate in Toronto is a notable exception; it was stimulated by concerns that Toronto might be gaining an advantage in economic competitiveness. There was less awareness in Toronto that Montreal was going through parallel debates about possible amalgamations and regional institutions.

This changing context provides a greater opportunity for constructive bridge building by national and provincial associations in the field of municipal affairs than in most other Canadian fields of activity. The constitutional context that governs municipal activities and responsibilities is similar in Quebec to that in the rest of Canada. The pressures on local governments are similar, as are many of the demographic, social, and economic trends. This is very different, for example, from the cultural area, where French-speaking Quebec and the rest of Canada tend to operate within two solitudes. For the past twenty years, municipal associations have largely avoided the temptations of engaging in high politics and have attempted pragmatically to meet the concerns of their members. Quebec municipalities have not engaged municipalities in the rest of the country to the extent that takes maximum advantage of common interests, but the ruptures that have occurred in other national associations have been avoided and cooperation has been steadily built on a few practical issues.

The current Canadian context leaves a large gap in dealing with and taking advantage of the potential of our urban and metropolitan centres, nationally and internationally. Much of the country's economic competitiveness, social cohesion, and environmental sustainability will depend on how its urban regions are managed. Reaching the potential of the urban regions will depend in considerable part on taking advantage of the best examples from elsewhere, and it will require an enabling and supporting approach by the federal and provincial governments.

In the absence of a formal centre of responsibility for urban affairs in the federal government, a strong municipal association may be needed to reinforce the Canadian presence internationally on the growing number of issues where action at the urban level will be essential. Increasingly during the 1990s, it seemed that implementation of the Kyoto climate change agreement could depend to a considerable extent on actions by municipal governments. If Canada is to live up to its commitments in a renewed Great Lakes water quality agreement, actions by local governments to deal with the impacts of population and economic growth in the Golden Horseshoe may be vital. Many of the issues being discussed in bodies such as the Organization for Economic Co-operation and Development (OECD) are issues for which the responsible governments in Canada will increasingly be municipal.

At the United Nations City Summit in 1996, Canada was at a disadvantage because it had no institution within the federal government with expertise in or responsibility for overall urban issues. That summit concluded that in the twenty-first century – the world's first urban century – the major challenge will be how the world's urban regions will be managed. The challenge for Canadian cities will be not only how well Halifax benefits from a successful experience in Victoria or Quebec City but also how its port arrangements can compete globally.

There is a great potential, therefore, for municipal associations in Canada to become stronger bridge builders across the language groups, cultures, and regions of Canada. The Federation of Canadian Municipalities will have to respond to its membership, but there is a great opportunity for it to fill a gap in the Canadian governmental structure by becoming not only the national voice of municipalities but also the centre of Canadian expertise on urban and municipal affairs. Influential and effective provincial associations of municipalities will increasingly be seen as the representatives of a level or order of government.

To live up to its potential, it will be necessary for the FCM to be a model of sensitivity in its approach to linguistic and federal-provincial issues and to take the lead in ensuring that Canada has a centre of expertise on urban and local issues in a decentralizing but globalizing world. National and provincial associations of municipalities will have to fashion their activities and practices to meet the needs of both their urban and their rural members as they represent and promote the interests of the municipal sector as a whole.

5
Associations in the Voluntary Health Sector: The Heart and Stroke Foundations of Canada and the Huntington Societies of Canada and Quebec

Richard Simeon

In this chapter, I examine patterns of association across languages and provinces in one of the largest, wealthiest, and most influential voluntary associations in the Canadian health care sector: the Canadian Heart and Stroke Foundations. The focus is primarily on the national body – the Heart and Stroke Foundation of Canada (HSFC) – and two of the provincial foundations – the Heart and Stroke Foundation of Ontario (HSFO) and the Fondation des maladies du coeur du Québec – and on the internal lives of these groups as they entered the twenty-first century.[1] These foundations are devoted to supporting research and public education on all aspects of cardiovascular disease, pervasive illnesses that will touch almost all Canadians in their lifetimes. Such diseases are no respecters of regional, linguistic, or ethnic boundaries; they transcend all such identities. Yet this study shows that even such a focused and apparently apolitical group reflects within itself many of the tensions in the larger federal system. As one former HSFO president put it, "the whole foundation is a microcosm of Canada." Indeed, the dissatisfaction of one foundation, that in Ontario, almost led to the breakup of the national foundation. The manner in which the dispute was resolved – including the development of a constitutional "federation agreement," complete with a division of powers, fiscal arrangements, and a dispute settlement mechanism – bears an uncanny resemblance to some of the recent Canadian constitutional debates.

Quebec has not been a driver of recent change in the life of the foundation. However, the study reveals a constant, if low-level, tension that reflects subtle linguistic or cultural differences and the inevitable consequences for the minority language participants in an association that, despite its genuine commitment to bilingualism, functions at the national level largely in English. These differences interact with the basic agreement on the goals and values of the organization and its commitment to professionalism. While anglophone members may often resent the time, energy, and resources that

go into maintaining a bilingual organization, it is the francophone participants who must bear the main costs of communication across the language
barrier; when they interact in national board meetings, they almost invariably must do so in their second language. The result is what may be described
as "asymmetrical bilingualism." In terms of organizational structure, while
there is some informal recognition of the distinctness of Quebec, the formal
structures of the organization reflect the constitutional principle of "equality
of the provinces."

The analysis suggests that, while there is a relatively effective partnership
between the national and provincial foundations in the achievement of their
basic goal of fighting stroke and heart disease, the actual and potential contributions of such groups to the broader goal of building "social capital" for
the wider society in the form of positive linkages and face-to-face communications among members of different linguistic and regional groups may be
limited. The linkages that exist occur primarily at the board and committee
level rather than in interactions among the thousands of volunteers who
make up the rank and file, in a group version of "elite accommodation."

A very different voluntary association devoted to a specific set of diseases
is the Huntington Society of Canada/Société Huntington du Canada (HSC/
SHC). It addresses the needs of a much less common malady yet one with
devastating effects on its sufferers and their families. The disease is a fatal,
inherited brain disorder, with a median onset at age thirty-eight. Fifty percent
of the children of those with the defective gene will inherit the disease.
About 1 in 10,000 Canadians will contract the disease, and many more are
affected indirectly as family, caregivers, and the like. The Huntington Society
is therefore a much smaller organization than the HSFC. Its professional
staff, resources, and public presence are much more limited. It is structured
as a single national association with local branches across the country, and
it is allied with the Société Huntington du Québec (SHQ), which has a separate legal existence but which remains dependent on the national body in
several crucial respects. It is discussed throughout the chapter as a counter-
point to the central focus on the larger Heart and Stroke Foundations.

Why choose these cases? As will be evident, the Canadian voluntary health
sector is enormously diverse; there can be no purely "representative" case.
The two studied here were selected on the advice of several advisers, who
believed that they reflected the tensions and issues faced by many groups
in the sector, with the HSFC sharing many characteristics with the other
large, visible health charities and the HSC/SHC reflecting many of the challenges facing smaller organizations. I recognize that using only two cases
makes it impossible to generalize in any more than speculative terms about
the sector as a whole. The trade-off I make here is that a detailed case study

permits a far more nuanced analysis of each case than would otherwise be possible.

Group Profiles

Heart and Stroke Foundations

The Heart and Stroke Foundations are among the most high-profile voluntary organizations in the health sector. In a survey of Canadians' attitudes toward charitable organizations, the HSFC ranked second only to the Canadian Cancer Society in public recognition. The mission statement of the HSFC indicates that it is "a national, non-profit organization whose mission is to further the study, prevention and reduction of disability and death from heart disease and stroke through research, education and the promotion of healthy lifestyles. In recent years, the Foundation has also taken a leadership role in advocating for heart healthy public policy."[2] These goals are shared by all the provincial member foundations. For example, the Ontario foundation states that it is "a community based volunteer organization whose mission it is to reduce the risk of premature death and disability from heart disease and stroke by raising funds for research and health promotion." Similar mission statements guide the activities of the Quebec foundation and those in all the other provinces.

All the Heart and Stroke Foundations thus share a common goal and similar patterns of activity. Funding research on cardiovascular disease is the "number one strategic priority."[3] It represented slightly over half of the combined spending of all eleven foundations in 1998 – $41 million. These contributions support about 60 percent of all heart and stroke research in Canada. Health promotion is the second major goal. This includes a wide variety of programs to educate the public about the risks of heart disease and ways to prevent it, programs that include February Heart Month and June Stroke Awareness Month, the HeartSmart Shopper, Health Check, and HeartSmart Women. Such programs represented 21 percent of total expenditures, or $16 million, across Canada in 1998, with a further $5 million going toward community development. Campaign and administration expenses accounted for the remainder of the overall budget. All the foundations also dedicate time and resources to advocacy in federal and provincial governments on a variety of health-related issues and to developing partnerships with like-minded groups to advance their goals.

The Heart and Stroke Foundations act as a bridge between the community and the research and treatment world based in hospitals and universities. In the community, they deploy an army of volunteers in a wide variety of fundraising activities, and they provide a broad spectrum of programs to promote healthy lifestyles. The funds raised in the community are then directed to the promotion of research.

The organization describes itself as a federation. In some respects, "confederation" is the more apt term. The HSFC is in many respects a creature of the provincial foundations. Representatives of the provinces constitute a majority on the Board of Directors. Provincial foundations hold independent charitable donation numbers from Revenue Canada. This is a major resource ensuring the autonomy of the provinces; it is counterbalanced by the fact that the foundation's familiar logo and trademark – another vital resource – are owned by HSFC. The vast bulk of fundraising occurs at the provincial level, and provinces contribute to the national foundation's budget. As will be discussed later, in recent years the provinces, led by Ontario, the largest and strongest of the provincial foundations, have exerted tighter control over national activities, even as the national foundation has sought with considerable success to clarify its role and demonstrate its value to the provinces.

To raise these funds, the foundations depend on volunteer boards of directors, highly professional staff organizations, and an army of more than 250,000 volunteers across the country. The bulk of the funds raised comes from those affected in some way by the diseases associated with heart and stroke; a much smaller proportion – 20-25 percent – can be seen as simply altruistic, though the distinction is often far from clear. Increasingly, fundraisers are looking toward building partnerships and sponsorships with private corporations. This appears to be a response to a static or declining revenue base in philanthropic or altruistic sources. "It is the huge growth area," noted one official. The HSFO has been particularly active in developing these new corporate relationships, though so far they provide only about 5 percent of revenues. Such initiatives raise the prospect of interprovincial conflict as different foundations target the same sponsors and as sponsors look for national exposure. For example, just as the Ontario foundation was working on a partnership arrangement with a major margarine company, Quebec was negotiating its own arrangement with another firm. As one official who was involved put it, "Ontario said, 'Quebec, what are you doing? XYZ wants exclusivity.' But they did not consult." Such competition also enhances the disparities between provincial bodies since major corporate sponsors are likely to be based in Ontario and, to a lesser extent, Quebec. The shift may also have some implications for the nature of civil society. To the extent that the foundation's activities are increasingly focused on a professionalized staff, working with a "business model" of internal governance, with volunteers who bring professional skills to the board, and with corporate donors whose participation is tied to advertising or corporate recognition, the idea of the role of volunteers in a citizen-based civil society may be diminished. Finding the right balance will be a challenge facing many charitable associations in Canada in the future.

The Heart and Stroke Foundation of Canada

As already noted, the HSFC is a creature of its provincial members. In the words of one provincial executive director, "it is a true confederation; it is not top down." The presidents of the provincial foundations constitute a majority of the board (although in board meetings they are expected to wear "national" hats rather than simply act as delegates for their provinces). A board workshop in 1996 concluded that board members "owe their duty to the HSFC, not to their respective provinces," and that their duty is "to determine what is in the best interests of the HSFC as a whole, not a part, or parts, thereof." This is, however, a matter of continuing tension. "This dichotomy is real and alive; it has only been papered over with words." One former provincial president reported that he was often torn between his role on the national board (where he might be accused of being too "provincial") and his role on the provincial board (where he might be accused of selling out to the national perspective). Partly in response to these difficulties, in recent years a parallel governance structure, representing the provinces as "shareholders," has begun to emerge (this is discussed in more detail below). The other members of the HSFC board include six officers of the foundation, together with three members at large. This group too is made up primarily of former provincial executives. In addition, the board includes three non-voting associate members representing cognate associations (Canadian Cardiovascular Society, Canadian Stroke Society, and Canadian Council of Cardiovascular Nurses) with which the HSFC is closely associated.

This board structure does create a number of difficulties. The equal representation of the provinces is in tension with the marked differences in size, effectiveness, and financial contributions of the member foundations. It does not give greater weight to the larger, stronger provinces or to Quebec. On occasion, "Ontario feels hard done by, by being undercut by the smaller provinces – and they in turn resent Ontario 'bullying.'" Since provincial presidents serve only two-year terms – and thus generally serve only two years on the national board – it is difficult to build long-term trust relationships within the board or between it and the provinces.

The national foundation has limited independent ability to raise funds – rather, it derives its financial base from provincial contributions. Most foundation programs are developed and delivered at the provincial level. It is thus considerably more decentralized than some of the other major national health charities, such as the Canadian Cancer Society, which functions on a more classically federal model, and the Canadian Diabetes Association, which is structured as a single national body, with provincial branches.

Nevertheless, the HSFC has a number of important responsibilities. It manages a single national peer review process for research proposals, so that the funding of research across Canada is based on merit rather than on provincial preferences. However, once these determinations are made, the actual funding flows through the provincial foundations. "They want their share, their visibility."

The HSFC also provides the authoritative voice on policy issues that are national and international in scope. In this role, it makes policy statements and representations to the federal government on many health-related issues. It organizes an annual Heart on the Hill Day, which in 1998 brought seventeen board members and senior volunteers, six of the provincial executive directors, and four senior staff members to discuss health issues with members of Parliament and cabinet ministers. National staff played a major role in supporting the development of a new federal initiative to create a Canadian Institute of Health Research, which began in 2000. The current executive director has played a leading role in developing closer partnerships among organizations in the health sector. For example, the HSFC is a member of and a leading participant in the National Volunteer Health Organizations (NHVO), collaborated with eight other voluntary health groups on a national survey in 1998, and plays a major role in the sixteen-member Council for Health Research in Canada. In recent years, the HSFC has co-hosted (with the Canadian Cancer Society) the first Health Charities Roundtable, bringing presidents and CEOs of twenty-five organizations together with government representatives. Its goal is to explore cooperation on shared concerns and coordination of representations to government on national health issues such as smoking, reinforce their ability to undertake concerted action, and improve transparency and accountability. In 1998, the president of the HSFC chaired a meeting of health charities with Minister of Health Allan Rock, designed to strengthen relations between Health Canada and the voluntary sector. The HSFC is also responsible for most of the international activities of the organization.

In addition, the national body sets national strategic objectives and policies and plays an important coordinating role with respect to the dissemination of materials, such as books, pamphlets, and promotional materials that are to be distributed nationally. It also manages pensions and benefits programs for foundation employees across the country. An important feature of the organization's work is that "national" projects approved by the board are not necessarily carried out by the staff of the HSFC. Rather, they are assigned to a "lead province," which develops the program on behalf of all the members, who contribute to the cost on a proportional basis. Reflecting its size and strength, five of the seven such projects in 1999 were led by Ontario. A major initiative to establish a comprehensive and interactive new website for use by all member foundations (unveiled 31 January 2000) was assigned jointly to Ontario and Quebec, with the primary design and development undertaken by Ontario. This is another example of the confederal structure. To conduct these activities, the foundation maintains a professional staff of about twenty-two members, headed by the executive director.

As will be discussed in more detail below, the HSFC appears to be entering a period of relative calm and increased effectiveness after a recent history of considerable turbulence. As one knowledgeable observer put it, "the HSFC has been under stress for years." "By the mid-1990s, the board was dysfunctional – four people had to be approached before one could be persuaded to agree to be president," noted one former president. Said another official, "by the 1990s, the foundation had been traumatized by internal and external problems and by declining revenues." The basic tension was between it and the member associations. The membership believed that the HSFC had been treading on provincial turf and that its national staff had become bloated and inefficient. These tensions were exacerbated by the presence of a long-standing executive director who was perceived to be unresponsive to provincial concerns. A short-lived replacement did not work out. In 1994, a new executive director, a former senior federal civil servant and a director of policy for the Canadian Medical Association, was recruited. He has been able to play a major role in renegotiating relationships among the foundations, clarifying the roles and responsibilities of the national body, and promoting partnerships and cooperation among health-related charities at the national level. Under pressure from some provinces, an Administrative Audit Committee was established, and its recommendations led to significant cuts in central staff and activities. "The fundamental challenge for the national board was to bring about a situation in which the provinces saw it not as a cost but as value-added." As evidence of a turn-around, one participant noted that today "there is competition for the presidency."

The Heart and Stroke Foundation of Ontario
As I have noted, the Ontario foundation is the largest of the provincial Heart and Stroke Foundations. It maintains thirty-six offices across the province, supporting 104 chapters. It employs a professional staff of over 200, depends on the work of 65,000 volunteers, and involves about 600,000 participants in its various activities. It supports about two-thirds of the research on heart and stroke in Ontario, and it believes that its educational and health promotion activities reach millions of people across Ontario each year. The HSFO raises about 60 percent of the total funds raised by all the Heart and Stroke Foundations in Canada ($51.7 million in 1998). It is little wonder, therefore, that Ontario often thinks that it is capable of going its own way, believes that it has little need for the services provided by the national body,

and resents the disparity between its contributions to the HSFC and its weight in national decision making.

La Fondation des maladies de coeur du Québec/Heart and Stroke Foundation of Quebec

In 1955, ten Montreal women, all anglophone, and chiefly the spouses of Montreal cardiologists, put up $4,200 to form the Quebec Heart Society. In 1965, the organization affiliated with the Canadian Heart Foundation, the predecessor to the HSFC. Today the Quebec foundation maintains a head office in Montreal and twelve regional offices across the province. It has about fifty employees, thirty-two based in the head office. Its mandate and goals are the same as those of the other provincial foundations. In recent years, it has been able to draw on the efforts of about 12,000 volunteers.

In terms of fundraising and volunteer activity, Quebec falls well short of some other provincial foundations, especially that of Ontario. This appears to be a pattern consistent with other associations in the voluntary sector. For reasons not easily explained, Quebecers appear to be less involved in volunteer activity and charitable giving than citizens in other provinces. On the other hand, a disproportionate number of the leading researchers and practitioners in cardiovascular medicine are concentrated in a few leading institutions in Quebec. The result is that Quebec appears to be a strong net beneficiary of the foundation's research spending: the research funds that flow to the province outweigh its financial contributions. This disparity is another source of tension within the organization. But it also reduces any thought in Quebec that it would prefer to go it alone.

Huntington Society of Canada/Société Huntington du Canada

The HSC's website identifies the society as a national network of volunteers and professionals "working to build a brighter tomorrow for everyone whose life is touched by Huntington's Disease." In contrast to the HSFC, its primary emphasis has been on providing counselling and treatment services to those afflicted by the disease and their families. Raising funds for research, however, has recently become a larger priority – as a result of major progress in understanding the genetic basis of disease and of newly understood linkages between Huntington's, Parkinson's, and amyotrophic lateral sclerosis (ALS).

The society was founded in 1973 in Cambridge, Ontario. Very much the inspiration of its first and long-standing executive director, it began as a "kitchen table operation." His own family, and one of his students, had been touched by the disease. "We realized a support group was necessary, because there was simply no information about the disease anywhere." A first local meeting drew eight people; shortly thereafter, a meeting in Toronto attracted 125 participants, and a $5,000 donation from one person triggered the formation of the national group. Quebecers were involved from the outset.

One of the original members soon moved to Quebec, and a leading researcher on the disease, based in Quebec, leant his support.

Today the HSC is a national body. It maintains resource centres, usually staffed by a social worker, in nine provinces (with Prince Edward Island being served from Nova Scotia). It has about sixty local volunteer groups, most very small, across the country. The board normally has about thirteen members, chosen largely for their dedication as volunteers or for their specific professional expertise. There are no stated rules about regional or provincial representation, with the exception of an arrangement between the Huntington Society of Canada and the Huntington Society of Quebec for representation on each other's board. A meeting each fall combines the annual general meeting, a board meeting, and a conference. It moves around the country, alternating between a meeting in central Canada, eastern Canada, and western Canada.

Quebec has the only distinct provincial society. Interestingly, it appears that the decision to establish a separate Quebec entity was driven by the need for registration in Quebec for the association to be able to tap funding support from the Quebec government. "We supported this. It was absolutely amicable; they had our full blessing." As will be discussed below, however, the relationship has not always been an easy one, largely because of the continued financial dependency of the Quebec society.

The Group Setting
There are approximately 150 national voluntary health organizations or charities in Canada. They are involved in a wide variety of activities. Some are addressed to a target population within the larger society, such as Aboriginal peoples, women, children, the disabled, and so on. Others focus on general issues facing the whole society – health and fitness promotion, monitoring population health, prevention of injuries, and the like. Still others are focused on specific diseases and their victims – heart and stroke, cancer, diabetes, and so on.

Their activities are equally diverse – supporting and complementing existing health services; exploring innovative and creative ways to provide such services; raising funds for research; providing assistance to victims, their families, and their friends; identifying emerging issues in the health field; and developing public policy.

They vary enormously in terms of size, resources, and visibility. The HSFC is at one end of the continuum. The HSC is much smaller, yet there remain many other associations closer to the "kitchen table" level of development. The two also differ in their primary focus – on research and development in the medical field for the HSFC and services to patients for the HSC. The relative balance between such goals is a common source of tension within health sector associations.

Organizational forms within the sector appear to vary widely – from the relatively confederal, such as the HSFC, to the classically federal, as with the Canadian Cancer Society, to more unitary forms, as with the Canadian Diabetes Association. Apparently, few of the federally organized bodies have clear federal "constitutions" setting out a clear division of responsibilities and funding for the group. There does not appear to be any clear rationale why one organizational form is chosen over another. It may depend as much on the organization's origins and history as it does on any calculation of the most appropriate and cost-effective institutional design. Most do appear, however, to have at least some elements of federalism in their designs, reflecting the political structure of the country, the concurrent responsibilities of governments in the health field, the need to retain a local presence, and regional and linguistic identities among their membership.

The federal Department of Health – Health Canada – regards the voluntary health sector as an important element of its constituency. A program of grants to assist national voluntary health organizations was established in 1983. However, this program was drastically cut back in the round of federal budget cuts, beginning in 1995, and only recently is a close working relationship between Health Canada and the sector being restored.

Health Canada has been especially interested in helping the many associations in the sector to coordinate their advice to government more effectively. There has been considerable progress in this direction, and the Heart and Stroke Foundation of Canada, especially through its executive director, has been a leader in these efforts. For example, at a meeting in April 1998 to strengthen relations between Health Canada and national health organizations, Minister Allan Rock stressed the need for government to have a single voice with which it could communicate effectively. The groups agreed in principle – but also expressed their desire to retain their ability to communicate with the government individually on their specific concerns.

Indeed, the work of the HSFC suggests that, as its president put it, "strategic partnerships are increasingly a tool of choice for organizations such as ours to maximize our reach while minimizing expenses."[4] Recent speeches and newsletters provide a number of examples, including co-sponsorship of the Twelfth Canadian Heart Health Network meeting together with the Nova Scotia Heart and Stroke Foundation, Heart Health Nova Scotia, Health Canada, and Nova Scotia Health; a partnership with the Canadian Cardiovascular Society and Health Canada to create a state-of-the-art database; and development of a Family Fun Pack produced with Health Canada and the TD Bank Financial Group.

Each of the provincial foundations also participates in provincial-level networks. For example, the Quebec foundation is a major player in the Quebec-based Forum québécois des intervenants en santé cardiovasculaire.

It now groups more than forty associations, health care agencies, government ministries, research centres, hospitals, and universities.

At the Canadian level, this sector appears to function chiefly in English. In one catalogue of national voluntary health organizations, only 12 of the more than 150 names of responsible officials were obviously francophone, or less than 10 percent. Only a few of the members of the Joint Working Group in the voluntary sector had francophone names. Virtually all the national associations in the field "function essentially in English." The major exceptions appear to be the associations focused on hemophilia and epilepsy, both of which have their headquarters in Montreal.

It is noteworthy that a major national study aimed at improving governance in the voluntary sector, the Panel on Accountability and Governance chaired by Edward Broadbent, emphasizes the role of the sector in building social capital. Moreover, "when such interaction occurs across different groups in society (for example across social, linguistic, cultural or geographic groups), increased tolerance and social cohesion are the likely result."[5] It adds that "communicating to members, stakeholders and the public," and providing easy access to information, are critical for "effective governance and accountability."[6] Yet the panel pays virtually no attention to the linguistic dimension.

The panel does discuss the need for inclusiveness and representativeness on association boards. It suggests that "every board discuss whether the representation of constituencies and users on the board is important to the organization's mission and credibility and, if appropriate, work towards increasing the diversity of representation on the board." Again, language is not singled out as a major dimension of diversity.

Health Canada, representing the Government of Canada, is necessarily somewhat more attuned to issues of language. Yet its diminished financial support for the sector means less money for translation services, and there is little indication that the department utilizes its leverage to require a greater commitment to bilingualism in national associations that it supports.

For the associations themselves, a weak commitment to bilingualism is not surprising. As we have seen, most are quite small and highly stretched in terms of both personnel and financial resources. They are focused on their specific task or purpose; building social capital across linguistic or regional lines is not central to their particular mandate. As one close observer of the sector put it, "full bilingualism has a huge cost. These small organizations have to struggle just to stay afloat. So it is really tough, really hard." And as for providing expensive facilities such as simultaneous translation in meetings, "the reality is that most of the francophones can speak English – so why do it for just one or two people?" The answer, of course, is that such a policy ensures that unilingual francophones simply will not participate.

Knowing that bilingualism is essential, only those who are bilingual will become involved, thus creating a self-fulfilling prophecy. Finally, voluntary associations in the increasingly diverse society find themselves under pressure to provide services in a variety of other minority languages – some with considerably greater political and economic weight – further reducing the energy devoted to French-English bilingualism.

Patterns of Association

Given this environment, how effective are the Heart and Stroke Foundations and the Huntington Societies of Canada and Quebec in their reflection of linguistic dualism in Canada?

The Heart and Stroke Foundation of Canada

The Public Face
The public face of the HSFC is fully bilingual. A visitor to the HSFC website can click on either official language and receive the full text available on the site. All publications – statements, pamphlets, and promotional or educational materials – are equally available in French and English. At news conferences and public events, press releases are available in both languages, and bilingual spokespersons are available. Such a public face, however, has not been achieved easily or without some controversy. For many years, it was common that publications would appear first in English, and only after considerable delay would the French-language versions appear. It is now HSFC policy that all publications appear simultaneously in both languages. "Now if there is a national program, or one produced by a lead province, there is a conscious decision that they should be published simultaneously." And this in turn has generated some frustration among the anglophone membership at perceived delays in making and approving the French-language translations. "To do everything together and at the same time is a big cost, especially if Quebec does not have the staff or resources to move quickly." Translation itself is not always easy. "There is the question of style. If you just translated word for word from English to French, it would look stodgy and dull. So we will go back and forth on the wording, then all sign off."

The language of publication thus remains a sensitive issue despite the overall commitment to bilingualism. For example, a draft policy and procedures manual, discussed at the October 1999 board meeting, referred to a commitment to simultaneous publication in both languages "wherever possible." When it was questioned, the phrase was "struck out, without a moment's debate on it." Similarly, when a new Internet site was being discussed, some board members wondered whether it should appear first in English. Said a Quebec staff member, "I was truly shocked; I told my president, how is this possible?" Again, the idea did not prevail, but the sense that constant vigilance was necessary to ensure a fully bilingual face was once again underlined. So too was the sense among non-Quebecers that bilingualism is a burden. "There is a debate about whether we could save money if we did not translate everything into French. But we accept that, if we want to make headway in Quebec, we have to produce the materials in French."

One result of this difference in perception is that language issues are seldom at the forefront of the minds of anglophone participants: "They never think spontaneously about it." It is the Quebecers who must keep reminding them of its importance. Hence, the Quebecers are perceived as the *demandeurs,* as looking for a favour or privilege. Yet, despite these difficulties, the HSFC deserves high marks for its bilingual public face.

The Private Face

However, English remains the overwhelmingly dominant language at the board level. The board and its committees function in English. Virtually all internal documents are in English only. This is a reflection of the reality that the great majority of those in attendance will be English speaking and that only a few of them will be bilingual. By contrast, the few French-speaking participants are almost invariably competent in English. For obvious reasons of cost, there is no simultaneous translation. This again means that the burden of adjustment must be made by the francophones. Even when a person appears to be fluently bilingual, there is the danger that subtle points will be lost and that participation will be more tiring. "Sometimes ... [the national executive director] has to help me out at meetings; I have to tell him that I do not understand everything." A unilingual francophone would find it almost impossible to function at the HSFC board level.

Nevertheless, it appears that Quebec members are active participants at both board and staff levels. One past Ontario president observed that, under its recent chairs and senior staff, Quebec "has become much more involved. They are not drifting away; rather, they are coming in." The Quebec-Ontario partnership in the development of the new website is one example.

The organizational structure of the board, with one member from each province, makes it impossible to consider any extra representation for Quebec interests. The norm is "equality of the provinces," not two nations. However, as I have noted, the board does include three members at large, providing the opportunity for some additional representation from both Quebec and Ontario as the largest provincial members. In addition, major committees will normally include a representative from Quebec.

The national staff have considerable ability to function and serve the membership in French. Senior staff are bilingual, and the present executive director is strongly committed to maintaining French-language capabilities.

The Heart and Stroke Foundation of Ontario
The HSFO is essentially an English-speaking organization throughout its operations despite the presence of a significant francophone population in the province. There are no francophone names among members of the board or among senior staff. "We have very few bilingual managers on staff; it is not a high priority." (A recent employment advertisement, however, noted that bilingualism would be an asset.) Regional offices in areas of northern and eastern Ontario, where there are significant francophone populations, are able to provide services in both languages. There is no standard practice of translating pamphlets, educational materials, and the like. "We work on the squeaky wheel principle – if some regional office calls for materials in French, we might translate or borrow from Quebec." The foundation does not sense "significant pressure" from the francophone community or governments to do more in French.

There appear to be two sets of reasons for this relative neglect of bilingualism in Ontario. The first set is financial. "We are very accountable to our donors for how we use their money. They want [it] to be used very directly on the activities central to our mission. If we spent our money on other things [such as bilingualism], they would ask, 'is this a responsible way of spending this dollar?'" This perspective is reinforced by the growing pervasiveness of a business model approach to the work of the foundation. "When you think like a business, you think return on investment, and there is not much of that with the francophone community."

The second set is societal. For Ontario – and other provinces such as British Columbia – linguistic diversity stems from the increasingly multicultural character of Canadian society. "Our language discussion revolves less around French than around Chinese or other languages." The HSFO already has councils representing the Chinese and South Asian communities. "But we realize the need to integrate these visible minorities much more into the mainstream of the foundation – they are wealthy, well –organized, and very skilled politically." One possible consequence is further marginalization of the francophone presence in the foundation.

If bilingualism is a low priority for Ontario, it is even less so for the other provincial foundations, with the possible exception of New Brunswick. Like that of Ontario, the BC foundation, for example, is far more concerned with its ability to respond to the growing Asian communities in the province than it is to the tiny BC francophone population. As in the wider political world, it is also the case that regional identities, and grievances against the perceived dominance of Ontario or central Canada, loom larger than language. "Regional differences are just as important as Quebec; those mountains do make a difference." One implication appears to be that in federally or confederally structured associations, it is the national body that will be most attuned to linguistic dualism in Canada.

La Fondation des maladies de coeur du Québec

Reflecting the origins of its founders, the Quebec Heart Society functioned largely as an English-speaking organization until the late 1970s. Gradually, the pressure for a greater French-language presence increased, especially from client groups outside Montreal. It appears that the shift toward functioning as an essentially francophone organization was accomplished with remarkably little friction or tension. Today in both its public and its private manifestations, the foundation appears to be fully bilingual in its operations. This is true for its website, for its telephone answering, and for all its publications.

The Quebec foundation has not been a strong proponent of change in the national foundation, nor has there been any pressure for it to secede despite the asymmetrical bilingualism evident at the national level. Two factors may help to account for limited pressure for change. First is the fundamental task-oriented focus on combatting heart and vascular disease and the realization that pooled resources significantly assist in this task. Second is the presence of an exceptionally skilled group of cardiovascular researchers and clinicians based in Quebec institutions. They compete very well with their peers in other provinces and share the same professional norms and values. And since access to HSFC research funds is strictly merit based, the Quebec research community receives a disproportionate amount of foundation-raised research funds. Given rates of charitable giving and volunteer activity in Quebec, it is highly unlikely that an independent Quebec foundation would be able to generate a similar level of funding.

The Huntington Society of Canada

Functioning effectively in both official languages is an even greater challenge for an association as small and stretched for resources as the HSC. As early as 1974, the board discussed the need to ensure that nationally distributed materials be available in both languages. Nevertheless, with important exceptions, such as the *Manual of Care*, national-level publications have continued to be primarily in English. The society's website, as of August 1999, provided an opportunity to click on the French language, but the viewer was told that "les pages de langue française sont en train d'être développés." Board and annual general meetings are conducted in English. Until recently, the national staff have been essentially unilingual, but the ability to speak French has now been introduced as a criterion in future hiring. Quebecers have served as presidents on two occasions. Professional staff in Ottawa and Sudbury, serving a francophone population, are bilingual.

However, the recently appointed executive director has made a strong commitment to improving French-language capabilities. "What we do now is small, but we are determined to increase it." For example, a new program of audio, video, and print announcements about the work of the society is a first major effort to develop a fully bilingual program, and Quebec repre-sentatives played an important role in developing the scripts. But, as with the HSFC, limited resources mean that "we must always demonstrate the value of translation to the board."

As I have mentioned, the HSC is structured as a single national organiza-tion, with the exception of a separately incorporated Quebec society. By 1985, a Quebec resource centre, headed by a coordinator, had been estab-lished to improve services and build a volunteer base in the province. The Quebec society was then incorporated under the Quebec Companies Act, in large measure to ensure that it could be eligible for grants from the Quebec government.

Relations between the two entities are governed by a memorandum of understanding signed in 1986. According to the agreement, the national association has the right to appoint one member of the Quebec board, and the executive director of the national society, or a representative, is a non-voting *ex officio* member of its Executive Committee. In turn, Quebec ap-points one member of the national board, who is also a non-voting member of its Executive Committee.

Under the agreement, the national body is responsible for the direction and administration of all national policies, priorities, goals, and objectives; is to be responsible for all support of research; and conducts all international links. The agreement recognizes that the distinct health and social services environment in Quebec will be reflected in the activities of the Quebec group. "But Quebec is to keep [the] national [society] informed of its activ-ities. Its activities will be coordinated with [those of the] national [society], so that duplication and activities at cross-purposes can be avoided." Quebec is responsible for raising funds from sources based entirely in Quebec but needs national approval if the sources are based partly in Quebec and else-where. The agreement also recognizes that the Quebec society is weak finan-cially and that it would take time to become self-supporting. In the meantime, the national society would continue to cover the shortfalls between the Quebec society's spending and revenues, subject to its approval of Quebec's operating budget.

However, financial weaknesses have continued in the Quebec association, leaving it partially dependent on the national body. Rather than being headed by an executive director, the Quebec body is headed by a develop-ment coordinator, who reports to the national executive director as well as his own board. The two bodies produce a consolidated budget, and the na-tional society continues to cover a portion of the costs of the Quebec organ-ization. At its annual general meeting in November 1999, the SHQ adopted a strategic plan that called for increased "convergence" between HSC and SHQ in terms of administration and management. The Quebec branch has had a high staff turnover, has been dependent on a very small leadership cadre, and is "chronically short of funds." The result is that "patients and families are much better served in the rest of Canada than they are in Quebec – though services in some other areas, such as New Brunswick and Newfoundland, are weak as well."

Some national leaders believe that these weaknesses in Quebec can be attributed to a general culture in which voluntary activity and giving are less developed than in much of English Canada. Another explanation is that small organizations are enormously dependent on the leadership of a very few people. As I have noted, the HSC was largely the creation of a single unilingual individual. No such leader emerged in Quebec. As the founder put it, "I could speak anywhere in Canada and get people involved. I could not do that in Quebec. There was no one to do this in Chicoutimi." The experience of the HSC thus reflects the special challenges that effective bilingualism poses for small associations with limited resources. They are heavily dependent on the skills, interests, and leadership qualities of a few individuals.

Federalism in the HSFC
Federalism, as expressed in the relationship between national and provincial branches of the organization, has divided the Heart and Stroke Foundations far more deeply than has language. In the 1990s, the organization faced a crisis in these relationships that came close to destroying it. The resolution was the signing of a "federation agreement," with an accompanying agreement on financial relationships, developed in a process with remarkable parallels to constitutional debates at the explicitly political level.

The crisis was precipitated by the Ontario foundation. A number of long-standing grievances came to a head, spurred by a succession of Ontario presidents determined to bring about a change in the relationship between Ontario and the HSFC. The grievances stemmed from a number of factors. Ontario saw the national foundation as bloated and overstaffed and believed that it provided little return to the provincial membership. Ontario officials believed that there was excessive duplication in the activities of the provincial and national bodies. While Ontario did well in winning research funding determined by the peer review process operated nationally, it felt underserved in terms of other national spending. Ontario was by far the largest and most effective of the provincial foundations, yet it carried only one vote among the ten provinces at the board level. But at the same time, Ontario, by virtue of its fundraising capacity, was generating more than half of the national budget. "And the more successful Ontario was in raising funds, the greater the proportion we ended up paying," said one Ontario official. "We felt we could not continue this way: we were spending too large a proportion of the donor dollar on national infrastructure for very little return ... It did not make sense for one member unit to be contributing over half (57 percent) of the budget yet not have a strong voice in the organization." Ironically, the more successful Ontario was in its fundraising, the greater the proportion of national revenues it provided. As the conflict escalated, driven especially by its president, "we got very close to the point that we said we would leave; it was more than an idle threat. We cannot have a situation where the other provinces have the incentive to increase spending at Ontario's expense."

Ontario won some support among other provinces in its complaints about the national foundation. However, its situation differed from others in the sense that only Ontario had the capacity to operate fully on its own as an independent body; other provinces were much more dependent on the assistance they received from the national level. As Ontario became more assertive in demanding change, it provoked resentment among several other provinces. Said one official from another province, "it tends to see itself as the centre of the universe; it is not so concerned with the other provinces ... "there was much ill will, most of which was directed at Ontario, which had become so obstreperous." Said another, "I was sympathetic to Ontario, but it did not know where to stop." And another, "they see themselves as number one and see both the national [body] and the other provinces as satellites – so they tend to act unilaterally but to be upset when they are not consulted on everything." The hostility was reciprocated: "Some of the other provinces were a real pain in the ass; they were really stoking the fire – they would not let Ontario get away with anything." Ontario sought to propose a number of alternatives, but "by then our credibility was shot – everything we proposed was seen as self-serving."

The result was a marked level of tension and conflict at board meetings. "The foundation had been traumatized," said one member. "It was a very difficult time; there were fights in the alley," said another. "It quickly ran to personalities and sometimes became quite irrational." The conflicts interfered with the basic mission of the organization. It was clear that something needed to be done.

A number of developments contributed to the process of eventual resolution. A new president in Ontario concluded that a more conciliatory approach was necessary. "We had to reach middle ground; ultimatums do not work." His bottom line was that, "in the end, we cannot let the federation break up ... we realized that, if the national federation did not exist, it would have to be invented." In addition, a new executive director in Ottawa was selected largely for his ability both to rationalize national office operations and to forge closer relations between it and the provinces.

The crisis unfolded as follows. In February 1994, the president of the HSFO met the president of the HSFC and informed him that "Ontario was seeking a new relationship with HSFC and that they were no longer prepared to pay for services that did not demonstrate added value."[7] In April, the HSFO indicated that it "wished to see a major restructuring of the national founda-tion" and that it was not prepared to pay for the old model in the new fiscal year.[8] Given the national body's dependence on Ontario funding, these were powerful threats.

There was an immediate response. A proposed budget called for a 22 per-cent cut in HSFC non-research spending. Members of the national and On-tario executives then began negotiations on the terms of a new "federation agreement" that would set out the roles and responsibilities for each level, alter the governance model, and redefine fiscal arrangements. Among the issues discussed were a significant reduction in the size of the national board and an equal voice on the board for each foundation – but with weighted voting proportional to the financial contribution of each province. The latter was a major sticking point, and by October 1994 six of the ten provinces had still not signed on.

The eventual federation agreement, signed in June 1997, was preceded by a board workshop held in November 1996. Members agreed that the chal-lenge was "to clarify and agree on how we can work together as a federation." The goal would be a "written, agreed-on, and believed-in federation agree-ment," with a common mission statement, reduced tension, and "transpar-ent, achievable, measurable goals." Everyone was "to pull in the same direction," the "baggage from past years was to be left behind," and there was to be a "streamlined information flow." Two committees were established. The first, including the presidents of Ontario, Quebec, and a smaller province, was to work on the federation agreement; the second, made up of the HSFC Finance and Administration Committee, with an added Quebec representa-tive, was to work on a new funding formula. "The fundamental challenge was to bring about a situation in which the provinces saw the national body not as a cost but as a value added ... We had to develop a rationale: why have a national board anyway; what were national's core competencies?"

Two documents emerged from the process. The first, the federation agree-ment, reads remarkably like an intergovernmental accord, even a constitu-tion. It sets out in writing "the spirit and the general principles governing their relationship and responsibilities as a National Federation." It contains a preamble, expressed in the language of confederalism: "Whereas the prov-incial Foundations have expressed their desire to confirm their alliance as a National Federation." It also expresses the values of cooperative federalism, echoing the 1999 federal-provincial Framework Agreement on the Social Union, expressing a commitment to "a spirit of unity, trust, cooperation and collaboration."

There is also a division of powers. The primary responsibilities of the na-tional foundation are to organize and conduct the peer review process for all research applications, whether made to national or provincial bodies. The national body is responsible for advocacy activities at both national and international levels and is to take the lead in coordinating and advancing the provincial positions on national issues. The HSFC is also responsible for maintaining a single benefits program for all staff, national and provincial. The national association will collaborate on a national health promotion committee "for the benefit of all provincial foundations" and will coordinate a committee on emergency cardiac care that is "to be implemented provincially."

Confederalism is reinforced by the declaration that activities with a national scope do not necessarily need to be carried out by the national foundation. Instead, the agreement sets out the concept of a "lead province" through which provinces can be mandated by the national board to carry out initiatives on behalf of the entire membership, funded by sharing costs on a case-by-case basis. In this case, the national foundation is responsible for coordinating the dissemination of materials that have been developed. All nationally distributed materials are to be produced in both languages.

The federation agreement also proposes a dispute settlement mechanism, though its details are to be spelled out in the by-laws of the federation. It also permits secession: any member province may withdraw after one year's notice.

Fiscal arrangements are spelled out in an addendum to the agreement itself. The power to raise revenues remains with the provinces – along with a stated commitment to avoid competition. National fundraising activities are restricted to an appeal to national corporations, with the resulting revenues to be shared. The HSFC itself continues to be funded by the provinces. The goal is a "simple, fair, and affordable approach" that will eventually lead to "equal per capita funding." The key objective here was to provide an Ontario "cap" to ensure that no province would be required to contribute more than half the national budget. It was set at 49.9 percent. An additional proviso states that no province is required to contribute nationally more than 13 percent of its own revenues. This means that the Ontario contribution will be reduced and that the contributions of financially weaker provinces, such as Quebec, will be raised. This is to be accomplished over a three-year transition period (for Ontario) and a five-year period (for those whose contributions are to be increased).

These arrangements do achieve a reduction of Ontario's contribution and mean that no single province is responsible for more than half of the total national funding. Yet Ontario continues to have only one member of the board even though its contribution continues to greatly exceed that of any other province.

The apparent solution is what might be called a two-tier governance process. The board remains structured on the basis of equal provinces. However, a new committee has been constituted. It represents the provinces as shareholders. Hence, their weight is proportional to their financial contribution, thus ensuring that Ontario can defend its interests; with 48 percent of the votes, it needs the support of only one other province. This committee remains informal, but it does mean that, if opinion on a major issue is not going Ontario's way in a formal board meeting, it can call a shareholder's meeting to overturn it. It appears not to have done so to this point, but the possibility clearly alters the dynamics of debate within the board itself. "The dynamic now is that, whenever a difference emerges, everyone tends to step back from conflict. If it ever got to the point where we actually had to have a vote, we might as well close the door." "It's really like a nuclear deterrent – it works best when it is not actually used." This two-tier model makes a distinction between "who makes the policy and who writes the cheques – the board is about policy and strategy, the provinces for the dollars." Hence, provinces, as the funders, have an effective veto over board decisions.

Adoption of the federation agreement and new funding arrangements appears to have greatly improved relationships within the Heart and Stroke Foundations of Canada. It was, as the HSFC president put it in her annual report, the "highlight of the year ... a critical step." The roles and responsibilities, especially of the HSFC, have been clarified. The HSFC now has considerable autonomy within its jurisdiction, but it is clearly seen as a body oriented primarily to serving the interests of its constituent members. Those members in turn appear to perceive the benefits that membership in the larger association can provide and are reassured that they will have the final say in any future expansion of the national association's activities. Hence, they have a clearer sense of ownership and see the national body – or coalitions of smaller provinces – as less of a potential threat. There has been no need to invoke the dispute settlement provisions in the federation agreement. Ontario has succeeded in its major goals of reducing its financial commitment, rationalizing the size and role of the HSFC, and ensuring its veto over major decisions. As the lead province in most joint activities, its central position in the overall life of the organization is assured. With this mind, "we now think, after huge hostility, that [the] national [association] is valuable."

Hence, "we believe that after these changes, governance is now working pretty well in Heart and Stroke – but it took the threat of a breakup to make it happen." In the end, said a provincial president, "we accomplished something few do. Ten partners signed off on the FA [federation agreement] in goodwill." "It was very stressful, but we had to realize what Canada is; it is part of our makeup." Several respondents emphasized both the necessity for and the growth of trust relationships. "The key is respect, trust, communications; you have to check your ego at the door; put it in writing, explain it, go over it." Indeed, the agreement's stated commitment to trust and cooperation is now printed on the backs of the name cards at board meetings to remind the members of their common interests and the need to cooperate. "Now when we speak, we try to use those words."

Thus, the Heart and Stroke Foundations have creatively resolved a major crisis of federalism. Yet the accommodation reflected in the federation agreement may well face new challenges in the future. One such challenge is the major new federal initiative for funding health research in Canada – itself a response to lobbying pressures from many groups, including the HSFC. The Canadian Institutes for Health Research (CIHR) will greatly increase federal funding in this area. The chosen model is one in which the federal government will form partnerships with health organizations, allowing them to significantly leverage the funds they are able to raise. Health Canada, however, is geared to working with national organizations – with the HSFC, not the provinces. Hence, to leverage these new funds, provincial foundations will need to pool their funds allocated to research. As an Ontario executive said, "we saw the writing on the wall. To be a player, we had to leverage federal dollars. There was no way that on our own we could double our research dollars, which the feds are proposing to do." Thus, the provinces have agreed to flow a major part of their research funds through the HSFC. The federal initiative "is an enormous change in our environment" and may well begin to erode the confederalism that the FA was designed to achieve. Change in the external institutional environment can thus have a major impact on the internal dynamics of associations.

Conclusions

I began this study by asking the broad question how and how well do these two sets of voluntary associations in the health sector accommodate, manage, and represent Canada's linguistic diversity? The Heart and Stroke Foundations of Canada have been immensely successful in their primary mission of raising funds for research into cardiovascular disease and promoting education and awareness and heart and stroke issues. They have a strong and positive public image. In a more modest way, the Huntington Societies of Canada and Quebec have also done much to assist victims and their families in managing a horrific ailment. Both have had to adapt and respond to a federal and bilingual Canada. They do so both because of their need to adapt to their environment if they are to perform successfully and because of their own commitments to these normative dimensions of their political communities.

In my judgment, both sets of associations have done well in terms of the broad question. They are present from coast to coast. In neither case have disputes over language threatened the very existence of the organization or placed its ability to serve its clientele in jeopardy – although interprovincial differences created major strains in the 1990s.

Both are able to respond to French-speaking citizens, though their capacity in this regard varies. In particular, the Canadian and Quebec Heart and Stroke Foundations appear to be fully capable of meeting the needs of speakers of the minority language. The HSFO appears to be somewhat less effective in its ability to meet the needs of French speakers in the province. The HSC has been less fully bilingual in its public face, though that has been improving. The organizational weaknesses in its Quebec wing appear to have hampered its ability to fully meet the needs of Quebecers.

These associations are much less fully bilingual in their internal affairs. As with the sector as a whole, within their boards and committees, in their internal communications, and in their staff operations the working language is overwhelmingly English. In this sense, these groups are far from demonstrating a pattern of linguistic equality. The term I use to describe this is "asymmetrical bilingualism."

In terms of organizational structure and the distribution of power, again the pattern is mixed. Given the confederal structure of the Heart and Stroke Foundations, Quebec, like each of the other provinces, has an effective institutional space in which to develop priorities and programs that meet the needs of its constituents, while at the same time benefiting from its linkages with its partners elsewhere in Canada. At the national level, little formal accommodation to Quebec as a distinct entity is made: it is one of ten provinces represented on the board. Informally, however, it appears that Quebec does have representation on most important board committees, and a number of Quebecers have played leading roles at the national level. But overall, at the national level, federalism dominates dualism as an organizational principle. In the Huntington Societies, the inequalities between language groups are somewhat more marked, especially because of the weakness of the Quebec society. Nonetheless, the leadership of the national association has devoted considerable resources to strengthening the SHQ.

The picture, while a mixed one, is on balance a positive one – these organizations work well across the linguistic divide. With just two cases, it is hard to suggest explanations for these findings. Yet two factors seem to contribute most to unity and effectiveness here. First, the issues around which these associations are formed are serious diseases that can strike any citizen regardless of region or language. This common goal distinguishes them both from associations organized around issues in which the material interests of different regions or language groups are in conflict and from those organized around issues in which "identity politics" play a greater role. Overwhelmingly, these groups are focused on a common task. Second, a high degree of professionalism characterizes both associations. The executive directors and senior staff share common professional goals and values, and their cooperation across provincial lines has been an important factor in assuring harmony at the board level. So has a relatively high degree of continuity in staff leadership, which can mitigate potential conflict at the board level, where the turnover is much greater. Moreover, in the HSFC, the professional clientele of researchers and clinicians also have strong commitments to common professional norms and standards of quality. This commitment does not eliminate, but it does reduce, the likelihood of divisive conflicts over the distribution of resources and influence.

Despite this positive assessment, this study also demonstrates how difficult it is to build social capital across linguistic (and to a lesser extent regional) lines. Four sets of factors underline this point.

First, associations such as these are naturally and properly focused on their substantive policy goals; indeed, as just noted, this focus helps to build unity and cooperation. But an explicit, self-conscious focus on questions of language and region, not to mention national unity and cohesion, are peripheral to their central concerns. Hence, they are likely to be seen as a set of costs, burdens, and constraints, which cannot be ignored but which do interfere with their central tasks.

Second, the idea of asymmetrical bilingualism suggests that the burden of language falls in different ways on different participants. For anglophones, the concern is primarily with the costs that it imposes – the need for translation, the need for linguistic sensitivity, the attention to securing agreement. They have been far more effective in responding in their public faces than they have in their internal operations, which remain almost entirely unilingual English. For francophones, the burdens are both more subtle and heavier. In any national setting, they are a minority. It is they who must adapt to functioning in an English-speaking milieu. They are not the victims of overt hostility and discrimination. As Jean Laponce argues, English speakers – the right-handers – are not aware that, "'when they communicate, they dominate'; hence their being easily annoyed by, and their impatience with, those who keep worrying about their minority languages ... Their very dominance makes English-speaking Canadians mentally ill-equipped to find administrative and political solutions that would reassure and appease the minority languages over which they keep trespassing without noticing them."[9] This dynamic puts francophones in the position of *demandeurs* even when their demands are modest and, not surprisingly, provokes a corresponding resentment – "what are they on about?" The result is that, for a francophone to participate actively in the affairs of the national association, she must be bilingual, and she will nevertheless continue to experience the subtle costs of participating in her second language. It is easy to understand the extra effort that this requires. What we do not know is how many unilingual francophones, or even those for whom English is a difficult stretch, decide not to participate at the national level and instead focus their involvement entirely within Quebec.

Third, institutional arrangements may stand in the way of full accommodation of linguistic equality. Federalism and bilingualism interact in interesting ways here. Federalism, as manifested in both these associations, does provide considerable autonomy at the provincial level, where francophones can and do operate as the dominant language group. This is especially true of the Fondation des maladies du coeur du Québec. On the other hand, federalism in Canada is predicated on the equality of the provinces, so that it is difficult if not impossible to structure a national board on binational rather than provincial lines. Federalism also means that provincial associations outside Quebec may feel little obligation to their own French-language minorities. This is a problem with the HSFO. The HSFC, oriented to a nationwide constituency, and to an officially bilingual federal government, is much more effective in reflecting linguistic dualism than any of the provincial foundations except that of Quebec. One implication of this point is that, when associations move toward a more decentralized or confederal pattern with a weaker centre, their interest in and capacity for linguistic equality may decline.

Fourth, there is an increasing tension between the goal of accommodating linguistic and regional differences – the traditional fault lines in Canadian public life – and the goal of representing, accommodating, and serving the other dimensions of cultural diversity characteristic of contemporary Canadian society. It is not easy to respond to them all simultaneously. Thus, provincial Heart and Stroke Foundations tend to argue that it is their specific regional needs that need to be taken into account by the national body; there should be no priority given to the demands of language. More important for the future is that several provincial foundations find it much more important to respond to the increasing cultural and linguistic diversity of their own communities than to the demographically weaker and declining francophone communities. From their own perspective, this is entirely rational, but it may have costs for the future ability to accommodate linguistic dualism in Canada.

This analysis may appear overly pessimistic. The story told here is not one of an organization torn apart by linguistic tension and dispute, much less one of overt discrimination and hostility. The Heart and Stroke Foundations work well together to promote the well-being of Canadians. They have not been paralyzed by language. The Quebec foundation has the right to go on its own but has strong reasons to continue its membership in the HSFC; the same is true for the SHQ. Some of these reasons are financial and organizational, but others reflect the deep personal and professional commitment to common goals.

Indeed, almost forty years after Meisel and Lemieux wrote, after multiple constitutional crises, and after two referendums on Quebec sovereignty, it may seem surprising that language in these associations seems to be less a source of conflict than it did when they wrote. If this is so, then it is interesting to ask why. There are a number of possibilities. First, the Royal Commission on Bilingualism and Biculturalism, for which Meisel and Lemieux were writing, also documented systematic inequality and disadvantage for francophones in many areas of Canadian economic and political life. These inequalities have been largely eliminated. Second, they wrote at a time when Quebec nationalism was in the process of mobilizing to define a Quebec identity and to challenge their subordination in many areas, including voluntary associations. It may be that most of the resulting adjustments have taken place – that in associations where identity and conflicting interests play a major role the organizational splits have now occurred; and that in associations like these, where the common interests are so strong, a *modus vivendi*, while not perfect, has been worked out.

The larger concern of this study has been the potential of voluntary associations such as these to act as vehicles for building social capital that bridges the linguistic and regional divides in Canada. Each of the provincial associations is a powerful builder of social capital within its own province through fundraising, promotional, educational, and volunteer-building programs. These associations are also bridge builders at the national level. Through the activities of their national boards and staffs, they exchange information, pursue common goals, and are brought face to face to negotiate their differences. However, only tiny fractions of their volunteer base will play a role in governance at the provincial level, and only a few of them will interact with their counterparts in other provinces or on the national board. The federal organizational structure, combined with the increasing professionalization of leadership, means that these associations are not equipped to build social capital at the level of ordinary citizens. Instead, the bridge building occurs at the elite level. This pattern of "elite accommodation" is indeed a characteristic of Canadian public life more generally.

It is no doubt too much to ask any of these associations to place accommodation of linguistic duality at the beginning of their mission statements. It is unrealistic to expect them to devote far more resources to translation and other such activities. Any changes will necessarily be marginal and incremental. On the other hand, within their mandates and resources, they have accommodated linguistic duality in Canada.

6

From Biculturalism to Bilingualism: Patterns of Linguistic Association in the Canadian Council on Social Development

Jane Jenson and Rachel Laforest

The Canadian Council on Social Development (CCSD, Conseil canadien de développement social) has been a major actor in the field of social policy since its creation under the name of the Canadian Council on Child Welfare in 1920.[1] It is a bilingual organization that has, since its beginning, faced the question of how to sustain representation and visibility for anglophones and francophones and for all parts of the country. As this analysis will document, the challenges and choices it has made have closely paralleled the disputes and directions in language and cultural policy experienced by the federal government and Canada as a whole. The CCSD, as the Canadian Welfare Council (CWC) before it, has escaped none of the big issues around patterns of association that have confronted Canadians in general.

Currently, the council is a bilingual organization based in Ottawa with a staff of ten.[2] In 2006-7 its Board of Directors was composed of fifteen Canadians from across the country. It has had thirty-two presidents in its more than eighty-year history, ten of whom have come from Quebec and six of whom have been French Canadian, according to CCSD historian Richard Splane.[3] Its mission statement, the most recent version of which was agreed to in 1991, says, in part, "the Canadian Council on Social Development is a voluntary, non-profit organization whose mission is to: develop and promote progressive social policies inspired by social justice, equality and the empowerment of individuals and communities through research, consultation, public education and advocacy."[4]

Our analysis cannot consider the CCSD without also presenting the Conseil québécois de développement social (CQDS). This short-lived organization was independent of the CCSD, headquartered in Montreal, and served the Quebec social policy community. Its mandate included providing public information, education, and support to community-level organizations.[5]

The CQDS is relevant to the CCSD story because it was created as a "breakaway" from the CCSD in 1994. The original split occurred for a number of reasons that we will document in more detail below. The most immediate one, however, was the decision taken for budgetary reasons to close the CCSD's Montreal office. These were difficult financial times following from a restructuring of the federal government's funding practices. These practices, as well as those of the Quebec government, forced the CCSD to make a series of hard choices about real estate and representation. These choices had subsequent consequences for the patterns of association within the organization.[6]

After 1994, the CCSD and CQDS developed a cooperative, if arm's-length, relationship that continued until the CQDS was recently disbanded. There was an operational entente between the two and a certain division of labour. The CCSD continued to be active in Quebec and to consider that the province was within its representational "jurisdiction." Quebecers, both francophone and anglophone, sit on its Board of Directors; in 2007, four of the fifteen members of the board were from Quebec, including a regional vice-president. While the CQDS operated and published only in French, the CCSD functions in both official languages. The CQDS worked only in Quebec, while the CCSD addresses French-speaking Canadians across the country. In 1999, moreover, the CCSD appointed, for the first time, a francophone as executive director.

This pattern of association, both linguistic and organizational, was only one in a series of compromises about how to accommodate the two language communities present in the numerous communities the Canadian Council of Welfare and then CCSD have served.

Patterns of Association: 1920 to the B and B Commission

This first slice of history, from the founding of the council until the mid-1960s, involved a good deal of decision making about how to manage linguistic and cultural relations. This process culminated in the decision to present a brief to the Royal Commission on Bilingualism and Biculturalism outlining the "experience of a national voluntary organisation operating bilingually and biculturally."[7] At the request of the Board of Governors, the brief refrained from making any recommendations about instituting bilingualism; in the mid-1960s, the board was in the midst of one of the periodic reconsiderations and reorganizations of linguistic representational practices.[8]

It was the French Commission of the CWC (this structure is described below) that recommended presenting a brief to the Laurendeau-Dunton Commission. The Board of Governors, meeting in March 1964, was also encouraged to do so by Mrs. S.B. Laing of Calgary, a member of both the board and the royal commission. On 27 January 1965, the committee presented its draft brief to the CWC board.[9]

The purpose of the brief was to present the royal commission with information about the experience of the CWC to help develop better collaboration between French- and English-speaking communities. The CWC traced the history of linguistic relations within the organization. It presented the French Commission as the key ingredient in its success at uniting francophone and anglophone members around welfare issues for over forty years. The French Commission was a gateway through which the preoccupations of the francophone members could be expressed.

In this section, we present the history of linguistic and cultural relations as represented by the CWC in 1965. In other words, we use the brief as a datum for reconstructing patterns of association in 1965. Therefore, there may be some divergence from the "real history" of the CWC.[10]

As documented in its brief, the CWC was originally founded to address the "needs of the English-speaking community."[11] It was created to aid the work of community funds and schools of social work in English Canada. It was there that the first community fund was created in 1933 and the first school of social work in 1938.[12] Various Catholic organizations, whether religious or lay, provided the bulk of services at the time. Initially, these institutions did not exist in "French-speaking Canada."

However, the Canadian Council on Child Welfare, as it was called at the time, soon took on the task of creating an organization connecting individuals and organizations right across the country. High rates of infant and maternal mortality and other child welfare issues were of growing concern in all provinces and brought a range of social policy actors together. In 1921, the first Child Welfare Conference recommended the creation of a "Canadian" council to interface with the Division of Child Welfare in the federal Department of Health and to promote the establishment of provincial organizations. The only provincial one at the time was in Quebec.[13]

Then, three years after its founding, linguistic relations were explicitly on the agenda. In 1923, the Fédération des femmes canadiennes-françaises proposed creating a French section within the council. By 1925, the council's constitution described a mixed structure, which allowed a focus on substantive issues on the one hand and on representation of one part of the membership on the other. Thus, the work of the council was carried out in sections:

- child hygiene;
- the child in employment;
- recreation and education;
- the child in need of special care;
- the spiritual and ethical development of the child; and
- the French-speaking section.[14]

The purpose of the French-speaking section at the time was principally to provide services in French. Originally, this provision involved a focus on educational work and distribution of publications about infant and maternal health in Quebec and Ontario.[15] Other activities ranged from expert testimony to the organization of bilingual conferences in Quebec City and Montreal, work with community funds, and involvement in the development of professional social work in Quebec. Indeed, the council seems to have considered the latter its major contribution in the 1930s and 1940s.[16]

The CWC also published a journal in English, *Canadian Welfare*. In 1941, it started publishing a French-language journal entitled *Missive*, renamed *Bien-être social canadien* in 1949. In its brief to the royal commission, the council pointed with pride to the fact that it was "the only national agency that sought to serve the French-language charities through bilingual services and publications."[17]

Running through these various activities and organizational choices was a recognition of cultural as well as linguistic issues and a clear tendency to see both French and cultural difference as of particular relevance to Quebec members. In this matter, it was speaking directly to the second term of the royal commission's name. The council was developing a bicultural vision.

Thus, the submission to the B and B Commission quotes the 1947-48 report of the Division of French Services, which made an argument for a functional sector that would be transversal in terms of substance while being representative of a cultural community. The other functional sectors were, at the time, becoming more autonomous in their actions, and the argument made by the Division of French Services (as reported to the B and B Commission) was the following:

> The implications of this trend have not been worked out fully although they have been considered by the Division's Committee. It is clear, however, that there will have to be within the Council a bureau or a department which is in a position to serve our Quebec members. Difference of language constitutes one factor, but also important are the cultural and religious differences which make the context of social work in Quebec different from that of any other area of Canada. Moreover, it is only to the extent that French-speaking workers, volunteers and professionals have the opportunity to meet together that they can bring their full contribution to the thinking of the Council and to the general planning of welfare in Canada.[18]

The brief to the B and B Commission also reported that the statement of the executive director in 1948 "exposed the dilemma clearly."

> There was a need to meet the wish of French-speaking Canadians to take part in *all* the activities, general and specialized, of the Council. But there was also a need to find some way to encourage them to meet among themselves, if they felt the need for it, and afford them the opportunity to draw

away from the specialized interests of sectors, to integrate themselves with the over all policies of the Council, and bring about an expression of opinion reflecting the general interest of the French group of the Council.[19]

The result of this introspection was the creation of the French Commission (Commission française). The commission did not build its own program but worked to promote the council's activities within the French-speaking community and simultaneously to influence the council's program in directions of relevance to the community in Quebec. According to the brief, the result was that "the role of the Commission is, all in all, quite delicate."[20]

Throughout the 1950s, it seems to have functioned with a good deal of autonomy, proposing names of francophones for the council's board, commenting on briefs after consultation with its own community, and so on. It also worked on rendering the council bilingual. For example, it was the commission that insisted in 1953 that the French name "Conseil canadien du bien-être" obtain statutory recognition.[21]

However, by 1960 the winds of change were already rustling through the CWC. The French Commission had become large and unwieldy. Moreover, the fact that all the French-speaking members were grouped within one department had isolated them from the other preoccupations of the council. Most of the work of the francophones was restricted to that of the commission, and there was little exchange with other areas of the council's work. Therefore, the French Commission undertook a structural self-reform in 1960-61.[22]

The number of representatives sitting on the commission was reduced to fifteen. The commission included representatives from each division and standing committee, and its principal function was to ensure liaison with the remaining departments. After the restructuring, the Board of Governors described the purpose of the French Commission this way: "to offer guidance concerning the Council's policy and action; to facilitate the participation of French speaking persons and organisations in its programs; to promote the mutual understanding of the two official language groups which are active in the field of social welfare in Canada."[23]

In 1962, the French Commission was instructed to study the practices of biculturalism within the Canadian Welfare Council. The aim of the study was to help develop policy with respect to publications, board membership, staffing, and planning of meetings to consolidate the bicultural character of the organization.

The French Commission recommended that bilingual staff be hired. In addition, it called for the creation of the post of associate executive director, to be held by a person of the other mother tongue than the executive director, who would be given "the special responsibility of seeing that the Council is in fact truly bi-cultural." There were also recommendations for proportionate representation of "both the groups who were partners in Confederation." Staff should not only be able to communicate "in both official languages of the country in conformity with the spirit of the two cultures" but also be given the opportunity to "acquire knowledge of the different social and geographical settings."[24]

It was this policy, as well as the other actions over its more than four decades, that allowed the CWC to represent itself to the B and B Commission as having "always deliberately promoted the integration of bilingualism and biculturalism within its structures," as well as to say that "the French Commission has been a vital and necessary agent in directing the Council's work in French Canada and in winning for it the cooperation of the French-speaking Community. The Council has thus been able to serve both of the main linguistic groups of Canada, taking into account their differences and the contributions each can make."[25]

In this formulation, the CWC was clearly presenting a dualistic vision of Canada, composed of two distinct communities. While language distinguished them, culture was even more important. Hence, biculturalism had precedence over bilingualism in the discourse of the CWC and in its organizational arrangements until 1963. This vision justified the separate representation of French-speaking members. It also led to an understanding that the two communities had different interests. For example, in discussing staffing, the submission to the B and B Commission made it clear that being bilingual was not sufficient; there were different worlds of social welfare, and someone coming from one might not know the other as well.[26]

However, even as the CWC was instituting the recommendations of the French Commission's study and reporting to the royal commission, its focus was shifting from culture to language.

A Shift in the Model: From Biculturalism to Bilingualism

Before the French Commission presented its report in 1963, the CWC chose a new executive director, Ruben C. Baetz. His first task was to launch a major revision of the structures and the membership of the organization. He was quite sympathetic to linguistic issues and proceeded to hire new staff who were bilingual. He stated that "council structures must also be responsive to and reflect the dominant characteristics of our country if it is to serve Canadians most effectively."[27] He further appealed to the francophone members to encourage them to help fill vacancies by suggesting names of candidates.[28] The board tried to ensure that, at the least, the heads of departments as well as individuals in other strategic staff positions, such as external relations, were bilingual. In addition, courses in French were offered to staff who wished to participate. A full-time translator was also hired to help with the publication of the francophone journal, as well as other official documents.[29]

The council did not, however, accept the recommendation of the French Commission to establish a second-in-command who would have special responsibility for biculturalism. As visions of two Canadian communities were giving way to visions of two language groups in interaction, the patterns of association within the CWC also began to change. In part, this shift can be attributed to the fact that the "cultural differences" that were most frequently mentioned as distinguishing French- and English-speaking members were those linked to religion and views of family and other social relations.[30] Thus, as post-Quiet Revolution Quebecers created a more secular and progressive society, they were less likely to recognize their "cultural difference" as the one the CWC sought to respect in the 1940s and 1950s.

The discussion within the CWC adopted new terms as well as new goals. Rather than ensuring representational forms that would allow francophones and anglophones to express themselves easily, and to address their own particular interests, the goal became to help forge a *Canadian* vision regarding welfare issues that would allow members to overcome linguistic divides.

Throughout these debates, the board always acknowledged the important role the French Commission had played in the past, just as it had in the brief to the royal commission. However, some members no longer supported a separate institution of representation, and debates were ongoing by 1966. Thus, for example, there was a suggestion to rename it the "Canadian Commission." There was also a proposal to broaden the French Commission to include English-speaking members. By doing so, it was claimed, the commission would accurately reflect its new role as a site where both major groups in Canada could be united. Some began to argue that, if the primary goal of the French Commission was to unite linguistic groups, then its ultimate goal should be its own disappearance. The French Commission was even described as being responsible for putting distance between francophones and anglophones.[31]

By 1967, a clear alternative was being advanced by, for example, Mrs. Laing, who told the board there was a "need for a different kind of integration of French and English interests in the country. It was of vital importance that a new look be given to ways in which both sectors would work together through the Canadian Welfare Council in the field of welfare in Canada."[32]

In response to such internal debates, the forty-seventh annual report (1967) noted the difficulties of functioning in a bilingual fashion:

Recognition for the implementation of French-language services though progressive, has not been easy. Bilingualism means very little if staff are not available to work effectively in French Canada. Ideally a body such as the French Commission should not exist but, in practice, it is needed if for no other purpose than to ensure that everyone associated with the organisation is aware of, and in some measure responsible for, the Council's relationships with all the parts of the country. Whether the French Commission should be radically challenged so that it embraces a much wider scope of activity and its composition made representative of the whole council is one of the problems that will be tackled in its self-study.[33]

Thus, as in its submission to the royal commission, the CWC spoke frankly of the difficulties it faced in trying to be a "national and bilingual organization." Therefore, as in the early 1960s, the board sent the commission to conduct a self-examination of its role within the CWC, including the issue of whether its very existence was necessary.

In the meantime, the life of the organization went on, and linguistic issues were dealt with in everyday practice. One issue that was always controversial and related to these organizational matters was that of bilingual or separate publications.[34] At the time, the CWC had two journals, and each made its own editorial choices. Therefore, they had different content, reflecting different realities and interests. Some claimed it would be more effective to combine them into one bilingual magazine because the current situation did not help to foster dialogue and stimulate debate between the linguistic groups on social policy issues.

As a board member, Mrs. Beirnes said that "the English-language publication is confined to what is largely going on in English-speaking Canada and is depriving people of the opportunity to know better what is happening in Quebec."[35] Given that few articles about Quebec were published in the English-language publication, a joint publication was seen as a better way of allowing policy interests and ideas to be shared across linguistic groups. Nonetheless, the policy on publications was maintained, although certain articles would appear in both languages.

An examination of the activities of the organization in these years shows that the French Commission had become largely inactive (eventually, it was formally abolished). Rather than having one body to oversee linguistic matters for the whole council, issues were managed within the particular departments on an ad hoc basis. This approach marked a major change within the structure of the organization, removing the space within which francophone members had met and addressed issues of particular interest to them while extending the visibility of French and francophones in other parts of the organization. In these years, francophone participation started to wane on the board. The CWC had always had difficulty recruiting members from Quebec, and therefore its representation had always been below the average that its population would have guaranteed.

At the time, the CWC was experiencing a major existential crisis related to a number of broad issues. Some members feared that the CWC had become a rambling and diverse body, without a clear focus. There was a growing concern that the council was merely reacting to events as they unfolded rather than developing its own policy agenda. There was also a desire by some within the organization to do more advocacy work. As the fiftieth annual report (1970) put it, this was a reflection of the greater presence of activists and advocates within the membership. The CWC was moving in the direction of social action and away from being a traditional forum organized mainly by and for social work professionals and informed lay people.

Consultations and then a Commission on Functions and Organization, chaired by Humphrey Carver, a member of the board for many years, had suggested a radical overhaul and a name change.[36] The relationship between the CWC and its membership was revised. Several bodies, including the Community Funds and Councils of Canada (CFCC; they eventually became the United Way), were given greater autonomy within the organizational structure, with some becoming affiliated organizations.

In 1970, the name of the organization was changed to the Canadian Council on Social Development. The change was meant to give a more positive view than "welfare" did; social development was seen as a more proactive conception. The renaming of the organization also echoed the desire to widen the mandate of the organization to encompass a broader array of social issues. Moreover, the new name was meant to reflect a greater commitment to research and policy formulation. Research soon accounted for over 40 percent of the budget, 90 percent of which was funded by outside sources. This change was fostered in part by a growing pool of available grants for research on social issues.

The Rising Costs of Doing Business [37]
Despite this new access to research funds, the CCSD story is one of almost constant financial strain. Without access to funding from the CFCC, the council's finances took a serious blow. This impact was coupled with the loss of a $50,000 grant the CCSD had received from the government of Quebec. The grant was cancelled after the election of the Parti québécois in 1976, and one from the government of British Columbia was similarly lost.

As income plummeted over $68,000 between the 1976-77 and 1977-78 financial years, and a further $115,652 the next year, cutbacks were inevitable.[38] Staff were laid off. This action set in motion difficult labour negotiations and culminated in a five-week strike by unionized employees.[39]

In response to these financial setbacks, the CCSD began to cut its operational costs. At first, it tried using more contractual workers to become more flexible. Then, in 1978, *Perception,* a bilingual magazine, replaced both *Canadian Welfare* and *Digeste social.* While the articles were not all published in both languages, summaries of the texts were provided in the other language. The board described the change as one driven by principle but also by financial constraint. It was "an attempt to foster better communications between parts of the country and may involve the translation of an article before printing it. Restraints in budget and the decrease in approved size of the magazine make it impossible to have all articles translated and available in both official languages."[40]

The financial difficulties of the council were further exacerbated by a growing dissatisfaction in the west. In 1984, funding from the government of Manitoba was halved, to $5,000. In addition, Alberta and Saskatchewan stopped providing core funding to "advocacy" organizations, although they continued to provide an equal amount to the council as project funding.

All of this meant that the CCSD was invariably in straightened circumstances. Indeed, it took a full ten years – until 1985-86 – before revenues again reached the level they had been in 1976-77. Expenditures, on the other hand, were below 1976-77 levels only three of those ten years. Deficits were, in other words, almost a constant.

Throughout this period, to receive federal funding, an organization such as the CCSD had to prove that it was pan-Canadian. This meant ensuring there was adequate representation from Quebec and a commitment to bilingualism. In spite of its financial difficulties, the CCSD did maintain its practice of providing documents in both French and English. The council received funding from the Department of the Secretary of State to ensure the translation of all documents, and it expanded the capabilities of the French-language unit within its publication branch. In 1980, a second translator was hired, using a $25,000 bilingualism grant from the Secretary of State's program.[41] That funding, however, ended in 1982.[42]

Elsewhere in the organization, bilingualism became less of a priority, although the official bilingualism policy still required that all public documents, posters, and letterheads be available in both French and English. In 1976, the sole translator had moved from Administration to Publication and Information, clearly signalling that the main department concerned with language issues was the latter. The second translator, when hired, also worked in Publication and Information.

Funding was affecting all aspects of the council's work, and in each financial crisis language services were again discussed. In 1982, the CCSD had to lay off more staff. It closed the print shop. It reduced the number of board meetings from three to two and the number of board members from sixty to thirty-nine, in part to save the costs of travel. In all of this, there was some discussion of discontinuing translation services. The decision, however, was to reduce in-house translation and contract out services to reduce costs. One permanent employee would be kept on as a translator in Publication and Information.[43]

Finally, in 1985 the CCSD saw its financial situation significantly improve. In the five years between 1985 and 1990, its revenues more than doubled.[44]

In part, this was because the CCSD was asked by the Department of the Secretary of State to run the Court Challenges Program. This was an initiative supporting groups bringing test cases concerning language (and later equality) rights under the Charter of Rights and Freedoms.[45] Not only did this funding help to re-establish financial stability for a number of years, but administration of the Court Challenges Program also gave the CCSD new visibility in the area of language rights. Two panels adjudicated the cases that would receive funding, and one of the two was a Language Rights Panel. It dealt primarily with the educational rights of linguistic minorities. Therefore, the 1992 cancellation of the Court Challenges Program by the Conservative government was a blow to the CCSD.[46]

An even greater blow came from federal government funding practices. The Conservatives sought to eliminate core funding for organizations and began to insist on project-based funding. The argument was that such project funding allowed greater accountability and flexibility to respond to new needs. Thus, the federal government announced its decision to terminate the CCSD's sustaining grant at the end of the 1992-93 fiscal year. Revenues were declining from other sources as well. The combined operating and capital deficit was close to $600,000 in 1991-92.[47]

At the same time, the government had abolished a number of bodies, including the Economic Council, for reasons some observers, including within the council, attributed to vindictiveness in the face of critical commentary on government policy. The CCSD, which had mounted a major mobilization of critics against the 1991 federal budget and Bill C-69 (the cap on transfers to the provinces under the Canada Assistance Plan), feared the "possibility that the Council would be deprived of all federal support for punitive reasons."[48]

Eventually, the council restructured its operations, in the process refusing an offer from the minister of health and welfare to become a "social policy and research institute." It opted to stress that "public education, advocacy and networking activities are equally important," and it therefore rejected the federal government's suggested format. Ultimately, CCSD research activities did receive new funding from the federal government, but the council had maintained its position as a social policy critic. The focus remained, therefore, on seeking project funding.

Throughout these years, the council was virtually bankrupt. It was trying to but had not succeeded in selling its Ottawa office at 55 Parkdale Avenue, its headquarters since 1956. It had again reduced the size of the board, cutting from thirty-nine to twenty-one. It had suspended simultaneous translation services during board meetings. As one of a series of measures taken to ensure the survival of the organization, francophone members on the board agreed to this decision. Nonetheless, they remained irritated by what they saw as the low value placed on services that served as recognition of the distinctiveness of francophone members. From their perspective, language services were most often the first on the agenda to be reassessed when financial choices were made.

A Breakup over Real Estate

The late 1980s and 1990s comprised a period of heated political debate surrounding the future of Canada. Despite the variety of political opinion housed within the council, and large divides across the membership, the council was able to avoid crisis by limiting discussion of these matters within the organization.

Nonetheless, as several interviewees recounted, some of the members of the CCSD had difficulty coming to terms with the fact that some representatives from Quebec could be nationalists but as progressive social critics they could also believe that the CCSD was a relevant actor and an important place to debate these issues. The expressed Quebec nationalist sympathies of some CCSD members and employees were a source of irritation to some board members.[49]

The cost, indeed existence, of the office in Montreal eventually became the focus of such conflicts. A building to house a Montreal office had been purchased in 1989, when the council had its highest revenue ever. The notion was, as interviewees described, that investing in the concrete symbolism of real estate would be a way to gain greater visibility in Quebec and to reach out to that constituency in a period of political tension. The idea of offices outside Ottawa was not totally novel; the CCSD had struggled throughout its history with the issue of whether it should encourage the establishment of satellite offices. Given the political context in Canada at the time, it was decided that an office in Quebec would be an important way to foster good relations with the membership in Quebec.

It was also convenient to open the office because the CCSD had just hired a new research officer, Jean-Bernard Robichaud, who wished to remain in Montreal. He was a francophone from Acadia and had strong links with francophone communities outside Quebec. He saw his mandate as building bridges across the francophone communities in Canada.

Quickly, however, circumstances changed. Between the 1989-90 and 1990-91 financial years, revenues tumbled a huge $1,090,138. In 1992, Robichaud was replaced by Marc-André Deniger, who regarded the office as addressing the needs of members in Quebec. As a reflection of this shift in vision, the "Montreal office" was increasingly referred to as the "Quebec office."

Members in Quebec were also engaged in practices that differed somewhat from the research focus being developed in Ottawa. They favoured research that was more action oriented and focused directly on the needs of the local community. They wanted to link up with community groups across Quebec and combine forces to strengthen their advocacy role.[50] Having the office in Montreal was therefore a crucial tool to enable them to reach local communities across Quebec. It was also a way to create and maintain political visibility in Quebec as debates about social policy issues loomed larger.

As the financial vice tightened, the board had to consider what to do with the building and its activities. Cost cutting was instituted, but the financial situation of the whole council was deteriorating rapidly. When the board determined in June 1992 that it would put 55 Parkdale Avenue up for sale, the decision about Montreal was delayed until a later date.[51] Finally, in March 1993, the decision to sell the Montreal building was made. It joined the Ottawa building on the market, but there were no purchasers in sight for either.

Despite deciding to sell the building, the council still had the option of maintaining an operation in Montreal. Conflict over the matter was high throughout 1993 and 1994.[52] In June 1993, there was a vote of eight in favour and five (the members from Quebec) opposed on closing the office unless it could be shown to the satisfaction of the executive that it could be fiscally viable. The report to the executive eventually determined that it could not be, and the decision was made to shut down the CCSD presence in Quebec. Interestingly enough, the report also claimed that an independent provincial organization would be eligible for funding from the provincial government. It might therefore be self-sustaining if it were not part of the CCSD.

In February 1994, the immediate past president of the CCSD, Jean Panet-Raymond, presented a jointly signed letter announcing the resignation of all five Quebec members of the Board of Governors. The letter mentioned a number of factors, but most of the argument hung on the decision to close the office. "It stated that the case for the continuation of the Bureau, and the role it played not only provincially but in Canadian social policy as a whole, had not been adequately recognized by the Board."[53]

Not surprisingly, the resignation of the five members has been dissected and rehashed many times over. For many members of the board, the departure of the Quebec members was an example of poor sportsmanship or a case of leaving a potentially sinking ship rather than staying to defend it. They resented the Quebecers abandoning the organization in the middle of a financial crisis and when the future of the CCSD was so uncertain. Others sought to explain the decision with reference to a number of factors. They ranged from sheer nationalist pique or preparations for an independent Quebec to utter disappointment in the failure of board members from outside Quebec to understand the importance, in terms of recognition and social policy outcomes, of having a presence on the ground in Quebec.[54] While various accounts of nationalist sentiments were popular, at least one person interviewed, who was not involved directly at the time and is not from Quebec, was skeptical of the "nationalist" explanation. Indeed, this interviewee suggested that insensitivity and leadership style of the CCSD executive meant that the decision "was done in a way that almost forced the members from Quebec to resign."

The infrastructure of a social policy council still existed in Quebec after the resignations. It laid the groundwork for a new organization, and Jean Panet-Raymond became the president of the quickly created Conseil québécois de développement social.

Through its participation in the consultations around the social security review of 1994, the CQDS was able to secure a grant of $30,000 from the federal government. The money allowed it to rent office space, hire staff members, and get a minimum of equipment in order to operate. Essentially, it operated out of the same office as in the CCSD days, with the same staff. The CQDS bought the computers and other equipment that had belonged to the CCSD in Montreal.

The resignations and the creation of the CQDS were deeply troubling for the CCSD for a number of reasons. Obviously, a high-profile secession is not something any organization welcomes, and when the context is one interpreted in terms of patterns of linguistic association, as this one was, it is doubly difficult. However, the CCSD concerns were not simply tied to Quebec.

Rather, the CCSD feared that the establishment of an autonomous social development council in Quebec would encourage other provinces to opt out of the main organization. Such bodies already existed in British Columbia and Ontario. Thus, in the annual report of 1993-94, the CCSD sounded a warning about the need to maintain a pan-Canadian presence at the centre: "While we wholeheartedly support the development of provincial planning and social development councils like those already established in British Columbia and Ontario, we do not believe that a provincial council replaces the need for a strong Canadian voice for social development. This need is underscored by the current social security review now underway and the proposed reforms by federal and provincial governments across the country."[55] Any further defections or fragmentation of resources could prove to be costly.

Patterns of Association after 1994

When the five Quebec members of the Board of Governors resigned in 1994, both the letter of resignation and the response from the CCSD board expressed the hope that collaboration would continue. For the CCSD itself, it took a couple of years to re-establish links with members in Quebec; it had to struggle to rebuild its representation in Quebec. For a whole year after the event, no one from Quebec sat on the board but finally new members did join it. At first, they were all anglophone, and more recently there has been a mix of anglophones and francophones.

Although when they resigned the members from Quebec hoped to create the CQDS, they also believed their work would complement that of the CCSD.[56] The CQDS did not succeed in taking off as a visible and active organization, however. And the CCSD continued to make serious efforts to establish its presence in Quebec. For example, a 2000 publication on urban poverty in Quebec appeared only in French and was widely promoted by the new executive director, Marcel Lauzière.

Thus, in spite of the resignation *en bloc* of the Quebec-based members of the Board of Governors and the creation of the CQDS, the CCSD has maintained its commitment to being a pan-Canadian and bilingual organization representing members throughout Canada. It continues to translate and publish in much the same way as in the 1980s, when the end of Secretary of State funding for bilingualism and federal sustaining grants forced it to make careful decisions about what to translate and under which circumstances. The CCSD is formally bilingual and provides some services in both languages and others in English only. It does not, however, as the CWC did, provide any particular recognition of two cultures.

And indeed it was this non-recognition that helped to lead to the split. Not only did members of the board from Quebec feel they had little linguistic recognition, but they also failed to convince their *confrères* and *consoeurs* that social policy in Quebec was local, community–based, and action oriented and that therefore a local presence was needed. In other words, the real institutional differences in the social policy practices of Quebec compared with the rest of Canada added to the difficulties the CCSD faced in the province.

Then there was the budgetary crunch. As the federal government promoted one set of expectations about funding social policy research and the Quebec government limited its funding to Quebec-based groups, both the decision to shed the Montreal office and that to set up the CQDS were reasonable.

An irony, of course, is that the federal social security review process, with which the former executive director of the CCSD, Patrick Johnston, was so deeply involved, also provided the "seed grant" for the CQDS. But perhaps this is not so ironic. The same people were still doing the same things; only their patterns of linguistic association had changed. The CQDS was trying to occupy a space in Quebec for addressing issues in the province; this was the same space that groups in Ontario and British Columbia sought to occupy. At the same time, social policy actors in Quebec continued to recognize the CCSD as an important locus for discussing issues of concern and a critical actor in the federal social policy field. Indeed, over the last half decade the CCSD has re-established a place within Quebec's social policy community by recruiting board members who are well-known and have strong ties across the province. Despite the difficulties, it has remained a pan-Canadian organization speaking up for social justice.

7

Managing Linguistic Practices in International Development NGOs: The World University Service of Canada

Cathy Blacklock

The World University Service of Canada (WUSC) is one of the major international development non-governmental organizations (ID NGOs) in Canada. As a country chapter of World University Service (WUS) International and based at university campuses across the country, WUSC from the early 1920s through the 1950s was to raise funds for WUS International's student-relief efforts in war-torn Europe. Now it is positioned in the small but highly vocal and visible ID NGO community as an experienced, professional, and streamlined organization dedicated to international development work in Africa, Asia, and Latin America and development education work with university students on Canadian campuses.

Like most of the ID NGOs, WUSC has had to struggle to accommodate and manage its linguistic relations. Since its incorporation in 1957, WUSC has been officially bilingual. In practice, however, it has been a predominantly anglophone organization, and English has been the working language. It has faced three moments in its history when language issues have been critical. Each of these moments of change was triggered by different causes: consequently, in each moment, different strategies or "solutions" were adopted to accommodate francophones in the organization.

The first critical moment came in the late 1960s when student radicalism swept university campuses across the country. The dominance of English in WUSC communications came under fire, and agitation for a separate WUS Quebec emerged. An autonomous organization was established in 1968 but had dissolved by the early 1970s. WUSC, too, had almost collapsed by 1973 due to the cancellation of its fundraising activities, such as the treasure van by student delegates to the 1968 national assembly. The period from 1973 through the early 1980s was critical in WUSC's history. During this time, several key individuals – notably "student recruitment officers" Jacques Lapointe and John Watson – worked to rebuild a fully bilingual and bicultural organization. The national office was moved from Toronto to Ottawa to be closer to federal government funding opportunities. Reflecting the influence of the national politics of the Trudeau era, WUSC leadership endeavoured to rebuild the organization to be fully bilingual in its operations, communications, and representation and to create a sense of ownership of the organization by both francophones and anglophones. With funding from the Department of the Secretary of State, a bilingualism program was started in 1977 that included French-language training for WUSC staff and domestic seminars designed to sensitize Canadians to minority language and cultural perspectives. The culmination of this "incorporative" moment came in 1981 when a second WUSC national office was opened in Montreal.

Under the executive directorship of Bill McNeil, WUSC expanded rapidly through the 1980s, and hiring during this period reflected an active effort to recruit an equally representative and effectively bilingual staff. Developing francophone programming – particularly in francophone Africa – became a priority.

The growth of the 1980s proved unsustainable, however, and in late 1990 WUSC had to declare bankruptcy. With bridge financing from CIDA and under new directorship, WUSC undertook the painful process of restructuring. This was the third critical turning point for language relations in the organization. For financial reasons, WUSC was forced to close its Montreal office and lay off many of its staff. By 1992, it began to rebuild as a streamlined professional organization. The pattern of accommodation from 1992 to the present reflects the professional culture of Ottawa, where the capacity to operate in both official languages is assumed. Nonetheless, a bifurcation also common in Ottawa is present in WUSC: while its support staff are predominantly female, francophone, and bilingual, English persists as the operating language at the programming and management levels of the organization. Due to the increasing diversity of Canada's immigrant communities and the increasingly "internationalized" business climate of the 1990s, WUSC has been able to respond proactively to the growing need for a multi-language-skilled professional staff to operate in the now intensely competitive international development environment.

The Early Years of WUSC

In 1999, a staff member of WUSC wrote a brief history of the organization. According to "A Narrative History of WUSC," the organization's "earliest beginnings can be traced to the period following the First World War and an international student organization, the World Student Christian Federation, out of which grew European Student Relief [ESR] – the operational arm of WSCF."[1] European Student Relief gradually evolved into World Student Relief (WSR), with an administrative agency called International Student Service (ISS). In 1950, WSR was dissolved, and ISS adopted the name World University Service. This transformation reflected a broadening of the mandate of the organization. The mission of student relief work in Europe expanded to encompass programs in the Middle East and Asia, and the membership base of the organization grew to include university communities as a whole.

From the inception of WUSC in 1920, Canadian students were involved in fundraising efforts in support of ESR. However, it was not until 1939 that an official Canadian committee was established. Participation in WUSC had always been on a volunteer basis, and it continued to be a voluntary organization until the 1970s. Throughout the 1940s, local WUSC committees formed on university campuses across Canada, including the University of Montreal and Laval University. In 1948, WUSC held the first international seminar in Ploen, Germany. The purpose of the seminars has been to provide Canadian university students with the opportunity to learn about different cultures and international development in a developing country context. In 1997, WUSC celebrated its fiftieth year of international seminars with the Peru seminar.

Throughout the 1950s, WUSC continued fundraising through the sale of crafts from other countries. The treasure van – a convoy of vans and students – travelled from campus to campus across the country; eventually, it became an annual event. On 1 October 1957, WUSC was incorporated. In the 1960s, the treasure van and the international seminar continued to be the mainstay activities of WUSC. As well, it played a fundamental role in promoting the cause of international development in Canada by co-founding in 1961 the Canadian University Service Overseas (CUSO) and in 1963 the Canadian Bureau for International Education (CBIE). WUSC was one of the strongest country chapters of WUS International through the 1960s and 1970s. Over the 1980s, as WUSC started to develop its own projects and consolidate its financial base through CIDA funding, it gradually detached itself from WUS International. Although representatives of WUSC did participate in WUS International proceedings until the dissolution of the parent organization in the early 1990s,[2] they no longer relied on WUS International for guidance.

The Universe of ID NGOs in Canada

The community of ID NGOs in Canada includes approximately 500 organizations. As such, it constitutes only a small segment of the voluntary sector, which counts approximately 55,000 registered organizations.[3] The vast majority are tiny volunteer-based groups. There is a small mid-range of organizations and a handful of large outfits.

The history of this community of NGOs mirrors to a significant degree the history of international development assistance and North-South and East-West relations since the First World War. Reflecting the spirit of charity generated by the Great Depression and/or the political idealism that spawned the League of Nations, most of the ID NGOs that formed in the years before the Second World War were church-based groups or affiliates of international organizations, such as the Save the Children Fund, Scouts and Guides, YMCA, and YWCA. Founded in 1939 as a chapter of WUS International, with the mission of aiding student refugees in Europe, WUSC belongs in the latter category. In the postwar years between 1945 and 1970, a number of the now large ID NGOs such as CARE Canada (1946), UNICEF Canada (1955), World Vision Canada (1954), Christian Children's Fund Canada (CCFC, 1960), Oxfam Canada (1963), and Canadian Executive Services Overseas (CESO, 1967) formed. In 1961, WUSC founded Canadian University Services Overseas (now known only as CUSO) and in 1963 founded the CBIE. CARE, World Vision, and CCFC reflected the continuing tradition of Christian charity behind many organizations concerned particularly with "relief" work and the plight of the world's children. UNICEF Canada reflected the continuing influence of idealism behind the institutional structure of the United Nations. Oxfam Canada reflected the growing awareness of the development needs of the "Third World." And CUSO, CBIE, and CESO reflected the growing recognition that the promotion of education was essential to development in the Third World. These organizations had substantial human resources and financial outlays. This period between 1945 and 1970 was the era of large-scale organizations.

The 1970s and 1980s saw relatively smaller-sized organizations emerge, many of which were involved in research on issues relating to international development, development project delivery, and development education in Canada. The North-South Institute (NSI, 1976), for instance, concentrated on policy-relevant research. Others, such as the Centre d'information et de documentation sur la Mozambique et l'Afrique australe (CIDMAA, 1982) and the Centre d'études arabes pour le développement (CEAD, 1982), expanded their activities beyond research to include "learner centres" and solidarity work or popular education, as in the case of the Cooper Institute (1984).

In contrast to the orientation of the earlier era of large-scale charitable "relief" efforts, the international development work of the 1970s and 1980s sought to incorporate and utilize local resources at the "grassroots" level, thereby involving and supporting local communities to meet their "basic needs." The notable organizations of this era are the Foundation for International Training (FIT), the Aga Khan Foundation Canada (AKFC), HOPE International Development Agency (HOPE), and South Asia Partnership – Canada (SAP). Thus, the period 1970-90 and beyond witnessed the establishment of organizations more focused in terms of specialization in geographical focus or sector of service provision and/or project execution.

Some of the major activities of ID NGOs today continue to be the provision of emergency relief, project delivery, and development education. However, many became increasingly involved in providing technical assistance and doing policy and advocacy work at both the national and the international levels. For instance, the Friends of the Earth (FOE) Canada leads FOE International's ozone campaign and works with the Centre for Science and Environment in India. Similarly, the International Centre for Human Rights and Democratic Development (ICHRDD) seeks to defend human rights and the promotion of democracy by providing support to Canadian and overseas organizations working on these issues.

The nature of international development work has, however, evolved significantly since the infrastructure-building period characteristic of the 1970s. As many northern countries experienced serious economic slowdown in the 1980s, official development assistance (ODA) budgets were cut as governments gave priority to domestic expenditure over international development assistance. In this new era of tight development assistance dollars, international development work refocused on social development. The so-called soft side of international development entails the promotion of sustainable development by building the capacity of local institutions and human resources and, more recently, by promoting democratization, human rights, and good governance. As a result, development work shifted from "project delivery" to aid recipients to provision of technical assistance in support of sustainable development initiatives through North-South partnership arrangements.

While the Canadian community of ID NGOs is very small in comparison to the overall size of the voluntary sector, it nonetheless plays a key role in Canada's international development activities. The high level of activity and project and service delivery undertaken by the community reflects, in part, the fact that CIDA recognizes the cost efficiency and effectiveness of development work undertaken by NGOs and values their ability to work at the "grassroots" level, a key to realizing sustainable development. Consequently, CIDA has actively cultivated the capacity of the ID NGO community to act as Canadian executing agencies (CEAs) for projects that deliver bilateral and region-dedicated flows of ODA money. Since 1995, CIDA has provided matching funds at a ratio of 3:1 to many ID NGOs.[4] The generally supportive relationship CIDA has with the ID NGO community also reflects the fact that the community as a whole – from which many of the professional staff of CIDA have been drawn – is composed of a tightly knit group of Canadians highly committed to international development and social justice issues.

WUSC has been fundamentally important to the formation of this community. Since the 1960s, it has undertaken development education work, including the much-acclaimed international seminars that WUSC has now been organizing for over fifty years. This work has contributed to the formation of several generations of international development activists. Many of the former participants of the international seminars note that their first experiences with both the substantive issues of international development – such as poverty and inadequate infrastructure – and their enduring respect for other cultures were formed through their participation in WUSC study tours and seminars.[5] Many of them subsequently went on to work in international development as members of other NGOs in Canada and elsewhere, some founding their own organizations.

The main representative vehicle of the ID NGO community is the Canadian Council for International Cooperation (CCIC), an Ottawa-based umbrella organization of approximately 100 ID NGOs. The mandate of the CCIC is to coordinate research, media campaigns, government lobbying, and so on for the community. According to its own description, the CCIC "is a coalition of Canadian organizations who seek to change the course of human development in ways that favor social and economic equity, democratic participation, environmental integrity and respect for human rights. Established in 1968, the Council conducts research, disseminates information and creates learning opportunities for its members, coordinating their collective efforts to shape new models for world development, press for national and international policies that serve the global public interest, and build a social movement for global citizenship in Canada."[6]

The members of the ID NGO community vary widely in size when measured by number of personnel. The number of staff directly employed in Canada by the organizations listed in the CCIC publication *Who's Who in International Development: A Profile of Canadian NGOs* varies from 2 to 150, with about half of the organizations employing fewer than 10 persons. The sizes of the ID NGOs also vary significantly when measured by annual budgets, which range from $20,000 to $74.85 million. With approximately sixty employees and an annual budget ranging between $20.95 million (1994) and $16.8 million (1998), WUSC falls in the mid-to-large-size range of ID NGOs.

The linguistic practices of the community of ID NGOs are reflected in whether they are listed with a French name in the 1995 CCIC list of ID NGOs and whether their websites contain a French version. While the majority of CCIC-member organizations were thus found to be bilingual, 18.5 percent (twenty-two) appear to be unilingual English. Another twenty-two organizations are also apparently unilingual English, although this fact could not be verified as they do not have official websites. Fourteen organizations in Quebec are primarily francophone. All of the large organizations are bilingual with the following few exceptions: the Canadian Cooperative Association (CCA), Oxfam Canada,[7] USC (Unitarian Service Committee) Canada, and World Vision Canada.[8] As this study demonstrates, WUSC is one of the bilingual ID NGOs and has demonstrated a pattern of linguistic accommodation since its inception.

Seeking Accommodation: The Vagaries of Linguistic Relations over Time

In its early years, WUSC was an organization comprised of local committees of students and professors from university and college campuses across the country. WUSC was created with the intention of being bilingual from its inception, at least in theory. In its statutes, it is mentioned that the official languages of the service shall be French and English, since the first incorporation in 1957. WUSC has also had francophone members throughout its history. From its beginning, representation in WUSC was ensured by organizational membership. Since there were few francophone institutions that were members of WUS, however, it followed that there was little francophone representation at meetings. Thus, in practice, membership was mainly anglophone and has remained predominantly anglophone. The organization operates and provides services in both languages and has taken a number of initiatives over time to ensure francophone participation. However, there has never been equal representation of both linguistic groups on the staff, the Board of Directors, or the membership.

From the general assembly held in July 1964, the WUS statutes state that "WUS aims at expressing and promoting international university solidarity and mutual service within and between universities and centres of higher learning throughout the world."[9] Throughout the 1960s, international development became a highly politicized issue, owing in part to the ending of colonial rule in many Asian and African countries. It was also a decade characterized by growing student radicalism, and Canadian university campuses were not exempt from this trend. In the late 1960s, WUSC experienced its first significant crisis as an organization and between 1967 and 1969 endured a period of intensive introspection. By 1967, WUSC was losing an increasing number of local committees that disagreed with the vision and mission of WUSC. This identity crisis was exacerbated by WUSC's communication problems: the organization had difficulty transmitting information to local committees and keeping them informed of their activities. This was particularly a problem with the local committees in the West.

Since WUSC relied on the efforts of its local committees to raise funds in support of its activities, it was highly sensitive to the demands and pressures that came from the student movement. At the annual general meeting of 1968 held in Edmonton, student delegates passed motions to end the treasure van fundraising, arguing that it was demeaning to individuals in developing countries and exploitative of their work. Furthermore, while WUSC had generally abstained from involvement in political debates, student delegates also passed motions at the 1968 national assembly that redefined the organization as a political organization and a social movement. The students insisted that WUSC serve as a vehicle to develop awareness of the problems of Third World countries and help to educate Canadians about developmental issues. Consequently, WUSC became political, for example by officially pronouncing itself against apartheid. The priorities of WUSC were redefined as follows:

> That WUSC give priority to developing an international political conscious-ness in the university community; That WUSC act as a pressure group on the government and the community in an effort to stimulate public concern regarding the problems of domestic and international development; That WUSC be prepared to take public stands on matters of domestic and inter-national political importance; That on a nationally organized basis the traditional programme of fund-raising project Treasure Van be ended within approximately 24 months and the national SHARE campaign immediately. It is recognized that local WUSC committees may wish to innovate alterna-tive campaign models, related to local and regional conditions, for the support of WUS International Programme of Action.[10]

Among the solutions to the communication problems and identity crisis contemplated at the time was the dissolution of the organization, an option outlined in a letter by George Tillman entitled "Whither WUSC?" In 1969, Manuel F. Neira, a member of the WUSC national committee, was commis-sioned to write a report evaluating the structures of the organization and propose reforms. His report was entitled *Report on Structural Reforms and Constitutional Revisions*. The main concern of the report was the lack of par-ticipation of faculty and students because of the lack of relevance of the issues WUSC addressed. It notes that "the problem manifests itself simply in low control at all organizational levels, relatively high control of the na-tional secretariat with respect to the national committee and practically a non-existent control by the local membership."[11]

Among the recommendations made was the revision of the structure of the Board of Directors to reflect the membership. In 1968, the statutes were amended, and the composition of the board was increased to twelve members, six of whom had to be in full-time programs of study, one representative of the Canadian Union of Students (CUS), one of the Canadian Association of University Teachers (CAUT), one of the Association of Universities and Col-leges of Canada (AUCC), one of the Union générale des étudiants du Québec (UGEQ), and two from each local committee, known as corresponding members. This composition of the board reflected the membership of the organization at the time. Neira's report also stated that "the previous con-siderations have been translated into operational terms by proposing WUSC field workers (one for each province to the West of Ontario, and one for the Maritimes)."[12] It was not until 1969 that representation was restructured along regional lines. Amendments were adopted so the Board of Directors would include field representatives, three international liaison officers (which reflected the importance of WUSC affiliations with other international organizations), and three members-at-large.

It was during this period that language relations first became a significant issue within WUSC. In 1965, there were already concerns within the organization about the need to develop an appropriate communications strategy to reach people from across Canada. A communications committee was created to deal with issues concerning communication strategies, such as the use of posters, pamphlets, and publicity, but issues of language were not raised during these meetings. Most often discussions on linguistic relations pertained to the availability of documents in both French and English and the quality of the translation.

Until 1966, most documents remained solely in English. Some of the reports had small components that were written in French, but only those sections that were related to issues uniquely of concern to francophones, such as the annual francophone meeting minutes. After the international seminar in Chile in 1966, great dissatisfaction was expressed with the French-language content of the seminar report. This feedback resulted in a motion designed to ensure satisfactorily high French content in future international seminar reports. These reports became officially bilingual from 1966 onward. In May 1967, a motion was passed for the publication of separate French and English WUSC leaflets, and most documents were made available in French. Around this time, WUSC also hired a secretary who spoke French.

Despite these efforts to operate as a bilingual organization, the francophone local committee members argued that francophone universities could better contribute to WUS International if they had their own chapters and headquarters in Quebec. This sentiment reflected in part an attitude widespread at the time that autonomous organizations were needed to represent the interests of Quebecers and respond to their particular needs.[13] Supported by UGEQ, the francophone local committees of WUSC decided to leave WUSC to create their own independent organization in Quebec.

This decision was made through a consultative process and was based on a consensus within the organization that autonomy was the appropriate direction for WUSC. Since the 1950s, WUSC has organized special meetings during the annual assemblies to accommodate linguistic representation. Separate meetings are held for local committees of French- and English-speaking communities to discuss issues of specific concern to their members such as communication strategies, recruitment campaigns, and project development. From as early as 1965, the French-speaking local committees have discussed the possibility of opening an office in Montreal, the costs of operating headquarters in Quebec, and budgetary provisions for those operations.

In 1967, a working group was established to further assess the possibility of creating a World University Service Quebec (WUSQ). On 2 December 1967, the UGEQ, a member of WUSC, resolved to encourage the establishment of an independent organization in Quebec, Entraide universitaire mondiale du Québec (EUMQ). After a joint meeting between the UGEQ and a delegation from WUSC held on 21 June 1968 to evaluate the possibility of creating a separate structure for EUMQ, the Board of Directors agreed to the creation of a provisional committee with total responsibility for WUS in Quebec.[14] Shortly after, the newly created EUMQ temporarily moved into the old offices of UGEQ, which it subleased.

Over the next few months, communication between the EUMQ and WUSC proved difficult to maintain. Although the EUMQ and WUSC agreed to collaborate on specific projects, there was little contact between the two organizations despite ongoing efforts by WUSC to establish firmer links with its sister organization in Quebec. Although WUSC attempted in vain to rebuild links with the EUMQ through written correspondence, the EUMQ did not reciprocate. It remained firm in its desire to have independence from the office in Ottawa. By September 1968, the bridge-building efforts were abandoned after the national committee of WUSC agreed "that Quebec committees would receive assembly minutes. Quebec was no longer the concern of the national committee of WUSC. The secretariat would respond with discretion to requests from EUMQ committees, but would not be actively involved in Quebec."[15]

The presence of two national organizations representing WUS International in Canada would raise several technical and financial issues around the organization of the annual assembly. For example, the minutes note that, "due to the nature of the relationship between EUMQ and WUSC and supposing EUMQ participation in the symposium, the technicalities of EUMQ's role in decision-making bodies of the Symposium must be clarified by the Symposium Executive Committee ... That in the event of EUMQ's participation in the 1969 symposium, the problems of cost-sharing between organizations, particularly the soliciting and use of federal government funds would be brought to the attention of the business and finance committees."[16] In light of the forthcoming 1969 annual assembly, efforts were to be made to ensure that simultaneous translation was available at the symposium to accommodate the EUMQ. It was believed that its participation was dependent on the presence of translation services.[17] Despite these efforts, however, the EUMQ did not participate in the annual assembly proceedings.

While within Canada the EUMQ was recognized as a "national" representative, it did not have a voice within the structure of the international parent organization. The EUMQ went to the general headquarters of WUS International in Geneva seeking recognition of its role as the representative of Quebec. In agreement with WUSC, representatives from Quebec were delegated to the international assembly in Leysin in May 1968 and made a plea for recognition. The WUS International assembly denied this request and explained its decision as follows:

> On the basis of the present statutes of WUS, it is not possible for a WUS Committee to be established in Quebec and recognized by the General Assembly. Present categories for recognition cover only committees established in "any country" which are "broadly representative." WUS has already a national committee in Canada recognized on this basis. If a regional committee were to be formed within the universities of Quebec for the purpose of supporting the WUS programme, direct contacts could be established with WUS Geneva (with the agreement of WUS Canada). WUS Geneva would supply material regarding the WUS Programme and would keep the committee informed of WUS activities. The committee could raise funds for WUS and be invited to take part in WUS activities such as the General Assembly. The committee could say that it was a body cooperating with WUS although it could not use the name of WUS as such. On the basis of experience, it would be possible to review the situation in a few years' time. However, it should be made clear to the committee that although it would be open to the General Assembly to change its statutes at any time, it is unlikely that any change would be made to cater for the particular situation of Quebec universities because of the precedent which this might create for other university communities.[18]

The EUMQ remained fairly inactive over the next few years and was not able to sustain its operations in Quebec. Separation of the EUMQ from WUSC and its eventual dissolution had important repercussions for WUSC representation in Quebec. Given that the EUMQ had been inactive for a couple of years, WUSC had to work hard to re-establish its presence on campuses across Quebec. It had to rebuild communications with local committees and universities to reinstate regional representation from Quebec on the Board of Directors of WUSC.

The next critical moment in WUSC's management of linguistic relations occurred hand in hand with the rebuilding of the organization that took place from 1972 onward. In general, the 1970s were characterized by a re-orientation of WUSC's organizational identity and character and, concomitantly, its activities, as an ID NGO. The major contribution WUSC made to international development work in this decade was in the area of education, a focus consistent with its history as a university-based organization. It was particularly active in the recruitment and placement of Canadian teachers overseas.

The reactivation of francophone participation and representation in WUSC was a concern early on in this period of rebuilding in light of the dissolution of the EUMQ. On 16 May 1972, during the annual meeting, the possibility of moving the Toronto office to Ottawa was addressed. Although concern was expressed over the potential of government influence on WUSC policies and projects, the desirability of being located closer to Quebec and the francophone community was recognized. Moreover, it was argued by the Board of Directors that such a move would facilitate access to federal government funding sources. On 7 October 1973, the national committee passed a resolution, moved by André Sirois, l'Université de Laval, and seconded by Dale Postgate, "that the executive committee employ a full time secretary in the national office who is fully competent in French. One of the secretary's responsibilities will be to check the translation of documents."

The major issue facing WUSC during the 1970s was, however, that of finances. One severe consequence of the crisis of identity and communication problems of the late 1960s was that the funding base of the organization was severely eroded, leaving the organization in financial shambles.[19] It was under the executive directorship of Bill McNeil that a solid financial base was established for WUSC. Gone were the days, however, when fundraising on university campuses supported the organization. Under McNeil's directorship from 1976 to 1990, the organization was reshaped to undertake, administer, and deliver international development projects, and measures were taken to ensure adequate funding of this work. McNeil put together project funding from a variety of sources but most importantly from the newly founded CIDA. In 1969, CIDA had insisted that its funds be tied to projects. But in 1971, WUSC received funding from CIDA for general operations. From this point to 1992, WUSC was increasingly reoriented as an organization geared to project delivery.[20]

The student base of WUSC membership was never completely forgotten, however, and two individuals, Jacques Lapointe and John Watson, played an important role in the reactivation of linkages with francophone universities and student participation more generally. Finding themselves sharing the same brief within WUSC – that of student recruitment – they were forced to encounter their respective cultural isolation as representatives of anglophone and francophone Canada. Working through this "encounter" led them to the idea of organizing a domestic seminar program to augment the international seminars. These seminars were "planned to provide a forum for learning about and understanding the lives of Francophone minority groups in Canada."[21]

The government of Quebec funded parts of these seminars to foster a better understanding of how francophone minorities were dealing with language issues. The domestic seminars were also encouraged with funding from the federal government through the Department of the Secretary of State since they corresponded well with the purpose of "the Trudeau era of citizenship." Despite the financial support from these various sources, the domestic seminars were still expensive for students, who had to contribute between $2,000 and $3,000 to participate. Consequently, the domestic seminar and francophone program were short-lived as they were not sustained when funding dried up. The Board of Directors decided that WUSC's mission was not to provide domestic services; rather, its activities should focus on international development.

The organizational structure of WUSC was also revised during this period. WUSC had also just signed a global accord with CIDA for a three-year program that included francophone programming and project development in French countries. This restructuring proved to have a modest positive effect on linguistic relations. In August 1976, the statutes were changed to include a seat for a Quebec representative on the Board of Directors. The composition of the board was then president, vice-president, treasurer, five regional representatives (Atlantic provinces, Quebec, Ontario, Manitoba and Saskatchewan, Alberta and British Columbia), and five members-at-large. The statutes further stated that, of the thirteen members, at least three were to be francophone, and two were to be from universities and CEGEPs (Collèges d'enseignement général et professionnel). In Quebec, regional representation was re-established. However, Quebec counted as one region of four, the others being the Atlantic region, Ontario, and western Canada. Again, francophone representation in WUSC continued to be low. Nevertheless, for the first time, a minimal representation of francophones was ensured. This structure of representation remains in effect today.

One of the major catalysts for the development of bilingual communications tools was the availability of funding from the Department of the Secretary of State for the sole purpose of facilitating access to information in both official languages. The funding made available was substantial: WUSC received $20,000. On 2 December 1975, a long-term bilingualism development program for WUSC was submitted to the national committee. It stated that WUSC "(relative to other organizations) is extremely unitary in its structure and operations. Except at the local committee level there is literally no activity or structure in which the Francophone members participate as a majority group. The proposal to make seminars alternatively unilingual French and English is a more positive step towards changing this situation."[22] At the national committee meeting, the program was agreed to in principle.

On 9 February 1976, the bilingualism development program was accepted, and on 31 May a new director of the bilingualism program, Jeanne Boiclaire, was named. In July 1976, WUSC's official bilingualism program was put into effect (with funding support from the Department of the Secretary of State). The aim of the program was to allow WUSC membership to have direct contact and thereby gradually eliminate the need for translation services.

The program had four main components, as outlined in the 1976 annual report:

(1) publication of a French newsletter with the aim of publishing two issues simultaneously (in French and English);
(2) creation of French material (the first project was to be a slide and sound show on the role of local committees);
(3) preparation of French material for all programs; and
(4) teaching of French to all national office employees.[23]

According to the Secretary of State project guidelines under which the bilingualism program was funded, all national office personnel were to attain bilingual capacity within three years. In the interim, translation for WUSC was to be done by a professional translator hired by WUSC on a part-time basis. This part of the larger program became the predominant feature when, in 1978, it was divided into the two main components, language training, which encouraged the acquisition of a second language, and translation, which ensured that every employee who wished to have a text translated could access the services of the translator. The program lasted two years, after which the funding was not renewed.

Several other changes in the WUSC operations indicate genuine desire and effort to build links with the francophone community as well as with other parts of Canada. For example, at the national assembly on 30 May 1980, it was decided that the annual meetings would be rotated each year across the regions (the east, Quebec, Ontario, and the west). In 1981, a second WUSC office was opened in Montreal to serve the needs of the Quebec constituency, with bilingual services provided. The activities of the Montreal office increased over its first year. It had administrative responsibility for the administration of the Canada Awards Program in Quebec,[24] it was entrusted with the organization of the Montreal part of the International Commerce Centre (ICC) United Nations Conference on Trade and Development (UNCTAD)/GATT held in April 1981, and it actively recruited francophones to participate in the francophone programs overseas. WUSC also maintained relations with the Quebec Association of International Development Organizations (Association québécoise des organismes de coopération internationale).

Discussions were also held in this period about the possible incorporation of the EUMC (Quebec Section) to gain access to funding from the Ministry of Education in Quebec. The ministry offered a statutory grant to cover 75 percent of the administrative costs and 25 percent of the operating budget of the WUSC office in Montreal. The grant was conditional upon the incorporation of WUSC in Quebec. The ministry also suggested it would negotiate a reduction in the tuition fees of foreign students sponsored by WUSC to study at Quebec universities. Josée Lafleur, director of the Montreal office at the time, noted that a "decision to incorporate WUSC at the provincial level would reflect WUSC's determination to establish itself permanently in the province of Quebec."[25] In the end, however, WUSC was not incorporated in Quebec, but the Montreal office continued as a going concern for the organization.

Over the next ten years, the organization went through an unprecedented period of growth under the continued directorship of Bill McNeil. It was during the 1980s that WUSC "spread its wings" as an ID NGO and expanded into the provision of technical assistance. WUSC became an active Canadian executing agency for CIDA bilateral technical assistance programs, undertaking, for example, the capacity building of educators and educational systems, the administration of training projects for professionals from developing countries, and the management of exchange programs. As well, it expanded both its sectoral and its geographical coverage[26] and increased its partnerships with other aid delivery agencies, including Canadian consulting firms and other national government ODA programs.

The third turning point in the management of linguistic relations in WUSC was triggered by the bankruptcy of the organization. The rapid growth of WUSC through the 1980s had produced a concomitant growth in staff. WUSC had grown too large for its office space and undertook to build a new office. In early 1990, the staff moved into the new office, and on 26 September the office was officially opened, with the ceremonies presided over by visiting President Mugabe. In December 1990, WUSC went into receivership. The sale of the old office on Scott Street was to have financed the new office. However, a combination of problems, including zoning regulations and a severe downturn in the Ottawa real estate market, made the sale impossible and forced WUSC into receivership.

CIDA agreed to provide WUSC with a bridge loan that allowed the organization to restructure. A skeletal staff was retained, and WUSC moved back into its old office space in the summer of 1991. Perhaps the most painful decision was the one to close the Montreal office. By 1991, the worst of the financial crisis was behind it, and WUSC was becoming active again in international development projects. This period of reorganization, which continued through the mid-1990s, was characterized by a reorientation of WUSC back toward its traditional strengths: education-related work overseas and development education on Canadian university and college campuses. In 1994, for example, it expanded its overseas offerings to postsecondary students to include exchange programs and overseas internships.

Through the early 1990s, WUSC worked actively to rebuild its financial base in local committees. Regional meetings were arranged to consolidate the network between local committees in different regions, and these meetings continued until 1995. Among the recurring subjects discussed in the Quebec regional meeting was the reopening of a regional office in Montreal. Although the issue remained on the agenda, a Montreal office was not financially possible for the organization.

In 1995, WUSC again examined linguistic relations, and that examination led to the institutionalization of an official language policy in 1995. While in the late 1980s and early 1990s the focus had been on the "product" and getting more projects, after receivership renewed attention was directed toward WUSC's membership and its needs. As part of this renewed focus, a conscious effort was made to offer services attractive to francophones. Reflecting this concern, the official policy adopted stated that all documents for external use were to be made available in both languages. While most of the translation is sent out to a professional translator, the bilingual staff in house often end up doing translation without verification of its quality. This work has placed additional pressure on the bilingual staff. Most of the staff members who do some of the translation work think that this situation is unfair and that the work entailed is underestimated.

A committee was set up in 1996 with the mandate of developing WUSC as a "francophone-friendly" organization. It has the responsibility of evaluating on an ongoing basis the state of bilingualism within the organization. The intention of the committee was to deal with both francophone participation and programming, including a review of projects and contracts, funding, and public relations. However, in practice, the committee has been mainly concerned with technical issues to do with translation.

The advent of electronic technologies has changed the communication strategies of WUSC. Information was to circulate faster among the members, the staff, and the board. In reality, the same factor has made it more difficult to circulate information in both languages simultaneously. Circulating information in French consistently takes longer because of the delays caused by translation. WUSC developed a website and a list-serve in both languages. In practice, however, because it is faster, information is routinely communicated through the English list-serve and not translated onto the French bulletin board. Most members have ended up communicating through the English bulletin board because doing so guarantees that they receive adequate information rapidly. WUSC later joined the two bulletin boards to create a bilingual one. However, most of the communications through this venue are in English.

Conclusion

Over the many years of WUSC's existence, its capacity to fulfill its own functional purpose has waxed and waned. In general, however, this capacity has not been affected negatively or positively by its management of linguistic relations. WUSC established itself early on as an important player in the ID NGO community, and despite the serious setback it faced in the early 1990s as a result of financial crisis it has rebuilt and restructured effectively and continues in its role as an organization active in international development work. While its purpose was somewhat modified in the 1980s during the heyday of expansion, it returned to its "roots" in the 1990s by refocusing energy on international development work on education-related projects and development education of Canadian university students.

Since its incorporation, WUSC has demonstrated a pattern of accommodation in the management of linguistic relations. However, the mode of accommodation has varied over time, from separatism in the late 1960s, to incorporation in the latter half of the 1970s, to efficient functioning in the mid-1990s. These different modes of accommodation reflect the ongoing effort of the organization to accommodate linguistic differences in three different socioeconomic environments: the rise of radical student politics and Quebec separatism in the late 1960s, the growth of the development "aid industry" and the Trudeau era from the mid-1970s onward, and the bankruptcy of the organization in the context of tight development dollars in the 1990s. At the leadership and management levels of WUSC, the need for the organization to be bilingual has consistently been assumed. Nonetheless, the meaning of "being bilingual" has changed over time. In the late 1960s, progressive anglophone university students accepted the cause of separatism. At the height of the Trudeau era, progressive university students shared a desire for the two solitudes to encounter each other, as the story of the friendship and working relationship of Jacques Lapointe and John Watson illuminates. Since the globalized and lean decade of the 1990s, bilingualism has been accepted as a requisite for doing business – especially in Ottawa. But schemes to bring all staff up to bilingual capacity are no longer imagined as the means to fulfilling this requisite. And in the world of international development in the first decade of the twenty-first century, a multilingual staff capacity is viewed as necessary to operational efficacy. It is important to note, then, that only in the second "moment" of the latter half of the 1970s – characterized by abundant funding both for international development work and for bilingualism and biculturalism initiatives – did the vision of bilingualism "imagined" within WUSC entail "ownership" of the organization shared as a partnership of anglophones and francophones. Had a distinct francophone organization persisted, the pattern of accommodation might have evolved into one of sovereignty-association. As it is, WUSC is a single national body that remains predominantly anglophone in its structure and operation.

8
Two Voices for Human Rights: Amnesty International
Michel Duquette and Sylvie Dugas

Since the foundation of the Canadian section of Amnesty International (AI) in 1973, relations between francophones and anglophones have evolved positively, although not without occasional periods of stress. After a major crisis in 1978, which resulted in the separation of the two groups, these relations have remained civilized and mutually respectful. Our research on the anglophone and francophone chapters of the Canadian section of AI has convinced us that the activists of this organization have maintained, independently of their culture, and after their separation into two linguistic chapters, the pursuit of common objectives. Their fidelity to the goal of defending human rights has allowed them both to transcend their different sensibilities and to collaborate closely on the central issue that initially brought them together. The common interest of both linguistic groups, seeking to attract the attention of governments and citizens, has predominated and reinforced their capacity to cooperate. Moreover, their joint membership in an international organization, the International Secretariat (IS) of AI in London, has closely linked them in all their activities.

This degree of cooperation has been achieved not through greater organizational unity or integration but through a "pattern of disengagement" resulting in a relationship that bears many similarities to the political model of sovereignty-association. Indeed, as we will show, this disengagement was a necessary condition of success. Linguistic tensions within a closer union had previously interfered with the common mission.

According to the hypothesis put forward by John Meisel and Vincent Lemieux,[1] linguistic and cultural differences in the binational Canadian context influence strategic choices with respect both to organizational operations and to efforts to influence public opinion. This was certainly the case of Amnesty International in Canada. Since the creation of AI Canada in 1973, anglophones have been a majority within the association. The language used at the IS in London has also been predominantly English, although translation services were made available in the 1980s. Francophones were a majority in the province of Quebec but remained a minority with limited representation on the Executive Committee and the General Assembly of the national section as well as on the International Council (IC). Because of their small numbers, they did not have the necessary resources to establish an independent office, as they desired, or to cover the costs of translating AI's documents.[2]

Therefore, within the Canadian section, francophones were often unable to work in their own language. Moreover, they had different preferences regarding the content and the form of public awareness campaigns, membership recruitment drives, the management of budgets, and the coordination of their activities. Friction between the Montreal branch and the Ottawa head office became constant, largely because the rules of the organization required that francophones (the minority) obtain the authorization of anglophones (the majority) for all decisions. The organizational efficiency of both the anglophone and the francophone branches was weakened because of time wasted in consultation, seeking approval of specific files, as well as in translation costs and simultaneous translation during national meetings.

Language and related issues, such as strategy, power, and autonomy, were thus threatening to paralyze the organization and to subvert its fundamental mission. The centralized administration placed the minority linguistic group in a weaker position because it could not develop on its own terms. The conflicting interests of the leaders collided: François Martin of the francophone branch wanted at any price to obtain the separation of the two entities, while the founder and former president of Amnesty International Canada, John Humphrey, strongly opposed a split. However, the president of the national section at the time, Laing Ferguson, demonstrated openness toward the claims of francophones, as did Sean Marbright, an Irishman who, along with Peter Benenson, had founded the international movement. There is no doubt that sovereignist ideology inspired the francophone leaders of AI to seek a more entrenched organizational autonomy, to which the anglophone leadership would have to respond. Fortunately, their shared commitment to international human rights enabled both sides to resolve their differences.

The division of the organization into two independent and pan-Canadian linguistic branches,[3] which are linked by the pursuit of the same objectives and by which both are subordinated to the International Secretariat in London, seems to have been a success and has been for the good of the AI movement in Canada as a whole. The sovereignty-association of the organizations – separate entities collaborating on shared interests – has contributed to the resolution of existing problems between the members of Canada's two linguistic groups. Their autonomous working arrangement combined with joint tasks has enabled the two chapters to earn the confidence of both the anglophone and the francophone populations and to increase membership. The ability of each to communicate in a single language with its supporters has reduced expenses and eliminated time-wasting activities. The separation into two chapters was made without bitterness, and the public image of AI was not tarnished. Both chapters continued to coordinate their efforts during public awareness campaigns dictated by the London head office. The Quebec leaders were able to exercise their leadership in francophone members' activities throughout the country, while the Ottawa-based section managed AI's affairs across English Canada. They were united not by language or political identity but by a common cause that transcended domestic ethnic and cultural divisions.

This did not happen easily or by accident. Leadership played an important role. The arrival of Roger Clark in 1988 and Michel Frenette in 1994, respectively, as the heads of the anglophone and francophone sections of AI ensured a high level of collaboration between the two organizations. Originally from Britain, Clark was fluently bilingual and maintained excellent relations with Frenette. Each section consulted the other regularly before press conferences and developed common strategies to exercise pressures on the federal government and foreign governments. The directors of communication of both organizations informed each other of their respective activities, as did the directors of the regional groups dispersed throughout the country. Nonetheless, this cooperation was limited: language and culture remained obstacles to deeper relationships[4] between the employees and members of the two chapters. In addition to the planning of common public awareness and political pressure campaigns, the two organizations worked independently, in a way similar to any two independent national sections within the global organization of AI.

The experience of the Canadian section of Amnesty International is interesting because it reflects the situation of other Canadian organizations[5] that are participants in an international entity. Throughout the 1970s, many Canadian branches of international associations followed the AI model by dividing into two pan-Canadian linguistic sections to improve their effectiveness. Within the human rights sector, many groups have established autonomous and distinct Quebec or francophone organizations, operating on a regional basis in their own language and according to their own culture, which are then able to work effectively alongside their anglophone counterparts.[6] They include Aide aux Aînés, Associations des Nations-Unies au Québec, Association mondiale des radiodiffuseurs communautaires, Carrefour canadien international, Centre international des droits de la personne et du développement démocratique, Comité pour la justice sociale, Cuso-Québec et SUCO,[7] Développement et paix, Entraide universitaire mondiale du Canada, Jeunesse Canada Monde, Oxfam-Québec, and YMCA (international program) of Montreal. Investigating the relations between the two Canadian sections of Amnesty International is advantageous as they illustrate the tendency of Canada's two linguistic groups within the human rights sector to adopt a model of sovereignty-association.

The AI Organization

The International Organization

Amnesty International was founded by Peter Benenson, a British lawyer, who published in the London *Observer*, on 28 July 1961, a seminal article entitled "The Forgotten Prisoners." The article was an appeal for amnesty, an attempt to mobilize public opinion in support of two Portuguese students condemned to seven years of imprisonment by the regime of dictator Salazar for having publicly proposed a toast to liberty. The idea of an international campaign for the defence of human rights and the liberation of people imprisoned for their political beliefs, race, skin colour, religion, or national origin was launched. The campaign's objective was to encourage volunteers to write letters to government authorities in the many countries where political prisoners were jailed in the hope that doing so would lead to their liberation. The campaign quickly received widespread support.

From this small beginning, AI soon became an international movement. Its legitimacy is based on its rigorous research of the facts and on its reliance on international treaties. Its mandate is rooted in the Universal Declaration of Human Rights of the United Nations, proclaimed through the General Assembly's resolution 217A of 10 December 1948. From the start, principles of impartiality and independence were established, AI's interventions were to be based entirely on individual human rights, and they were not to be influenced by ideological, partisan, or geographical considerations. AI's mission consists of rapidly obtaining a fair trial for prisoners, preventing torture or execution, and ensuring the liberation of prisoners of conscience. This form of intervention, centred on individuals rather than on countries or political systems, rapidly achieved tremendous success.

Since the 1960s, at the local level, members formed what were called "adoption groups," which were later identified in the 1980s as "local groups." Their task was to mobilize efforts on behalf of a specific adopted prisoner and to lead a specific campaign in his or her country. To ensure the security of members and to maintain the impartiality of the movement, it was ruled that activists would only interfere in countries other than their own.

AI was awarded the Nobel Prize in 1977 and the Human Rights Prize of the United Nations in 1978. This recognition gave the movement its *lettres de noblesse*. The association has tremendous prestige at the international level and is among the most respected and influential human rights organizations in the world. AI now numbers more than a million members throughout 150 countries. The head office of the organization is in London, also the location of the International Secretariat and the Coordination and Research Centre. Amnesty International brings together over fifty national sections. Their role is to mobilize public opinion and to pressure governments to act. The IS oversees the activities of the movement by researching the cases and establishing the files of political prisoners. It supports national sections by providing publications and information for public awareness campaigns and urgent actions designed to help prisoners in imminent danger. Each section uses this information to exert political pressure in its designated territory. Thus, the local groups of AI constitute the foundation of its organizational structure and activities. Members meet locally and receive from the National Secretariat the information and the assistance required for their training and their work.

Every two years an International Council brings together the delegates of all the national sections to fix the general orientations and the priorities of the movement. Besides deciding questions of strategy, organization, and finance, the IC examines the work done by the London-based International Executive Committee (IEC) and elects eight of the nine members of that committee. Its decisions are then sent to the IEC in London, which executes them through its Board of Directors. Finally, the IS implements the decisions of the IEC and the IC.

The Canadian Section
The Canadian section of Amnesty International was founded on 13 May 1973. The first Canadian president, John Humphrey, was one of the authors of the United Nations Universal Declaration of Human Rights. The mandate of the Canadian organization is identical to that of the international organization. At the time of its founding in 1973, AI Canada was a unitary organization that brought together local groups spread across Canada. From its foundation,[8] the National Secretariat was established in Ottawa, reflecting the fact that the anglophone groups constituted a majority.

Canada is a country where two official languages and two cultures, French and English, live together. We begin with the hypothesis that Canadian NGOs attempt to reflect that reality. Yet the Canadian section of AI, as a mainly anglophone institution, did not work optimally with respect to bilingualism. The representation, communication, and coordination capacity of the organization were affected by the logic of unequal membership between anglophones and francophones, tensions between sovereignists and federalists, and differences between advocates of national bilingualism and those of a francophone Quebec.

From 1973 to 1976, activist groups were created throughout the country. The first francophone group[9] of AI emerged in 1974. The majority of the members of the management and of the national Executive Committee were therefore anglophones. AI in Ottawa referred to the International Secretariat in London for its main orientations and to obtain information in English on defended prisoners. All of the documentation was written in English, and national meetings were largely held in English. In fact, only the designation of the organization and the title of its bulletin were bilingual.

Confronted with the difficulties of operating in their own language, Montreal francophone activists in 1975 obtained approval from national headquarters to create a regional francophone secretariat with a head office in Montreal that would cater to all of Canada's francophones.[10] More broadly, the objective of francophones in AI was to create an independent francophone National Secretariat to possess full power to act according to their cultural priorities.[11]

In the context of Canada-wide bilingualism that resulted from the adoption of the Official Languages Act in 1969, the National Secretariat in Ottawa proceeded, from 1974 to 1978, to translate its main written documents and to provide simultaneous translation at its general assemblies. Nonetheless, due to the delays and costs of translation, and the impossibility of translating all communications,[12] a gulf was created between the two linguistic communities. In addition, the minority position of francophones on the Canadian board, resulting from the smaller number of francophone adoption groups, fed tensions between the two linguistic groups. Since anglophone membership in AI Canada was three times larger than that of francophones, the latter had only a third of the total Canadian vote at the International Council of AI. The Montreal bureau received a much smaller budget than Ottawa's, even though the francophone bureau was carrying out the full mandate of AI.

Following the establishment of a regional office of AI in Quebec in 1975,[13] which became the francophone National Secretariat, francophone members developed their own techniques to influence public opinion. They made better use of publicity campaigns[14] and popular education, and they publicized fundraising better, than did anglophones. Churches, schools, businesses, professional corporations, and labour unions were contacted by both organizations. But students and teachers have contributed more to the growth of AI in Quebec than in the rest of Canada, through the work of school chaplains. Cultural differences between the two linguistic groups were notable with regard to the composition of their membership, the ages and social classes of their members, and their management styles, definitions of objectives, and operational techniques. These differences made effective coordination of activities difficult and contributed to a rise in tension and conflict.

Furthermore, the sovereignist political context in Quebec contributed to the emergence of a group of Quebec leaders who put pressure on the Ottawa National Secretariat to grant greater autonomy for Quebec, both for the diffusion of information and the development of public awareness campaigns and for the administration of the budget and the coordination of its activities. The election of René Lévesque in 1976, and the larger process of political assertion of Québécois, influenced the strategies and objectives of francophone activists in many sectors, even if they were not officially active in a political party. The internal political dynamics of AI both reflected and contributed to change in the broader political context. The international leaders of AI, concerned more with their global mission than with internal Canadian politics, acted as an honest broker, seeking to help their Canadian members to resolve their differences in ways that would not impede the cause. The effect was to support the Quebec initiatives. Similar developments influenced other Canadian movements, such as the Boy Scouts and the Optimist Club, which were headed by an international organization.

For all these reasons, the national section was split in 1978 into two linguistic chapters, anglophone and francophone, both serving the entire Canadian territory. They work autonomously,[15] but they belong to the same national section working under the international bodies of the organization: the International Secretariat and the International Assembly. Each chapter has its own National Secretariat, one in Ottawa and the other in Montreal, and Board of Directors. Regional centres of coordination linked to the anglophone secretariat are in place in Toronto and Vancouver. Through the support of numerous volunteers, the two secretariats (anglophone and francophone) are responsible for their own activities, including public information campaigns and services such as communications, urgent response support networks, representations to governments and embassies, and fundraising.[16] Each linguistic chapter is responsible for its management, administers its budget, and manages its activities independently. But with respect to coordination of their actions, both remain bound by the decisions of the International Secretariat and the International Council: they simultaneously carry out their awareness campaigns targeted to the public and the media.

The increase in membership since 1978 demonstrates the benefits of the division of AI into two separate chapters in Canada. Today AI Canada is composed of more than 67,000 members[17] – a third of whom belong to the francophone chapter – and thousands of active supporters in communities, schools, and networks across the country. The members of the different sections intervene in the countries of their choice, with the Quebec section more likely to intervene in francophone countries.

Francophones outside Quebec represent less than 5 percent of the French-language membership, but they are integrated into the National Secretariat based in Montreal. They have been relatively well served by the francophone section of AI, and cooperation between the two chapters, in support of francophones outside Quebec, whether in Toronto, Winnipeg, or Moncton, has remained harmonious since the separation.

Parameters of Association

The sharp tensions before 1978 and the peaceful resolution of conflicts between the leaders of both linguistic communities were the result of non-structural factors, which have influenced the formal and informal practices of the movement, as well as the modes of representation, communication, and coordination that are currently in place. Among these non-structural factors that contributed to the harmonious breakup of AI in Canada are

- the willingness of francophone leaders to create an independent entity, a solution supported by a majority of anglophone leaders;
- the common objective of both groups to defend human rights, their membership in the same international organization, and their interest in preserving the image of the movement; and
- the natural tolerance and openness of human rights activists.

Moreover, the structural procedures and the formal and informal practices of the organization also contributed to the effective resolution of the conflict.

- The asymmetrical representation of francophone activists on the Board of Directors of the Canadian section of AI before 1978, and the centralization of power in Ottawa before 1978, were regarded as inefficient by most francophone and anglophone members who were interviewed.
- The regular consultation between the heads of the diverse services of each organization before and after the breakup, the coordination of their activities during national public awareness campaigns, and the constant dialogue between the directors of the two linguistic communities, before and after the split, provided a reconciliation desirable for both parties.

According to Meisel and Lemieux,[18] the pursuit of a common objective among Canadian members of voluntary associations may affect the wider relationship between the members of Canada's two main ethnic groups, francophones and anglophones, in organizational practice, representation, communication, and coordination. This study demonstrates how the mechanisms of representation, communication, and coordination of AI in Canada have evolved over the years to adapt to the needs of the anglophone and francophone groups within the movement.

Domestic and International Representation

According to Meisel and Lemieux, representation in a pan-Canadian association is a microcosm of provincial-federal political representation. Before 1978, the representation of AI in Canada was the subject of infighting between anglophones and francophones because of the weakness of francophone, especially Quebec-based, representation in the decision-making bodies of the movement. This situation clearly reflected the under-representation of francophones in other Canada-wide institutions. In the revised minutes of the foundation of AI in St-Lambert, in May 1973,[19] it was ruled that, in the Canadian National Council, to be the governing authority of AI in Canada,[20] only one vice-president would represent the francophone community. The role of the National Council[21] was to coordinate the activities of all the Canadian groups as well as to promote the interests of AI in Canada to form public opinion and to influence governments, primarily the Canadian government. Among its responsibilities were fundraising and the development of new groups, the coordination of publicity in Canadian media, the distribution of AI documents in French and English, the publication of a monthly bulletin, the organization of awareness campaigns, the promotion of cooperation with other national sections, especially the American section, as well as the collection of individual and group subscriptions.

Under the guidance of the National Council, it was resolved that the Canadian Executive Committee would consist of a general director, group representatives, the president of the Ottawa group, and three representatives[22] of the general membership. With regard to the members of the Canadian Executive Committee,[23] it was understood that it must "reflect a large range of the Canadian society."[24] This committee was in charge of the recruitment of members and of the management of groups. To pursue these tasks, the committee could rely on headquarters in Ottawa as well as a team of permanent employees. It too would have only one francophone member. On a national level, representation at the annual general assembly (AGA) was proportional to the number of adoption groups in both languages, each group exercising three votes. The AGA voted on the main resolutions, oriented the movement, and appointed the national representatives. In 1974-75, with only one group[25] in existence, francophones had one vote compared to seven for anglophones. To increase the francophone representation at the AGA, the Montreal group was divided into three. This gave francophones nine votes compared with the anglophones' thirty-six, or one-third of the total. By 1977, the number of francophone groups was seven, and AI-Québec[26] had acquired between 25 percent and 30 percent of the vote. This was indeed close to proportional representation. But that did not mean proportionality on the critical executive bodies, nor did it reflect the "two–nations" view increasingly dominant in Quebec.[27] Francophones increasingly blocked the decision-making system through procedural amendments to demonstrate their different perspective. These conflicts threatened to paralyze the organization and divert its energies and resources away from the common task. The result was that, between 1974 and 1978, an anglophone majority made their decisions in English. Because of the small budget of the National Secretariat, francophones were at a disadvantage because each representative had to pay travel expenses to Ottawa.

At the end of 1975, the Quebec section created an alternative to the weak representation of francophones at the national level. AI-Québec put in place a separate francophone Board of Directors and a General Assembly to link representatives of the members and the Board of Directors. Subject to the decisions of the Ottawa head office, this regional structure was to send money from members' subscriptions to Ottawa. Francophones therefore constituted a separate entity, but initially no legal recognition, despite almost entirely fulfilling the mandate of AI. They wished to be perceived as a second equal section rather than a regional secretariat. The director of the Quebec section between 1976 and 1981, François Martin, did not speak or understand English but would be an important actor in the split. After two years of constant pressure, a dozen Quebec delegates[28] forced the 1977 AGA held in Guelph to recognize their right to act as an independent section.[29] A constitutional revision committee[30] composed of three anglophones and four francophones (one from outside Quebec) was mandated to draft a new constitution.

In June 1978, fifteen delegates from the francophone Canadian section attended the AGA in London, Ontario, to establish the terms of separation between the two linguistic groups. The founding general assembly of the francophone chapter of AI was held on 18 August 1978, where the basic rules were established. Later nine representatives[31] of the two chapters were sent to the Cambridge International Council of 1978 to gain the acceptance of AI for the division of the Canadian movement.

At the IC of AI, the right to vote is proportional to the number of groups and members in each country. The IC is the sole decisional entity allowed to modify the status of the organization. From 1977 to 1988, Canada possessed three votes, two for the anglophones and one for the francophones. It was at the IC that the conditions of separation between the two linguistic chapters were adopted. It was stated that the francophone executive committee would from then on accredit[32] each adopting group; that the two chapters would have separate AGAs to which representatives of each executive would be invited; that the two branches would have to be in continual contact; and that approaches to the Canadian government would have to be concerted. A member[33] of each Executive Committee was named to ensure a link to the other linguistic chapter.

Coordination Mechanisms

Coordination, according to Meisel and Lemieux, concerns the transmission of orders or directives in an organization and the internal governance of the different sectors. The main coordination mechanisms at Amnesty International are at the national level; until 1978, this meant the national

Executive Committee, the AGA, and joint committees established to co-ordinate a working relationship between the two linguistic groups and to promote regional cooperation. At the provincial level, only Quebec had formed its own Board of Directors and AGA. At the international level, the decision-making bodies are the International Secretariat and the International Council.

Most of the actions and the organizational and functional priorities of AI during this period were decided at the IS[34] in London on the basis of resolutions adopted at the IC. The Executive Committee, directed by Pierre Sané and formed by nine elected members from different countries, implemented the decisions of the CI. Thanks to its research team, London provided basic information to the national sections, which then translated the information into concrete actions. But it was local sections that interpreted these decisions. They prepared the strategies, the interventions, the material used, and the supervision of volunteers.

As specified previously, the Canadian National Council had the responsibility of coordinating the activities of all groups in Canada and of promoting the interests of AI in the country. This council oversaw the activities of the anglophone regional bureaus of Toronto, Vancouver, and Ottawa as well as the Montreal bureau through the AGA, which brought together delegates from all the regions of the country.

Within this framework, representatives of the two cultural communities experienced a cultural shock because of the different perceptions of their mission. Despite the introduction of a francophone Board of Directors at AI-Québec, the AGA continued to approve the decisions of the Montreal bureau, including the financial decisions,[35] the vote, and the elections to the Board of Directors. Other decisions, such as the calendar of actions and the public awareness campaigns, were decentralized. From 1975 to 1978, francophones almost fully carried out the AI mandate independently: that is, they coordinated francophone groups, accredited support groups (where the approbation of London was not necessary),[36] and organized information, fundraising, and public awareness campaigns. The participation of anglophones in the decisions of francophones was perceived as interference and contributed to the increase in tension since the two communities had different ways of executing their mandates.

Shortly before the constitutional revision, administrative changes were introduced, anticipating the 1978 separation between the two chapters. According to Document 3, approved by the Executive Committee of AI Canada at its 26 June 1977 meeting, all documents originating from the Ottawa national bureau and intended to apply to francophone groups were to be sent to members of the Montreal office. For the accreditation of groups, anglophone requests made to the Montreal office were automatically sent to Ottawa, whereas francophone requests were sent directly to the IS, with a copy to the national bureau in Ottawa. Moreover, all groups formed in Quebec were allowed to pay their subscriptions to Montreal, which transferred the funds to London while informing the national bureau in Ottawa.

The Communication Function

Meisel and Lemieux's theory is that the language in which communications are drafted[37] is as important, if not more so, than the content. Language and culture cannot be separated. Consequently, the language in which discussions are held and publications written has important consequences both symbolic and practical.

The Canadian section of AI, founded by anglophones, represented all Canadian groups and members whether they were francophone or anglophone. Nonetheless, because of the majority of anglophone groups and members and the existing link with the International Secretariat, all written communication was in English, and the national AGAs were held in this language primarily.[38] In reality, it was usually only the name of the movement[39] and the title of the monthly bulletin[40] that were bilingual. Quebec francophones were and remain the only organization in the world to have adopted the francophone designation Amnistie internationale.[41]

From 1973 to 1978, according to a tacit agreement, the correspondence of each group or office was made in its own language. Interpreters, paid through subsidies granted by the Department of the Secretary of State to promote bilingualism in NGOs, ensured simultaneous translation for francophones in national AGAs. Yet informal conversations were essentially in English. Only priority documents (statutes and rules) originating from the Ottawa National Secretariat were translated from English into French. The predominance of English in written and oral communications of the organization isolated francophone activists, who were already in a minority during the AGAs.

Since less than 30 percent of documents[42] from London were translated into French, a volunteer team of translators in Montreal managed the translation of the remaining documents. Unlike anglophone groups, francophone groups did not accept subsidies from the state, wanting to preserve their independence vis-à-vis public authorities. The voluminous work[43] of translation of French-language materials was often useless since certain French documents already existed in the translation department of the London office or in the francophone sections of France and Belgium. The problem was that these documents were not being sent to Ottawa. On the other hand, the Quebec secretariat organized congresses, meetings, or press conferences in French on themes such as the abolition of torture or the death penalty. The different style of public awareness campaigns[44] by francophone activists was essential to reach the francophone public and to promote the expansion of AI in Quebec. All of these reasons led to the creation of an autonomous francophone structure capable of serving its members and activists in their language.

Thus, by 1978, tensions between anglophone and francophone AI activists were growing. A number of accommodations had been made, but they had not resolved the fundamental differences. That resolution would require more basic constitutional change.

The Parameters of the Association since 1978

In October 1977, the committee charged with the writing of a new constitution recommended that the International Secretariat be notified of the creation of two chapters of AI in Canada. According to its memorandum of agreement[45] released on 25 February 1978, AI Canada recognized the necessity of creating two independent sections, which would continue to cooperate. At the end of its proceedings, the committee stated that it was impossible to create two autonomous sections within the same organization. There would have to be a more formal split.

At a special general assembly in London, Ontario, on 2 June 1978, the Canadian section of AI was thus divided into two autonomous chapters, in accordance with the statutes of AI. These two chapters are respectively named Amnistie internationale – Section canadienne francophone, and Amnesty International – Canadian Section (English speaking). While remaining linked to the head office in London by their national section status, each is sovereign and has its own constitution, Board of Directors, budget, and membership, and each is responsible for its contribution (*cotisation*) to the IS. Because of the AI principle that only one section per country can be recognized, the two entities collaborate on numerous activities in a partnership that can only be described as sovereignty-association.

At the International Council held on 22 and 23 September 1978 in Cambridge, England, the Canadian delegates tried to ensure the adoption of the separation of the Canadian section into two branches, following the resolution approved at the 2 June 1978 London general assembly. The proposition was discussed in workshops, but the motion was rejected at the plenary session. Given the threat of the resignation of all the francophone delegates[46] present at the council, negotiations[47] were held with the international authorities, who finally accepted the constitution of a Canadian section divided into two autonomous chapters. A member[48] of each Executive Committee was then mandated to ensure liaison between the two linguistic chapters.

This arrangement established new rules of representation, coordination, and communication between the two linguistic chapters of the Canadian section of AI. The relations between the two linguistic communities have significantly improved since the separation. Each linguistic group is unilingual francophone or anglophone, but frequent contacts occur between the executives (but not rank-and-file members) to coordinate the activities of the two chapters. With regard to communications, each linguistic chapter, as a unilingual entity, works in its own language. An informal bilingualism marks their exchanges, which are conducted in each person's language of choice, although English predominates. This arrangement has led to a greater independence of the two chapters from each other in day-to-day operations.

Domestic and International Representation

The 1978 memorandum of agreement – *protocole d'entente* – creating two branches of AI in Canada states that each linguistic chapter is to be represented at the national and international level (embassies, UN international agencies, and the International Council of AI) by a committee called the Canadian National Section. At the IC and in its relations with other international authorities, the Canadian section remains only one section. Consultations between the two sections precede the adoption of any common position and the dispatch of delegates. Before 1988, Canada had three votes (two for the anglophone section and one for the francophone section). Since 1989, the number has been four (three for anglophones and one for francophones), with a common voting right. There are eight Canadian delegates, three francophone and five anglophone. This ratio reflects the anglophone majority but does come closer to equal representation than numbers of members alone would suggest. At the end of the 1980s, the francophone section demanded an additional vote if Canada was to be awarded a fifth vote, a demand that was accepted by the anglophone chapter.

Political approaches to the Canadian government and ambassadors are also coordinated, a product of regular contact between the general directors. For reasons of proximity, the anglophone representatives have more contact with Ottawa and the foreign embassies located in this region. A national meeting is held every year between the two sections before the international human rights meeting in Geneva, the two sections dividing current files between themselves. With regard to public awareness campaigns,[49] the representations are orchestrated according to the knowledge and availability of representatives. At the national level, the two sections are full members of the Network International Human Rights Organizations/Réseaux international des ONG sur le plan humain. Each section has a separate vote at the AGA of this network, with no limit to the number of participants. When AI Canada is represented in other organizations, votes are equally split between the two sections.

Coordination Mechanisms

After the separation, agreements were signed regarding action campaigns and the sharing of resources. In 1979, the francophone branch[50] adopted the idea of an agreement between the two national structures to share the countries of the world and separately intervene, in the name of AI Canada, based mainly on language. From that moment on, tensions between the two linguistic communities declined. Francophone adoption groups have been able to focus on prisoners living in the countries of their choice, using mainly the French language.[51]

The general assembly facilitated the constitutional change. In 1978,[52] it ratified the creation of two linguistic chapters under certain conditions:

- for coordination purposes, the minutes of each meeting of the two Canadian executives are sent automatically to the other executive, as are the agenda and activity and AGA reports;
- the two entities consult each other before all positions are taken before Canadian and international authorities; and
- the contribution to the international budget is fixed according to the number of members and the budget of each branch.

The national contribution that Canada provides to the IS is the sum of revenue accumulated in each branch, anglophone and francophone, considered as two sections. It is important to highlight that the budget of each section reflects the different sizes of the two organizations.[53]

To improve coordination, joint delegations[54] were created to discuss issues that are to be debated in international meetings. Working joint committees meet before governmental meetings,[55] International Councils of AI, congresses, or international conferences. In 1980, a joint committee was put in place to prepare for an IC in Montreal in 1981. No documents mention any specific conflicts related to that event. This occasion not only gave international recognition to the francophone section of AI but also fostered growing respect among anglophones. Nonetheless, the francophone Canadian section was the only one to collaborate with francophone countries, planning international events such as the parallel summits of francophone NGOs, held at the occasion of the Sommet de la francophonie in Moncton.[56]

The main features of the collaboration between the francophone and anglophone coordinators were defined at a joint meeting[57] of the executive committees in 1982. Each branch is authorized to develop its own system of coordination in conformity with its needs and its resources. According to tradition, the general directors of the two sections have the responsibility to ensure liaison between the two sections, a role that Roger Clark and Michel Frenette assumed with enthusiasm.

Relations between the anglophone and francophone chapters have always been respectful, both before and after the separation. In 1988, a joint committee was formed in anticipation of the consultation preceding the International Council of AI. At a meeting of the anglophone branch on 8 January 1988, it was suggested, to resolve all latent conflicts, that a liaison committee be formed between anglophones and francophones consisting of three members of each branch. However, because of a lack of common ground, the committee has never been active.[58]

Indeed, issues of status and identity continued to arise. For example, between 1988 and 1990, anglophones insisted that the designation of the Canadian movement be changed. The anglophone section argued that employing "Amnesty International Canada" and "Amnistie International Canada" would be clearer for the different actors and would allow a better government representation. Because of the multicultural context of Canada, anglophones[59] wanted a name that would include all the linguistic communities of the country, not only those whose language is English. However, francophones terminated the process, arguing that the term "Canada" would be too encompassing and put off the sovereignist clientele of Quebec. Anglophones reintroduced the issue, but the discussion has been closed, since London will not permit a unilateral change of designation.

The Communication Function

Since the split in 1978, there have been no obstacles to the unilingual operation of each of the two chapters of AI in Canada in written and oral communications. Although the linguistic relationships were strained before, the two chapters now work more efficiently in the overall operation of the AI movement. Even though English is predominant, language is not an obstacle to a good relationship. In fact, at the International Secretariat in London, French and English are both spoken, even more so since the nomination of the North African Pierre Sané to the position of secretary general of AI.[60] In the IC meetings and among section directors, English is the common denominator.[61] At the national level, communication, which is principally in English, is constant between the communication directors, and so are exchanges of information between the two Canadian sections.

Documents[62] released by the secretariat of the Canadian anglophone section are entirely in English. The language of communication in national meetings is English, but the two current presidents occasionally use French during their annual meetings. Similarly, French is sometimes used during communications with government officials and ambassadors if there is a joint action with the francophone section. A new Internet site refers to the French website (and vice versa). Each general director addresses the media in the language of his respective section, although the director of the anglophone section, Roger Clark, gives some interviews to the francophone Montreal media, with the consent of Michel Frenette, when the latter is unavailable or does not know a specific topic well. The only rule is to make the other section aware of any actions targeted toward government actors.

Creation of the francophone branch in 1978 facilitated the use of French in all aspects of communication. It has made participation in the Éditions francophones d'Amnesty International (EFAI) possible. Francophone member countries[63] of AI founded the EFAI in 1980. A representative of each francophone country sits on its Board of Directors, which then elects a president.[64] Participation in the activities of the EFAI contributed to bringing the francophone branch closer to francophone countries than to the anglophone branch.[65] Today approximately 70 percent[66] of AI official documents released are translated by the EFAI and sent to francophone sections. Documents sent in English from London deal with directives sent to tourists, communiqués of reactions to unforeseen events, with limited distribution, and descriptions of prisoners adopted by different groups. Because of translation delays at the EFAI, volunteers from the francophone section translate urgent documents as well as information concerning prisoners.

All of the documents[67] released to the public by the secretariat of the Canadian francophone section are therefore written in French, with the exception of postcards and petitions to governments and embassies, which are generally bilingual (in English, Chinese, Arabic, or Spanish), according to the language of a specific country. Documents intended for the media are in French since press communiqués have been systematically translated by the EFAI since 1996. The francophone section, which adapts press releases to its own context, only covers francophone media, mainly those located in Quebec. The anglophone sphere of action is geographically much larger and has offices in Ottawa, Toronto, and Vancouver. In the late 1990s, a French Internet site was created by the francophone section of AI, complementing the English site of the anglophone section. E-mails have also contributed to the transmission of information in French.

Linguistic conflicts between the two Canadian chapters of AI have been reduced because of the use of only one of the official languages in each organization. The members of the two main linguistic groups are now served in their own language. Despite the unilingual working of each organization, the leaders of each section have demonstrated a willingness to cooperate efficiently in the defence of human rights and to enhance the image of AI in Canada.

The Impact of Non-Organizational Factors on Anglophone-Francophone Relations

The causes of the rupture of the two organizations of the AI movement in Canada were not only linguistic. Government language policies and the sovereignty debate contributed to the separation of the two organizations. It was also caused by the cultural gap that separated the francophone and anglophone communities with regard to the membership and the strategies used to ensure the development of AI in Canada. These divergences continue today, confirming the existence of two distinct entities working nonetheless for the same common objectives.

Two Cultures, Two Philosophies

Despite their common desire to defend human rights within an international organization, the two Canadian linguistic communities have been confronted with deep cultural differences. Hence, the separation occurred both for cultural reasons and for questions of efficiency.

These cultural differences appeared in management styles, objectives, marketing strategies, membership,[68] and language. The methods[69] used to ensure the liberation of political prisoners were different. With anglophones, fundraising was largely the result of word of mouth; francophones, on the other hand, used the media more often as well as cold mailings. AI Canada was the expression of two solitudes. The means used to achieve the objectives of the movement were not the same. For example, francophones have developed programs supporting AI in the school system of Quebec and thus have learned to appeal to the young. But the fundamental difference lies in the combination of numbers and language. In a single organization, Quebecers would always be a minority, and the predominant language and culture would always be English. Recruiting is bound to be a failure in such an organization. Only the formation of the francophone Canadian section has allowed AI to become established in Quebec. Its membership[70] progressed until the 1990s. It was indispensable to address a francophone audience in French.

Today the two chapters try to develop common strategies to pressure the different governments of the world by combining their sensibilities in a systematic way during international campaigns dictated by the IS. But differences remain even if the content of the message is the same. For example, during the campaign on violence in the United States in 1999, the francophone campaign was more visible and media oriented, with more shocking posters and advertisements. Anglophones, on the other hand, remain more afraid of American reaction. Female genital mutilation, gay rights, and Aboriginal claims[71] are themes perceived differently between the two sections. Coordination remains essential since the two groups have different priorities and different ways of seeing the world.

In accordance with these different cultural perceptions and a different vision of the Canadian reality, certain frustrations remain in the anglophone section. Some of its members, underestimating the importance of cultural and language questions, lament the fact that francophones have created their own organization. Their dream of unity remains very much alive. Inspired by the new Canadian philosophy of the 1990s, which presents Canada as a multicultural nation, anglophones have revealed the ambiguity of the AI Canada designation. They have asked for a sole designation, translated into two languages, Amnesty International Canada and Amnestie internationale Canada, to end references to the terms "anglophone" and "francophone." They argue that these terms do not correspond anymore to the

Canadian multicultural reality. Since the past decade, the demographic reality of Canada has been transformed, and NGOs increasingly want to be representative of this multiethnic reality. The anglophone branch has in fact constituted a working committee on cultural diversification to represent all Canadians. No step has been taken to that effect by the francophone section.

Relationship with Government Policies

It is undeniable that, in addition to the differences engendered by the bilingualism policy of the Canadian government, the growth of the sovereignist movement precipitated the split of AI Canada. From its foundation to 1978, the Canadian section had a bilingual status. NGOs were encouraged by the state to serve all citizens of the country in their own language. In conformity with the Official Languages Act adopted in 1969, the Department of the Secretary of State provided grants to the Canadian national section to promote bilingualism in its organization. But translation efforts were insufficient to transform AI Canada into a fully bilingual organization. The failure of bilingualism made the situation contentious.

The resentment of francophones, a minority in the Canadian section confronted with the predominance of English, was also reinforced by the rise of the sovereignty movement in Quebec throughout the 1970s. This situation favoured the formation of an active group of members in Quebec that pressured Ottawa to obtain an autonomous status to control the diffusion of its information, the creation of its public awareness campaigns, the administration of its budget, and the coordination of its activities.

The election of the Parti québécois in 1976 and the political affirmation of Québécois influenced the strategy of AI's francophone activists, even if they did not officially belong to a political party. Anglophones were overwhelmed by the claims for autonomy by the Québécois, and the political wave of the period was favourable to francophones.

Despite the numerical disproportion between the two organizations, the leaders and the activists of the francophone section of AI have been able to assert their existence to the anglophone community. They continue to do so with the same conviction. Neither of the "no" victories in 1980 and 1995 or the failure of the Meech Lake Accord has changed this affirmation. The anglophone organization has adapted to this situation. Yet the new concepts of multiculturalism, promoted by the Canadian federal government, could modify the linguistic practices of the anglophone branch of AI. Other languages frequently used in Canada, such as Chinese or Ukrainian, could be added to the publications and national conferences. Ironically, perhaps, the separation has not only permitted the francophone organization to respond better to its constituents but also allowed AI in the rest of Canada to respond better to its environment.

The International Organization Factor

The existence of an international organization has also been an important factor; in fact, the support of the francophone cause by one of AI's founders, the Irishman Sean MacBride, contributed to the harmonious separation of the two Canadian groups. His role was crucial since John Humphrey, a founding member of AI and one of the authors of the Universal Declaration of Human Rights, initially supported the principle of a single section per country. AI leaders were not immediate parties to Canada's internal debates, but they were fearful of the collapse of one of its most important member countries. Hence, they wished to facilitate any Canadian reorganization that would best sustain AI's fundamental goals, including, if necessary, separation.

Despite the fact that AI Canada was split into two distinct branches, one unilingual French and the other unilingual English, the separation has not been as radical as some francophones would have hoped or as some anglophones would have feared. In fact, because of the rules of the movement that allow only one section per country, the international authority forbids a total rupture. It imposes coordination mechanisms that ensure a national and international representation and the nomination of agents of liaison between the two branches.

Conclusion

Relations between the two linguistic groups of AI in Canada have always been cordial despite the difficult moments they have been through. For most members of AI, francophones and anglophones, the chosen solution has been judged as satisfying. Everyone won in terms of functionality, organization, and efficiency. Once the disagreement between the two sections was solved, the leaders and members of the two linguistic sections were able to focus on the defence of political opinion prisoners. AI emerged in Canada in 1973 because of the good relationship between the two main linguistic communities, which allowed them to develop the movement according to their own cultural characteristics. There are now 300 Canadian groups, including more than 100 in Quebec. This separation did not damage the image of the movement and has not compromised the collaboration between francophones and anglophones. It was done in good faith, with respect from the two sections and with the consent of the International Council in 1978.

This harmonious arrangement offers to pan-Canadian NGOs in this sector of activity a model of organization that is remarkably functional. The harmonious working of AI in Canada, where the chapters consult each other to obtain common objectives and communicate to their clientele in their own language, has convincingly demonstrated its efficiency in the context of a defence of human rights that transcends the differences of sensibility or the organizational traditions of the different actors. The case of Amnesty International suggests that the pursuit of a common goal, with a strong ethical and international component, decreases the impact of the linguistic variable and increases the level of collaboration between related organizations.

9
Accommodation at the Pinnacle: The Special Role of Civil Society's Leaders

Richard Simeon and David Cameron

Let us summarize what we found. How and why have linguistic relations within these groups changed over time? How and why do they vary across groups in the thirty years or so covered by our study? What factors – internal to the groups themselves and in the wider environment – are at work in shaping the relationships? Which of the theoretical models noted in the introduction seems to provide the most persuasive set of explanations? And, finally, what lessons can be learned? Do the experiences of these groups in civil society have something to say to politicians and to those concerned with ensuring social cohesion and harmony at the level of politics and governance?

Patterns of Association Thirty Years Later

"Canada, without being fully conscious of the fact," wrote the commissioners of the Royal Commission on Bilingualism and Biculturalism in their preliminary report, published in 1965, "is passing through the greatest crisis of its history."[1] This crisis was played out in many of the groups studied by John Meisel and Vincent Lemieux at the time.

Associations in the voluntary sector – like the rest of Canadian society – were subjected to pressure for change with a double thrust. The first was a drive for nation building within Quebec or, in the language of social capital, an effort to create "bonding capital" within a distinct Quebec society. The second was to achieve greater equality between French and English within pan-Canadian institutions, to build bridges between members of Canada's two language groups. The first called for greater autonomy for the Quebec collectivity, even secession and sovereignty; the second called for greater representation of individual francophones at the centre and in Canadian institutions. Both required basic change in national associations: would Quebecers break away from national institutions, or would they gain stronger representation in those institutions? The answer was some of each.

But getting there would not be easy for either language community, as many chapters in this book show. All relationships were up for renegotiation; what had once seemed settled was now up in the air. Francophones would no longer tolerate anglophone privilege, and anglophones, however well intentioned, often found it hard to give it up. The world had "jumbled its catalogue."

Today, in most associations, the landscape is much more peaceful. None of the associations we studied is riven by disagreements over language use and practice. Associations that were working well in the 1960s – for example, the Canadian Federation of Agriculture and the various business associations – continue to work well today. Those, such as the Federation of Canadian Municipalities or Amnesty International, which were deeply divided in the past, have worked out the necessary accommodations. In few is language a barrier hampering their work. In most of the associations we studied, a mutually acceptable *modus vivendi* has been established. Linguistic relations have become routinized and normalized. This is not to say that all are models of ideal linguistic equality and functional bilingualism, much less that they are vehicles for the development of close personal interaction between large groups of anglophones and francophones. The day-to-day lives of these associations are far more complex.

What We Found
Federalism, as Daniel Elazar famously observed, is simultaneously a regime of "shared rule" with respect to common interests and "self-rule" for the constituent units – or, put more bluntly, a "coming together" and a "coming apart." It is premised on the value of "engagement" on common concerns and "disengagement" where values or identities differ. In different federations, the relative emphasis on shared rule and self-rule varies. So too in our associations: virtually all have employed both strategies, but the balance between them varies considerably. Indeed, we were struck by the variety and inventiveness in the choices made by different groups.

The most common pattern is one where the "national" (pan-Canadian) level has become officially bilingual, while the Quebec-based units have functioned increasingly as unilingual French-speaking groups, which have substantial autonomy in conducting their own affairs. This pattern substantially reflects the accommodations that have been worked out at the formal political level in Canada.

External Communications
Virtually all the associations studied adopted "official bilingualism" in their national offices, especially in their public faces. They have made considerable investments in providing extensive translation. Their publications and websites are bilingual (though in some associations francophone members

complain about delays in providing French-language materials), their receptionists answer in both languages, and their services are provided to members in the two languages. Only small, underfunded groups, such as the Huntington Society, have difficulty meeting these minimal standards.

Quebec-based units, reflecting the impact of Bill 101, function essentially in French. Other provincial units or branches tend – with the notable exception of bilingual New Brunswick – to function primarily in English, a result of the overwhelmingly unilingual character of their constituencies, of a lack of resources to provide bilingual services, and of their increasing need to respond to the linguistic reality created by new immigrant groups, especially in cities such as Toronto and Vancouver, where Chinese, Korean, Tamil, and Portuguese speakers, for example, are more numerous than francophones.

The Internet is a powerful new tool for communication between associational leadership and members and among members themselves. But developing a powerful website in both official languages is a challenge. Mailing lists and chat rooms appear to attract mainly English-speaking participants. And Internet communications place a high premium on speed and immediacy, working against the time and effort required for translation.

Internal Communications and Practices

When it comes to the internal lives of Canada-wide associations – the language used among staff, in board committee meetings, and around the coffee machine – things are very different in most of the associations we studied. Here the language remains predominantly that of Canada's linguistic majority – English. More formal settings, such as annual general meetings, may provide simultaneous translation and bilingual programs, but less formal and less public activities, such as committee deliberations, are normally conducted in English. This is no surprise. The Canada-wide constituency is majority English speaking; most provincial leaders are unilingual in English, as are most staff members; and translation is very expensive. These are the sources of "asymmetrical bilingualism." It means that the Quebec representatives in most national associations must be fully bilingual if they are to participate effectively. Even those who are fully bilingual carry the extra burden of working in their second language. There is no such requirement for anglophone leaders, though in some associations facility in the second language is a significant criterion for selection to senior positions.

Representation

All the national associations have some representation of Quebecers on their boards of directors. In some cases, representation is spelled out in formal constitutional documents; in others, it appears to operate through informal norms, as with the Canadian cabinet. In some organizations, francophones

play important leadership roles; others have difficulty in recruiting francophone board members.

Several models of representation contend in Canada. Do we think of representation in terms of provinces and regions, of reflecting two equal nations,
or of quite different categories (gender, Aboriginal peoples, sectors within
particular areas, such as producers of different products in the agricultural
sector, or large and small cities in the municipal sector)? Whatever the categories, should representation be proportionate or equal?

In the Canadian national associations we studied, the most common
principle in the selection of board members is province and region, though
this criterion is often supplemented by other considerations specific to the
group itself. Many associations are also increasingly concerned about their
ability to respond to the "new" multicultural Canada. As a result, with the
exception of the Federation of Canadian Municipalities, none of the associations has a board that mirrors the proportion of francophones or Quebecers
in the population as a whole, much less equality between "two nations."

We do not have data on the general membership of these associations.
But the case studies suggest that, in most, Quebecers and francophones are
less likely to attend annual general meetings or other such events than are
anglophone members.

These data suggest that, while greater responsiveness to francophone needs
and concerns has preoccupied many associations, and while all have made
considerable progress in this direction, the outcome has primarily been not
to institutionalize greater representation on pan-Canadian bodies but to
support greater autonomy for the francophone membership in Quebec-
based bodies: decentralization rather than increased representation at the
centre.

Structure and Organization

Our cases demonstrate a wide range of institutional or associational forms.
In social policy, we see a virtually complete separation between the work of
the Canadian Council on Social Development and the Conseil québécois
de développement social; in others, we see confederal relationships prevail,
as in the Heart and Stroke Foundation of Canada and the Fondation des
maladies de coeur du Québec and in several business associations. The relationship between the anglophone and francophone branches of Amnesty
International closely mirrors the idea of sovereignty-association, with separate groups collaborating where mutually desired. Finally, there are more
conventional federal arrangements, as with the Canadian Federation of
Agriculture or the Federation of Canadian Municipalities. In the federal and
confederal cases, we find in practice a high degree of "asymmetry" or "distinct society" status for the Quebec units.

This variety of organizational solutions reflects the internal dynamics of each group. The general tendency to increased autonomy for the Quebec-based units seems to work for both sides of the linguistic divide. For francophone members in Quebec, it permits affirmation of national identity, networking with other elements of Quebec civil society, and close relationships with the Quebec government, even as they continue to benefit from the ability to link to national networks and the federal government on matters of shared interest. For the national associations, it permits them to claim to act for all segments of Canadian society while minimizing some of the costs of adjustment that would be necessary in a more centralized model. The specific institutional arrangements may differ, but the common goal is to reconcile Quebec's desire for autonomy with the need for a minimum degree of cohesion at the national level.

Working Together

The most striking conclusion to emerge from these case studies is how well these associations have learned to collaborate on shared goals. None of these groups is hamstrung or paralyzed by internal conflict over language – as was the case with several when Meisel and Lemieux conducted their study. Nor does the ability to cooperate appear to depend on the organizational forms that have been chosen. Overwhelmingly, the level and degree of cooperation depend on the interdependence among the groups and the extent of their common concerns. Where interests are shared, we tend to find cooperation; when they are not, the groups tend to go their own ways. Indeed, in several cases, it seems clear that "disengagement" at the organizational level has facilitated cooperation on shared goals in practice by removing – or diminishing – language and representation as issues of contention, which get in the way of substantive issues. Disputes over language use and representation can easily divert groups from their basic objectives, as Meisel and Lemieux discovered. Moreover, these patterns facilitate interaction with the governments of Canadian federalism. In most policy areas of concern to these groups, responsibilities are shared between federal and provincial governments. Participation in national groups helps to strengthen the Québécois voice in the federal bureaucracy; while autonomous Quebec units have access to the Quebec government, such access is not available to pan-Canadian groups.

So the general picture is one of relative success. Most of the anglophone elites in these associations have recognized the importance of bilingualism; many of the francophone leaders have developed a highly pragmatic approach to their role at the pan-Canadian level. We do not, however, wish to paint too rosy a picture. In associations such as the Canadian Federation of Agriculture, there is remarkable harmony across the language groups. In others, there are significant resentments on both sides, with some francophones feeling unrepresented and ignored in the national association and some anglophone leaders still resenting the push for greater responsiveness to francophone partners, which they see as getting in the way of the pursuit of their substantive goals or diverting attention away from other dimensions of difference to which they must respond. Cultural and philosophical divergences between Quebecers and other Canadians still sometimes pose barriers to cooperation.

Most of the relationships we have explored are grounded in down-to-earth considerations: that is, they appear to be based not on strong common values, culture, and identity but on shared interests. They are pragmatic. Few leaders on either side see their groups as having a major role in building or promoting "national unity." Not only are they down-to-earth, but they are also structurally limited. They provide few opportunities for face-to-face contact and exchange among rank-and-file members. Instead, in most groups, the pattern is of "elite accommodation" on the consociational model. This is largely a product of the sheer size of the country and the geographical distribution of French and English speakers. Indeed, elite accommodation is in most cases the best way of describing associational arrangements across English-speaking Canada itself. This tendency is strongly reinforced by the increased role of professional managers in the lives of Canadian associations. Grace Skogstad's conclusion with respect to farmers is characteristic of other groups too: "The interaction ... does not penetrate very deeply and not much beyond the level of the senior leaders and permanent staff."

Despite the considerable progress since the 1960s, relationships at the level of pan-Canadian associations remain asymmetrical in many ways. In very few are French speakers able to participate fully and effectively in their own language. It is the francophones who must adjust to a predominantly anglophone environment rather than vice versa. This has little, if anything, to do with conscious discrimination or exclusion; rather, it is primarily a simple consequence of numbers.

Finally, the accommodations we see today were often hard won. Many of these groups went through major crises as they moved along the path to linguistic accommodation.

Explaining Difference
These broad generalizations obscure the variation that emerges from these cases. The accommodation to linguistic difference has occurred in different ways, with different timing, and with different results, across the groups we have placed under our microscope. What explains these variations? The evidence in our case studies suggests that two sets of factors are important. First are the characteristics of the groups themselves – their goals and values, their leadership, their resources, and their links to wider networks. Second

is the wider political and social environment in which these associations are embedded and in which they pursue their goals.

Internal Factors

Perhaps the single most important factor here is the character of the interests the associations represent and the goals they pursue. Put most simply, how important is cooperation across the linguistic divide to meeting the needs of their members? If the benefits of cooperation are great, then there will be strong incentives to overcome linguistic differences and find ways to work together. Where there are few benefits to be gained, there is little incentive to work at cohesion. Where the legitimacy and reach of the national association require that it demonstrate support in Quebec, there will be a greater need to ensure effective bilingualism. Where Quebecers gain a great deal – perhaps from greater access to Ottawa – they may be more willing to tolerate some lack of representation in the national office. Such considerations help to explain why groups with clear economic interests, such as agriculture and business, appear to have the most settled and harmonious relations.

On the other hand, where there is little to be gained from cooperation – or even more when the policy goals of Quebec and the rest of Canada diverge – there is less reason to work together. One example of policy divergence is found in groups concerned with social policy. In Quebec, "progressive" movements have tended to be linked to the PQ and nationalism; their English Canadian counterparts, by contrast, have looked to the federal government and relied on the Canadian Charter of Rights and Freedoms. This difference led to major differences in strategy.

Nevertheless, even when there are "objective" reasons to collaborate, language may still get in the way. This suggests a second critical internal factor: the character and commitments of the group leadership. In several of our cases, we saw groups struggling with linguistic conflict that was resolved only when strong, committed leaders emerged to take matters in hand. On the anglophone side, this often meant new leaders who recognized the importance of bilingualism not only as a national value but also as essential to the continued success and legitimacy of the group. On the francophone side, it has meant the development of a newer generation of young leaders for whom the project of national affirmation has largely been achieved and who are thus more focused on doing what is necessary to achieve common goals. In some cases, success involved partnerships between leaders on each side, both willing to make the necessary compromises.

Finally, while we argued above that the specific organizational design does not seem to have had a major impact on the ability to cooperate effectively, the organizational framing, in a larger perspective, has been important. The common achievement that we have seen is that, in virtually every case, the

Quebec-based sections have gained greater autonomy since the 1960s – whether in the form of decentralized federalism, confederalism, sovereignty-association, or separation. Organizational changes have responded to the aspirations of Quebecers for greater autonomy, and this has been a powerful agent for diminished conflict.

External Factors

Voluntary associations have their own constituencies, values, and objectives. But they are also embedded in a wider society, culture, and institutional setting, with profound consequences for their organization and strategies.

To start with, the environment in which they exist consists both of broad trends in values and of more specific government policies and programs. At the most general level, we have seen how all these associations have had to come to terms with the drive for self-affirmation and autonomy in Quebec following the Quiet Revolution. Not only does our analysis of the groups show considerable change since the period studied by Meisel and Lemieux, but it is also the case that the larger political economy in Canada today differs from the picture painted by the Royal Commission on Bilingualism and Biculturalism. The economic inequalities between anglophones and francophones have been eliminated; the Official Languages Act is in place; under-representation of Quebecers in the federal bureaucracy has been considerably attenuated. In the same period, the Quiet Revolution in Quebec has played out in Bill 101, increased state capacity, distinctive social and economic policies, and a unique role for Quebec in Canadian federalism (even if not constitutionally entrenched). All our associations have lived through these changes and have been deeply affected by them.

Similarly, all these associations have been profoundly shaped by the institutions of federalism. The country's political structure is mirrored in the organization of voluntary associations – especially those with clear policy objectives. Groups whose interests lie chiefly in provincial jurisdiction will have strong provincial organizations and a weak centre; those oriented mainly to concerns in federal jurisdiction will have a more centralized structure. But none of the groups we studied has a unitary structure: all, in various ways, are federal.

Yet federalism is a broad church. Our strong impression is that these associations have been more innovative and flexible in redefining relationships than have the governments in Canada in their successive efforts at constitutional renewal.

Government – the federal and provincial manifestations of the state in Canada – looms large in the lives of our associations. Indeed, on occasion, the groups are caught in the crossfire between rival governments. In the period under study, the federal government was aggressively pursuing a policy of promoting official bilingualism at the national level. This policy created a strong incentive for Canada-wide groups to demonstrate that they too were effectively bilingual. Their legitimacy and access to the federal government could depend on it. Moreover, throughout much of this period, Ottawa offered subsidies for translation that alleviated the costs of greater bilingualism. When these grants were largely eliminated in the budget-cutting 1990s, it became more difficult for groups to sustain their bilingual communications.

Quebec governments at the same time were seeking to bind NGOs into unilingual provincial policy networks, and thus fostered stronger Quebec-based associations. It was a major reason why the Huntington Society established an autonomous Quebec branch. Conflict within the Federation of Canadian Municipalities was resolved only when it dropped constitutional change from its policy agenda.

Associational life, then, plays out in the dance between the internal dynamics of the associations themselves and their interactions with the larger political, social, and institutional environments in which they are located.

Social Cohesion and the Canadian Voluntary Sector
These observations suggest some additional insight into the sources of cohesion in divided societies. We identified four approaches in the introduction. Cohesion can be facilitated by maximizing contact among members of different groups; by building "bridging" social capital across associations; by cooperation and accommodation at the elite level; and by more materialistic calculations of the costs and benefits of interaction. These approaches, of course, are not mutually exclusive.

To the extent that the contact thesis rests on the assumption of broad social interaction, it is of relatively minor significance in understanding the phenomena we are examining, for the simple reason that none of our case studies describes a truly mass membership organization. Canada's huge size and dispersed population, its low levels of bilingualism, and the extent to which associations are now largely run by professional managers all reinforce this minimal effect.

Similarly, while all the associations we have studied are certainly – though to different degrees – examples of bridging social capital and do indeed help to knit Canadians together in positive, mutually rewarding ways, the fact that these are not mass-membership groups means that the major benefit posited for bridging capital – building trust and the ability to compromise through fostering face-to-face relationships – plays only a minor role at the level of the citizenry as a whole.

Yet each theory is helpful in accounting for the concrete pattern of relationships that is revealed in the case studies. The voluntary sector leaders and the professional staff who are centrally responsible for managing these organizations develop social networks and norms of reciprocity and trust that facilitate the process of establishing joint enterprises and of making them persist over time. The impact of positive social contacts and the mutually respectful interaction of organizational leaders are significant in sustaining these civil society groups and the values they represent. They are a lubricant that assists in the ongoing process of linguistic accommodation.

The theory of elite accommodation – our third approach – discloses a major dimension of the reality we have been examining in this book. This is not simply because most modern voluntary associations are managed by their executives and senior staff. It is also because these organizational elites are likely to have the deepest commitment to the group's goals, the strongest interest in the survival and growth of the organization itself, and a broader awareness of the political and institutional environment in which the group is working. Lijphart's model is conditional on the desire of elites to sustain the system and on the willingness of followers to defer to the guidance of the elite. In our study, the elite's commitment is to the basic purposes of the group, and there is little evidence of membership challenges. Members of the elite have wide discretion in conducting their affairs with each other and with wider networks.

However, the theoretical approach with the greatest purchase in explaining the behaviour of the groups we have studied, we believe, lies in our fourth approach, which we call the "political economy of linguistic relations." The starting point is shared, common interests – whether in economic growth and profitability, the health of the farming industry, saving those facing torture and oppression, or preventing heart attacks and strokes. Common interests are what bring associations together, and these interests are what keep them together. What motivates people to take the time and energy to work through the language issue and related questions? Why, on the one hand, would anglophone leaders make the effort to ensure that their organizations become more effectively bilingual and to concede more autonomy to their Quebec partners? And why, on the other hand, would the leaders in Quebec decide to continue to participate in associations in which they remain under-represented?

The answer, we believe, lies in their shared substantive goals, in their common interests. It is this commitment that supplies the motivation and the incentives that make the effort to work together worthwhile. Each side of the language divide decides that the benefits of continuing to work together exceed the costs of not doing so.

Negotiation of the relationship in each association will then depend on the perceived coincidence of each side's goals with the goals of the other, on the resources each brings to the relationship, and on the incentives and disincentives that emanate from the larger political environment. How these calculations of costs and benefits, advantages and disadvantages, play out will largely determine the organizational outcomes and levels of cooperation that result.

This focus on the calculus of costs and benefits is very helpful in explaining the patterns of associational life that we have traced. It helps us to understand the calculations that leaders made as they led their associations through difficult times. It helps us to understand how constraints and incentives in the larger environment – in shifting values and attitudes and shifting government policies – affected the outcomes. It helps to explain a puzzle: why did predominantly anglophone organizations adopt, more or less fully, bilingualism? And why did largely francophone organizations continue to participate? And it helps us to understand the most common pattern of accommodation in these associations: in every one, the solution was some combination of increased recognition and accommodation of Quebec in central bodies combined with increased autonomy for the Quebec-based institutions.

Conclusion

We end on a cautious but positive note. It is made possible by what we learned from the pioneering work of Meisel and Lemieux. They found a landscape fraught with tension; we found a world in which Canadians, anglophone and francophone, have been able to work out their differences and find ways of cooperating that transcend the linguistic difference. The patterns are varied, the atmosphere is by no means harmonious in all respects, but the practical arrangements are by and large effective. This outcome is achieved not by denying difference but by recognizing and accommodating it. It is achieved not by positing a fundamental conflict between integration in common institutions against separate institutions but by accepting both – by building bilingualism into national institutions and by providing autonomy to Quebec-based bodies. The former reflects the continued presence of Quebec in pan-Canadian politics; the latter recognizes the sense of national identity in Quebec and the reality of the French language's minority status in the rest of the country. Asymmetrical bilingualism in national bodies is, at least to some extent, mitigated by asymmetrical federalism in organizational life.

What larger lessons can we draw from this? Two lessons stand out.

First, the *vouloir vivre ensemble* is about much more than a common identity, though that is important; it is equally, and perhaps more importantly, about a sense of shared fate, about an interdependence in needs, interests, and concerns – *devoir vivre ensemble*. It is this beacon that has helped our associations to navigate through turbulent times. "Whatever our linguistic, cultural, or other differences, we have these shared goals and concerns. For the sake of what we have in common, let's figure out a way to cope with what divides us."

Second, the question *comment vivre ensemble?* has no definitive answer. We are impressed by the creativity that the groups we studied have displayed. But the common thread is the construction of institutions and practices that enable cooperation on shared goals where that is necessary and facilitate autonomy and freedom of action where they are desired. There are no right models but many variations on a theme.

Both of these broad conclusions may have lessons for Canadians more generally. The case studies suggest that, yes, face-to-face contacts are highly desirable, as is attention to the building of bridging social capital. But they also suggest that successful accommodation in divided societies does not rest simply on shared visions, common values, and national identities. It rests as heavily on much more pragmatic considerations: the implicit acknowledgment of the existence of a common constitutional and political framework and, within that framework, the recognition of interdependence and of shared substantive problems. Mutual need, our case studies show, matters as much as, and perhaps more than, shared values.

This is a message with real resonance in the Canadian political debate. We Canadians have learned to tread carefully when we enter the symbolic world. During the past four decades, Canadians have had their share of conflict occasioned by the manipulation and deployment of symbols that divide the country's citizens and communities from one another. These matters have been shelved, at least for the moment, and what has come into bolder relief as a consequence is a very successful country – a peaceful and prosperous land from which most people benefit greatly. Also brought into bolder relief is the Canadian capacity, when not distracted by the things that divide us, to work together pragmatically, tackling problems, making incremental improvements, elaborating arrangements that accommodate the differences that are part and parcel of life in this corner of the world. A virtually unknown chapter in this larger Canadian story is the voluntary sector, whose associations and institutions, if our case studies are any indication, have been getting on with their jobs in just this way for several decades now. We hope that this volume will not only deepen our understanding of these associations and how they go about their business but also contribute to a fuller appreciation of what makes Canada itself work.

Notes

Chapter 1: Language and the Institutions of Civil Society

1 John Meisel and Vincent Lemieux, *Ethnic Relations in Canadian Voluntary Associations*, Studies of the Royal Commission on Bilingualism and Biculturalism, Document 13 (Ottawa: Queen's Printer, 1972), 4.
2 Ibid. The research was conducted in 1964-65.
3 *Voluntary Associations*, Reports of the Royal Commission on Bilingualism and Biculturalism, Book 6 (Ottawa: Queen's Printer, 1970), 143.
4 Ibid., 158-59.
5 Ibid., 143, 217.
6 Quebec's Tremblay Commission, which reported at the end of the historical period of which we are speaking, offers the most comprehensive articulation of French Canada's distinctive culture and the perceived difference between it and the culture of English Canada.
7 In 1953, the high-ranking public service was 84 percent anglophone and 13 percent francophone. By contrast, in 1973 the proportion was 65 percent anglophone and 24 percent francophone. See Raymond Breton, Jeffrey G. Reitz, and Victor F. Valentine, *Les frontières culturelles et la cohésion du Canada* (Montreal: Institute for Research on Public Policy, 1981), 219.
8 In fact, the roots of modernization are buried deep within the old regime. Quebec was experiencing urbanization and industrialization throughout most of the twentieth century.
9 Ramsay Cook, *Canada, Quebec, and the Uses of Nationalism* (Toronto: McClelland and Stewart, 1986), 94-95.
10 This paradoxical situation was highlighted in the preliminary report of the Royal Commission on Bilingualism and Biculturalism: "It is almost ironical to recall now the opinion of people who expected that as a result of 'modern' education and industrialization there would be an increasing assimilation of Quebec to the rest of Canada. In one sense it is true that North American technology is bringing the two groups closer together and is developing similar patterns of behaviour, a fact which everybody admitted to us; but the greater closeness makes the competition that much keener and strengthens the determination to live and work under the new conditions 'in a French way.'" See *Preliminary Report of the Royal Commission on Bilingualism and Biculturalism* (Ottawa: Queen's Printer, 1965), 110.
11 "Les résultats obtenus en 1961 ... font apparaître une différence notoire, pour l'ensemble du territoire, entre le revenu moyen des Canadiens d'origine française et celui des Canadiens d'origine britannique. Les Canadiens d'origine britannique occupaient le second rang pour la moyenne de leurs revenus totaux et gagnaient 1000$ environ de plus que ceux d'origine française, qui, pour leur part, se plaçaient avant-derniers parmi tous les groupes ethniques. En d'autres termes, les Canadiens d'origine française gagnaient 80 percent environ du revenu moyen de ceux d'origine britannique." Breton, Reitz, and Valentine, *Les frontières culturelles*, 170.

12 It is estimated that in 1951, 92 percent of the economic elite in Canada was from Anglo-Saxon background, while less than 7 percent was from French background. Ibid., 178.

13 Between 1931 and 1961, the linguistic retention rate among francophones outside Quebec fell from 80 percent to 51 percent. Ibid., 222.

14 Donald Smiley, "Language Policies in the Canadian Political Community," in *Être contemporain: Mélanges en l'honneur de Gérard Bergeron*, ed. Jean-William Lapierre, Vincent Lemieux, and Jacques Zylberberg (Sillery, QC: Presses de l'Université du Québec, 1992), 287.

15 Harvey Lazar and Tom McIntosh have argued in a recent book that "whatever one makes of Canada's place in the international cultural marketplace, on the domestic front the greatest failure has been in bridging the language divide among Canadians. The cultural output of English-speaking Canada remains largely unknown in Quebec and vice versa. At all levels, but especially in the realm of popular culture, there appear to be few common points of reference." Harvey Lazar and Tom McIntosh, "How Canadians Connect: State, Economy, Citizenship, and Society," in *Canada: The State of the Federation 1998/1999: How Canadians Connect,* ed. Harvey Lazar and Tom McIntosh (Montreal: McGill-Queen's University Press, 1999), 19. See also Frederick J. Fletcher, who notes that "it has long been said that Canada's two major language groups live in separate, or 'distinct,' media worlds. This observation applies to the entire range of cultural products – from books to popular music – and has led observers to conclude that Canada is divided into two distinct cultural markets, with relatively little interpenetration, which are largely open to external penetration, especially from the United States." Frederick J. Fletcher, "Media and Political Identity: Canada and Quebec in the Era of Globalization," *Canadian Journal of Communication* 23, 3 (1998), http://www.cjc-online.ca. Fletcher also remarks that "it is striking that the French- and English-language services of the CBC are, for many purposes, best seen as separate institutions despite attempts to operate the corporation as a single broadcasting system. Over the years, the CBC has attempted to produce programs in both official languages, through dual shooting or dubbing, but has rarely achieved substantial audiences in both communities." Ibid. Finally, it is interesting to note here that the linguistic divide also extends to the realm of journalism. David Pritchard and Florian Sauvageau note that "anglophone and francophone journalists practice their profession in separate worlds, as their media consumption habits show. Neither group pays much attention to what happens in the other's culture. In this sense, the two solitudes are alive and well." David Pritchard and Florian Sauvageau, "English and French and Generation X: The Professional Values of Canadian Journalists," in *Canada: The State of the Federation 1998/1999: How Canadians Connect,* ed. Harvey Lazar and Tom McIntosh (Montreal: McGill-Queen's University Press, 1999), 283.

16 Lazar and McIntosh, "How Canadians Connect," 26.

17 Breton, Reitz, and Valentine, *Les frontières culturelles,* 302.

18 A 1978 Centre de recherche sur l'opinion publique (CROP) poll tried to evaluate how English and French Canadian attitudes had evolved since the 1965 preliminary report of the Royal Commission on Bilingualism and Biculturalism and noted the following: "Questions along the lines of the old would-you-let-your-sister-marry-one? variety showed some interesting quirks. More Francophones now have Anglo friends (19 percent from 13 percent), but the contact hasn't been a huge success because fewer (46 percent from 57 percent) say they actually want Anglos as friends. Worse, only 39 percent (from 50 percent) want Anglo relatives and far more don't care one way or the other. On the other hand, while Anglos don't want or don't have more francophone friends than before, those opposed to one in the family went down to 9 percent from 15 percent. It seems Canadians have still not succeeded in converting the 'two solitudes' into an equal working partnership – personal or otherwise." See "Can't We Be Friends? A Special Report," *Maclean's,* 6 February 1978, 20.

19 H.D. Forbes, *Ethnic Conflict: Commerce, Culture, and the Contact Hypothesis* (New Haven: Yale University Press, 1997).

20 H.D. Forbes, "Integration, Contact, and Linkages," paper prepared for the Privy Council Office (Ottawa, Government of Canada, 2001), 18-19.

21 Ibid., 10. See also Breton, Reitz, and Valentine, *Les frontières culturelles,* 310-11.

22 Forbes, "Integration," 10.

23 Robert Putnam, *Bowling Alone: The Collapse and Revival of American Community* (New York: Simon and Schuster, 2000), 7.
24 Raymond Breton, "Social Participation and Social Capital," paper presented at the second national Metropolis Conference, Montreal, 1997, 8-9.
25 Putnam, *Bowling Alone*, 5.
26 Ashutosh Varshney, *Ethnic Conflict and Civic Life: Hindus and Muslims in India* (New Haven: Yale University Press, 2002).
27 Deepa Narayan, *Bonds and Bridges: Social Capital and Poverty* (Washington, DC: World Bank, 1999).
28 Louise Marmen and Jean-Pierre Corbeil, *New Canadian Perspectives: Languages in Canada: 1996 Census* (Ottawa: Minister of Public Works and Government Services Canada, 1999), 42.
29 Ibid., 39.
30 Ibid., 45.
31 Ibid., 41.
32 See Paul B. Reed and Valerie J. Howe, *Voluntary Organizations in Ontario in the 1990s* (Ottawa: Statistics Canada, 2000).
33 As Martin Hering argues, "segmented societies are characterized by extraordinary political cleavages. The distinct subcultures are separated from each other. They are virtually self-contained groups which have their own cultural and political life ... Being isolated from each other, the subcultures articulate and aggregate their interests separately. Interests in homogeneous political systems are transferred from citizens through mediators to the state, similar to the image of a pyramid, as a process from the bottom to the top. In consociational democracies this mediating process is multiplied depending on how many subcultures exist. There is no pyramid, but there are many separated pillars. Between each of these pillars is a gap. At this point, one can see which function the elites perform: elite cooperation is the bridging mechanism at the top of these pillars, or the separated subcultures respectively." Martin Hering, *Consociational Democracy in Canada*, 1998, 3, http://www.archiv. ub.uni-marburg.de/sum/84/sum84-6.html."
34 Will Kymlicka makes a relevant comment: "Democratic politics is politics in the vernacular. The average citizen only feels comfortable debating political issues in their mother tongue. As a general rule, it is only elites who have fluency with more than one language, and who have the continual opportunity to maintain and develop these language skills, and who feel comfortable debating political issues in another tongue within multilingual settings." Will Kymlicka, "Citizenship in an Era of Globalization: Commentary on Held," in *Democracy's Edges*, ed. Ian Shapiro and Casiano Hacker–Cordón (Cambridge, UK: Cambridge University Press, 1999), 121.
35 For instance, Meisel and Lemieux noted that in pan-Canadian voluntary associations "the monetary costs of publishing all of an association's materials in both languages tend to be borne by all the members equally but the beneficiaries of this service are a relatively small number of Francophone members." Meisel and Lemieux, *Ethnic Relations*, 312.
36 Phillippe Van Parijs, "Must Europe Be Belgian? On Democratic Citizenship in Multilingual Polities," in *The Demands of Citizenship*, ed. Iain Hampsher-Monk and Catriona McKinnon (London: Continuum, 2000), 6.
37 Jean Laponce, *Languages and Their Territories* (Toronto: University of Toronto Press, 1987). Van Parijs speaks of the tendency toward linguistic homogeneity: "Languages can coexist for centuries when there is no or little contact. But as soon as people start talking, trading, working with each other, courting each other, having children together, one language gradually drives out the other one." Van Parijs, "Must Europe Be Belgian?" 7.
38 Laponce, *Languages*.
39 Jean Laponce, "Reducing the Tensions Resulting from Language Contacts: Personal or Territorial Solutions?" in *Language and the State: The Law and Politics of Identity*, ed. David Schneiderman (Cowansville, QC: Éditions Yvon Blais, 1989), 175.
40 This may explain why – historically – francophones have had a lower propensity than anglophones to engage in associational membership and why they have been more likely

to join associations whose membership is predominantly French speaking. See Laponce, *Languages*, 311. See also the discussion in Gary Caldwell and Paul Reed, "Civic Participation in Canada: Is Quebec Different?" *Inroads* 8 (1999).

41 See Jean Laponce, "The Case for Ethnic Federalism in Multilingual Societies," in *The Territorial Management of Ethnic Conflict*, ed. John Coakley (London: Frank Cass, 1993), 27-28.

42 Breton, Reitz, and Valentine, *Les frontières culturelles*, 312.

43 The Canadian Centre for Philanthropy estimates that there are 77,000 registered charities in Canada and 100,000 non-profit corporations, which together have 21 million individual donors and 7.5 million volunteers. See http://www.nonprofitscan.org/sizescop.htm.

Chapter 2: French-English Relations in Comprehensive Business Associations

Part of the data in this chapter is discussed and analyzed in another context in William D. Coleman and Tim A. Mau, "French-English Relations in Business Interest Associations, 1965-2002," *Canadian Public Administration* 45, 4 (2002): 490-511.

1 William D. Coleman, *Business and Politics: A Study of Collective Action* (Montreal: McGill-Queen's University Press, 1988); Charles Lindblom, *Politics and Markets* (New York: Basic Books, 1977).

2 Coleman, *Business and Politics*.

3 John Meisel and Vincent Lemieux, *Ethnic Relations in Canadian Voluntary Associations*, Studies of the Royal Commission on Bilingualism and Biculturalism, Document 13 (Ottawa: Queen's Printer, 1972).

4 Coleman, *Business and Politics*, 87.

5 William D. Coleman, "Federalism and Interest Group Organization," in *Federalism and the Role of the State*, ed. H. Bakvis and W. Chandler (Toronto: University of Toronto Press, 1987), 171-87; Coleman, *Business and Politics*; P.C. Schmitter and Luca Lanzalaco, "Regions and the Organization of Business Interests," in *Regionalism, Business Interests, and Public Policy*, ed. William D. Coleman and Henry J. Jacek (London: Sage: 1990) 201-30.

6 Chambre de commerce de Montréal, *Un siècle à entreprendre: La Chambre de commerce de Montréal 1887-1987* (Montréal: Éditions Libre Expression, 1987), 17-18; authors' translation.

7 Vincent Lemieux, "Le conflit dans les organisations biculturelles," *Recherches sociographiques* 24, 1 (1973): 41-57.

8 Meisel and Lemieux, *Ethnic Relations*, 209.

9 Ibid., 202.

10 Ibid., 185, 190.

11 Ibid., 209.

12 At one point, the CCQ won a North American award for being the only state or provincial organization to have 100 percent participation by the local chambers.

13 Meisel and Lemieux, *Ethnic Relations*, 195.

14 Ibid., 206.

15 See http://www.ccq.ca.

16 Meisel and Lemieux, *Ethnic Relations*, 186.

17 Statistics Canada, "Population by Knowledge of Official Language," Ottawa: Statistics Canada, 1996.

18 This particular problem was rectified during the time of the study with the selection of Perrin Beatty as president of the CME.

19 This is no longer the case as the CME now has a fully bilingual website. See http://www.cme-mec.ca.

20 Chambre de commerce de Montréal, *Un siècle à entreprendre*, 19.

21 Meisel and Lemieux, *Ethnic Relations*, 180.

22 William D. Coleman, *The Independence Movement in Québec: 1945-1980* (Toronto: University of Toronto Press, 1984), 72.

23 Ibid., 72-74.

24 Ibid., 100.

25 Chambre de commerce de Montréal, *Un siècle à entreprendre*, 117.

26 Jean Paré, "Merger Shows the Persuasive Power of Money," *Financial Post,* 16 March 1992, S2.
27 Chambre de commerce du Montréal métropolitain/Board of Trade of Metropolitan Montreal, "Les services en français et en anglais à la Chambre de commerce du Montréal métropolitain: Bilan et recommandations," juin 1995.
28 Chambre de commerce du Montréal métropolitain/Board of Trade of Metropolitan Montreal, interview, February 1999.
29 Peter H. Russell, "The End of Mega Constitutional Politics in Canada?" in *The Charlottetown Accord, the Referendum, and the Future of Canada,* ed. Kenneth McRoberts and Patrick Monahan (Toronto: University of Toronto Press, 1993), 211-21; Peter H. Russell, *Constitutional Odyssey: Can Canadians Become a Sovereign People?* (Toronto: University of Toronto Press, 1993).
30 Meisel and Lemieux, *Ethnic Relations,* 11.
31 Lemieux, "Le conflit dans les organisations biculturelles."
32 Canadian Federation of Independent Business, "Québec's Small Business Sector Rejects Sovereignty Option," press release, 18 October 1995. Interestingly, when CFIB members were surveyed on the 1980 referendum question, a smaller percentage (63.4) of the respondents voted no. Forty-five percent, or 3,231 of the federation's then 7,200 members, responded to this survey.
33 For an abbreviated version of this brief, see Chambre de commerce du Québec, "Canadian Federalism Is an Economic Failure," in *Canada, Adieu? Québec Debates Its Future,* ed. Richard Fidler (Halifax: Institute for Research on Public Policy, 1991), 82-89. See also Conseil du patronat du Québec, "The Dangers of Sovereignty," in *Canada, Adieu? Québec Debates Its Future,* ed. Richard Fidler (Halifax: Institute for Research on Public Policy, 1991), 114-19. Like the CCQ, the CCMM supported continued membership in the Canadian federal system but argued that all provinces should have increased powers.
34 Ted Glenn, "The Calgary Declaration," *Backgrounder B-19* (Toronto: Ontario Legislative Library, Legislative Research Service, 24 April 1988), provides an overview of the Calgary Declaration and the response of the federal, provincial, and territorial governments to this process.
35 Confederation 2000, "Today and Tomorrow: An Agenda for Action: Ideas and Recommendations of the Confederation 2000 Conference Participants," 3-4 May 1996.
36 Business Council on National Issues, memo to Frank McKenna, premier of New Brunswick and chairman designate, Council of Premiers, 15 July 1991, 1.

Chapter 3: Canada's English and French Farm Communities
I would like to thank the several leaders and officials in the Quebec and Canadian farm organizations and an editor at *La terre de chez nous* who generously shared their knowledge of the workings of farm organizations in Canada and Quebec with me. I am also grateful for the research assistance of Elizabeth Moore and Gunilla Leroux.

1 John Meisel and Vincent Lemieux, "L'union catholique des cultivateurs and the Canadian Federation of Agriculture," in *Ethnic Relations in Canadian Voluntary Associations,* Studies of the Royal Commission on Bilingualism and Biculturalism, Document 13 (Ottawa: Queen's Printer, 1972), 286, 288 respectively.
2 The number of Canadian farms and farmers is declining, with the number of operations down 1.3 percent in 1996 from 1991. Agriculture and agrifood industries comprise about 9 percent of Canada's GDP and account for some 2 million jobs.
3 Quebec ranks fourth behind Ontario, Saskatchewan, and Alberta in number of census farms and size of its total farm population.
4 The provincial organization must be a general farm organization representative of agriculture in the province and to which all farmers may belong either directly or through organizations. Both the commodity and the cooperative members must be interprovincial in their operations. There is also a provision for associate member status for national or interprovincial organizations of producers that are not otherwise eligible.
5 Following William D. Coleman and Grace Skogstad, logic of membership factors refer to "the interests and motivations of individuals and firms that bring them to join a group" and include "such factors as the size of the potential membership domain, the geographical

distribution of members, their resource base, and the nature of primary, informal social relations." See William D. Coleman and Grace Skogstad, *Policy Communities and Public Policy
in Canada: A Structural Approach* (Mississauga: Copp Clark Pitman, 1990), 23. Logic of influence factors are those that affect the organizational development of groups but that are
extraneous to membership characteristics and include, principally, the structure of the state
and state policies.

6 While 12.4 percent of Saskatchewan's GDP derives from agriculture and agrifood industries,
these industries account for only 4.2 percent of Quebec's and Ontario's GDP. However, the
latter two provinces together account for 56 percent of Canada's agrifood production and
71 percent of its food processing. See the CFA website at http://www.cfa-fca.ca.

7 Together these products account for over 60 percent of agricultural production.

8 The distinctions are not quite so clear since Ontario has a strong cattle industry geared to
export markets and Quebec has a large pork sector, which is becoming increasingly export
oriented.

9 Grace Skogstad, "Canadian Federalism, Internationalization, and Quebec Agriculture: Dis-
Engagement, Re-Integration?" *Canadian Public Policy* 24 (1998): 27-48.

10 Grace Skogstad, *The Politics of Agricultural Policy-Making in Canada* (Toronto: University of
Toronto Press, 1987), chapter 6.

11 In 1999, the Agricultural Producers Association of Saskatchewan was formed, and it has since
provided Saskatchewan farmers with membership in the CFA. Before then, the Saskatchewan
Association of Rural Municipalities played a *de facto* representational role to some extent,
but its mandate is to represent rural municipalities, not agricultural producers. The Saskatchewan Wheat Pool represented Saskatchewan at the CFA for several years as well, but
as its name suggests its mandate is to represent the interests of its pool shareholders. It
ceased to be a CFA member after it became a publicly traded company in 2004.

12 The organizational weakness stems in large part from the fact that there is no legislation
in Alberta requiring farmers to pay a "check off" when they sell designated farm commodities (as prevails in Manitoba for KAP), or to pay dues to a farm organization of their choice
(as in Ontario for the Ontario Federation of Agriculture), or to pay dues to a designated
organization that has the support of a significant majority of farmers (as in Quebec with
UPA).

13 The twenty-one members of the CFA in 2007 no longer included the Saskatchewan Wheat
Pool and Agricore, which merged in 2007, or the Canadian Aquaculture Industry Alliance.
The Canadian Wheat Board, the Canadian Horticultural Council, and the Western Farm
Leadership Council are now members.

14 The Canadian Pork Council withdrew from the CFA in the early 1980s, following the CFA's
support of continuing grain freight subsidies (which drove up the cost of grain-fed hogs).
It rejoined in 1999 out of the belief that the CFA had emerged as the dominant national
farm organization and was recognized by the Canadian government as the dominant voice
of Canadian farmers on a multiplicity of issues, including multilateral trade policy.

15 This followed passage of la Loi sur les producteurs agricoles in 1972.

16 Following the 1972 recognition of the UPA as the sole representative of Quebec farmers,
the 828 local groups that existed under the UCC were amalgamated to yield 178 local
syndicats.

17 Note that an organization representing Quebec English-speaking farmers, numbering some
500 members, was also a member of the Canadian Chamber of Agriculture and the CFA.

18 Before 1940, the UCC was a member of other Canada-wide organizations, including the
Canadian Federation of Milk Producers and the Canadian Horticultural Council.

19 Meisel and Lemieux, "L'union catholique des cultivateurs," 283.

20 Ibid., 275.

21 Ibid., 279.

22 Ibid., 280.

23 Ibid., 279.

24 Ibid.

25 As noted earlier, Alberta pays a lower membership fee to the CFA than the funding formula
would warrant and therefore enjoys only associate member status. As a result, even though

Alberta's farm sector is larger than Quebec's, Alberta farmers have less representation on the CFA governing bodies owing to WRAP's financial weakness.

26 At the annual meeting, non-Atlantic provincial federations, including Quebec's UPA, have twelve delegates each. This number compares with four delegates each for the Atlantic farm federations, two each for national or interprovincial members, and one apiece for associate members.

27 The National Council consists of the president; two vice-presidents; three councillors from each non-Atlantic provincial member; and one councillor for each Atlantic provincial member, national or interprovincial member, or associate member to represent women in eastern Canada and to represent BC, Alberta, and Manitoba women.

28 The Board of Directors consists of the CFA president, its two vice-presidents, plus one director from each member association, one woman director from eastern Canada, and one woman director from western Canada.

29 The Executive Committee includes the president, two vice-presidents, plus five other directors, one of whom represents commodity members. The five directors are elected from the National Council. The Executive Committee manages the work program of the CFA and assists the president and vice-presidents to carry out their responsibilities.

30 This description of preferential status is linked to Quebec's hold on the position of first vice-president of the CFA (which is held by the president of either the UPA or the Coop fedérée). Nonetheless, one UPA observer noted that there has never been a CFA president from Quebec. He added, however, that it would likely not be feasible for the UPA president to be the CFA president since the presidency of the UPA is a full-time job.

31 Meisel and Lemieux, *Ethnic Relations,* 279.

32 Ibid., 275.

33 Ibid., 280.

34 Ibid., 283.

35 Ibid., 168. Meisel and Lemieux report that, when the CFA attempted a French translation, the results were "disastrous" (268). While the UCC was willing to pay itself for a better translation, the need to do so was a source of resentment since the UCC was already contributing about 20 percent of the CFA budget.

36 The discussion that follows is based on interviews with two current and two former UPA officials, an editor at *La terre de chez nous,* a former CFA president, and a current CFA official.

37 One female translator was apparently at Jacques Proulx's side so frequently during formal events, including banquets, that for several years many CFA members erroneously believed she was his spouse.

38 In 1999, four of the seven support staff at the CFA national office were either bilingual or able to function in French.

39 The UPA reports that about 80 percent of all CFA documents are in French and received simultaneously with those transmitted in English. The exceptions are when decisions must be made quickly and the English version is transmitted first.

40 The Ontario Federation of Agriculture tries to ensure that one of its delegates to the CFA speaks French.

41 Less than 5 percent of the UPA's members are English speaking. The UPA does provide some documents in English, including a summary of the policy resolutions to be debated at its annual meeting as well as other "critical" documents. As well, the UPA produces an English insert for the monthly English publication the *Quebec Farmers' Advocate,* a publication of the English-speaking Quebec Farmers Association. Oral English services are available from those regional federations whose constituencies include English-speaking farmers. Nonetheless, the UPA's meetings are conducted solely in French. Its main secretariat includes individuals fluent in English; one estimate is that 50-75 of the 400 staff in the Longueuil office can manage in English. And some presidents of specialist federations, such as those representing the dairy, hog, and poultry sectors, who interact with their English-speaking counterparts outside Quebec, are becoming more bilingual.

42 One UPA official, who described himself as more sensitive to the linguistic situation than many, voiced the sentiment that, despite its best efforts, the CFA is not fully cognizant of

the importance many francophones place on being able to communicate in their native tongue. The example offered by way of support was that technical difficulties with translation services always produce CFA apologies but never are deemed significant enough to terminate CFA meetings. The sense of disappointment was, nonetheless, muted and accompanied by a recognition that, outside Quebec, English is the language of communication. Separately, a CFA spokesman observed that the CFA will never show overheads in English only, if the French overheads are unavailable.

43 Several individuals interviewed for this study stressed the importance of securing interpreters who serve an organization over the long term. Continuity in individual interpreters sensitizes the latter to farm leaders' and officials' use of a language and the nuances of their modes of expression and enables them to develop a good grasp of the intricacies of the agricultural sector itself.

44 First elected in 1999, Bob Friesen was in his eighth year as CFA president in 2007.

45 In 2007, Laurent Pellerin, who replaced Proulx in 1993, had served even longer as UPA president.

46 Since the reorganization in 1994, Ontario and Quebec each have three members on the fifteen-member Board of Directors, while other provinces have one member each. On the fifty-three-member General Council, Ontario and Quebec have twelve members each, compared with six members each for British Columbia and Alberta; four each for Saskatchewan and Manitoba; two each for the Maritime provinces and the Canadian Dairy Network; and one for Newfoundland. Quebec and Ontario have the most voting delegates at the annual policy conference in January and the annual July meeting, which approves the budget and elects the General Council.

47 These executive positions are president, first vice-president, second vice-president, and executive member.

48 In 1994, the Dairy Bureau, the marketing arm of dairy producers, merged with the Dairy Farmers of Canada. All communications of the marketing and nutrition/promotion office in Montreal, staffed with approximately twenty individuals, are in both languages.

49 The general manager of the FPLQ reports that she sometimes receives the English version of a communication first, followed by the French version within twenty-four to forty-eight hours. This delay does not occur frequently, only when a communication requires urgent action. As well, being fully bilingual, she will often function in English at meetings where the discussion is purely technical, thus obviating the need for simultaneous translation for her non-French-speaking Canadian counterparts.

50 The board room at the Dairy Farmers of Ontario is equipped for translation services.

51 The FPPQ was called the Fédération des propriétaires de porcs from 1966 to 1970. In 2007, hog-marketing boards in all provinces except Newfoundland were members of the CPC. British Columbia, which had withdrawn in the 1990s, has rejoined. The Canadian Swine Breeders Association holds an *ex officio* place on the CPC.

52 Martin Rice described himself as able to be understood in French but not able to understand all spoken French. Interview, 15 June 1999.

53 One UPA official noted that the CFA's budget is equal to that of the smallest UPA regional federation.

54 The UPA's financial and personnel resources far outstrip those of all provincial federations.

55 The Ontario Farm Federation has approximately thirty staff in its head office and another thirty distributed in offices throughout the province. Its annual budget is approximately $8.5 million.

56 A 1998-99 example is a multilateral trade negotiation simulation (the Great Globalization Game) designed to teach Canadian farmers the language and impact of trade negotiations. The simulation is under the auspices of the CFA in Canada and the UPA in Quebec. Another example offered by UPA officials was CFA leadership in obtaining support from the Canadian Farm Management Council to assist Quebec farmers with applying for emergency assistance during the 1998 ice storm.

57 The only prairie pool left in existence in 2007, the Saskatchewan Wheat Pool, was no longer farmer controlled and no longer a CFA member.

58 Meisel and Lemieux, *Ethnic Relations*, 283, identified the UCC's greater militancy and syndicalism, compared with the CFA, as a factor accounting for the two organizations' periodic conflicts.

59 I use the term in Coleman's sense to refer to the capacity to represent and integrate the diverse interests in an economic sector, while possessing the resources of adequate finances, bureaucratic expertise, and coordination mechanisms to serve as the sole voice for the sector. See William D. Coleman, *Business and Politics: A Study of Collective Action* (Montreal: McGill-Queen's University Press, 1988).

60 Senior UPA individuals stated in interviews that Proulx's withdrawal threat was never seriously considered and did not have the support of other UPA leaders.

61 Union des producteurs agricoles, "Mémoire présenté à la Commission parlementaire québécoise par l'Union des producteurs agricoles: L'avenir politique et constitutionnel du Québec," in *Canada, Adieu? Quebec Debates Its Future*, trans. R. Fidler (Lantzville, BC: Oolichan Books; Halifax: Institute for Research on Public Policy, 1990), 11. In an interview with the author, on 28 July 1999, Jacques Proulx retracted his earlier statement, declaring that the CFA had defended Quebec farmers' interests because of the major role that the UPA had played in the CFA throughout the negotiations.

62 In an interview with the author, 28 July 1999, Jacques Proulx traced these different approaches to the anglophone community's Anglo-Saxon background compared with the francophone community's Latin origins. In his view, these origins result in anglophone farmers preferring not to raise their voices and wanting "to get along," while francophone farmers are inclined to vigorous debate and aggressive pursuit of their aims.

63 Meisel and Lemieux, *Ethnic Relations*, 273.

64 See Union des producteurs agricoles, "Mémoire."

65 This pragmatic philosophy is also reflected in the effort of younger Quebec farmers to build links to their English-speaking counterparts throughout Canada. Their objective is to increase their influence with Ottawa. See Ed White, "Quebec Farmers Extend Hand to Counterparts," *Western Producer*, 22 February 1996, 1.

66 A good example is Agriculture and Agri-Food Canada's adaptation funds, designed to compensate for the termination of federal freight rate subsidies, which are being distributed in Quebec by the UPA.

Chapter 4: Municipal Associations
We are indebted to staff of the Federation of Canadian Municipalities and several provincial-municipal associations for generous access to documents and numerous interview opportunities. We are also grateful for many other interviews we conducted during this research, including with several present and past members of boards of municipal associations and with academics and consultants working on municipal issues.

This chapter and a journal article ("Coping with Canadian Federalism: The Case of the Federation of Canadian Municipalities," *Canadian Public Administration Journal* 48, 4 [2005]: 528-51) overlap a little because both had their origins in an earlier unpublished report. The Institute of Public Administration of Canada has kindly given us permission to reproduce the parts of the chapter that also appear in the article.

1 John Meisel and Vincent Lemieux, *Ethnic Relations in Canadian Voluntary Associations*, Studies of the Royal Commission on Bilingualism and Biculturalism, Document 13 (Ottawa: Queen's Printer, 1972), 4.

2 According to Statistics Canada at http://www12.statcan.ca/english/census06/analysis/popdwell/charts/chart5.htm, the urbanized share of Canada's population rose from 67 percent in 1956 to 78 percent in 1996.

3 For a detailed history of the CFMM-FCM, see Federation of Canadian Municipalities, *FCM 1937-1987: 50 Years Making History* (Ottawa: FCM, 1987).

4 Meisel and Lemieux, *Ethnic Relations*, 234.

5 For two contemporary accounts of the CFMM-FCM in the 1970s, see Charles Bens and Anne Golden, *The Federation of Canadian Municipalities: In Search of Credibility*, Comment No. 161 (Toronto: Bureau of Municipal Research, 1976); and Lionel D. Feldman and Kath-

arine A. Graham, *Bargaining for Cities: Municipalities and Intergovernmental Relations: An Assessment* (Montreal: Institute for Research on Public Policy, 1979).

6 For a discussion of the membership of the CFMM-FCM, see Appendix A of Don Stevenson and Richard Gilbert, "Coping with Canadian Federalism: The Case of the Federation of Canadian Municipalities," *Canadian Public Administration Journal* 48, 4 (2005): 528-51.

7 Meisel and Lemieux, *Ethnic Relations*, 234.

8 Ibid.

9 Harvey Lazar and Tom McIntosh, "How Canadians Connect: State, Economy, Citizenship, and Society," in *Canada: The State of the Federation 1998/1999: How Canadians Connect,* ed. Harvey Lazar and Tom McIntosh (Montreal: McGill-Queen's University Press, 1999).

10 Denis Bédard, *Pacte 2000: Rapport de la Commission nationale sur les finances et la fiscalité locale (Bédard Report)* (Québec: Les Publications du Québec, 1999).

Chapter 5: Associations in the Voluntary Health Sector

1 This work is based largely on interviews with executives and staff of the organizations, which were conducted on a non-attribution basis.

2 The wording is slightly different but makes the same points in 2008. See http://www.heartandstroke.on.ca.

3 Heart and Stroke Foundation of Canada, president's newsletter, winter 1999.

4 Ibid.

5 Panel on Accountability and Governance in the Voluntary Sector, "Building on Strength: Improving Governance and Accountability in the Canadian Voluntary Sector: Final Report" (Final report, Ottawa, Voluntary Sector Round Table, 1999, 6).

6 Ibid.

7 Heart and Stroke Foundation of Canada, board minutes, 11 June 1994, 1.

8 Ibid., 3.

9 Jean A. Laponce, "Minority Languages in Canada: Their Fate and Survival Strategies," in *Languages: Cultures and Values in Canada at the Dawn of the 21st Century,* ed. A. Lapierre, P. Smart, and P. Savard (Ottawa: Carleton University Press, 1996), 78-83, 77. See also Jean Laponce, *Loi de Babel et autres régularités des rapports entre langue et politique* (Québec: Presses de l'Université Laval, 2006), 157-64.

Chapter 6: From Biculturalism to Bilingualism

1 The name has changed several times. The Canadian Council on Child Welfare (1920) became the Canadian Council on Family and Child Welfare (1929), the Canadian Welfare Council (1935), and finally the Canadian Council on Social Development in 1971. To simplify matters, we will use the name Canadian Welfare Council to refer to all the councils from 1920 until 1971.

2 These numbers are from the CCSD website, http://www.ccsd.ca, and from interviews.

3 See Richard Splane, *75 Years of Community Services in Canada: Canadian Council on Social Development, 1920-1995* (Ottawa: Canadian Council on Social Development, 1996).

4 Available at http://www.ccsd.ca/aboutus.html#ar.

5 The mission of the CQDS was "Promouvoir l'intégration sociale et économique des Québécois et des Québécoises et le développement des communautés et des regions au Québec, par un support actif aux groupes du milieu." This quote from its mission statement is in Jean Panet-Raymond, "Le Conseil québécois du développement social est né!" *Nouvelles Pratiques Sociales* 7, 1 (1994): 197.

6 The story is told in Panet-Raymond, "Le Conseil québécois du développement social est né!"

7 Lucien Massé, Chairman of the Special Committee to Develop a Submission to the Royal Commission on Bilingualism and Biculturalism, to the CCSD Board, 27 January 1965.

8 See minutes of the annual meeting, 19 March 1964, 7-8.

9 We are using the version of the submission transmitted to the board by Lucien Massé on 27 January 1965. Canadian Welfare Council, "Submission by the Canadian Welfare Council to the Royal Commission on Biculturalism and Bilingualism."

10 The official history of the CWC and CCSD is in Splane, *75 Years of Community Services in Canada.*
11 Canadian Welfare Council, Brief to the Royal Commission, 3.
12 These dates are from the submission to the royal commission, and it is not clear what constituted "French-speaking Canada" (ibid.). Given the institutional focus, Quebec is probably the point of reference.
13 Canadian Welfare Council, Conference Report, 1921, 8.
14 Canadian Welfare Council, Constitution, 1925, 9.
15 Canadian Welfare Council, Brief to the Royal Commission, 10.
16 Ibid., 11, 12.
17 Ibid., 9.
18 Ibid., 12, 13.
19 Ibid., 13.
20 Ibid., 16.
21 Ibid., 15.
22 Minutes, Meeting of the Board of Governors, 31 May 1961.
23 Minutes, Meeting of the Board of Governors, 1 December 1961.
24 Report of the French Commission, 11 June 1963.
25 Canadian Welfare Council, Brief to the Royal Commission, 18.
26 Ibid., 25.
27 Minutes, Annual Meeting, 27-29 May 1963.
28 Minutes, Meeting of the Board of Governors, 22 October 1964.
29 Minutes, Annual Meeting, 27-29 May 1963.
30 The Board of Governors in the 1960s contained a number of ministers and priests. See Splane, *75 Years of Community Services in Canada,* 176. One member who played an active role in the French Commission in these years was M. l'abbé R. Riendeau of Montreal.
31 Minutes, Meeting of the Board of Governors, 17 March 1966.
32 Minutes, Meeting of the Board of Governors, 15 March 1967.
33 Canadian Welfare Council, *47th Annual Report,* 1967.
34 Indeed, in 1964, when the CWC decided to send a brief to the royal commission, some members of the board insisted that "no reference [be] made to future action which had not been decided upon, e.g., the possibility of establishing one bilingual official publication." Minutes, Meeting of the Board of Governors, 19 March 1964.
35 Minutes, Meeting of the Board of Governors, 1 November 1972.
36 See Splane, *75 Years of Community Services in Canada,* 37ff.
37 Much of the rest of the analysis is based, in addition to internal documents and other publications, on interviews with past members of the executive and directors of the council. The interviews, conducted by Rachel Laforest, were with Susan Carter (10 December 1999), Terrance Hunsley (8 March 2000), Patrick Johnston (1 February 2000), and Jean Panet-Raymond (22 February 2000).
38 Calculated from Splane, *75 Years of Community Services in Canada,* Appendix 4.
39 Ibid., 54-55.
40 Minutes, Meeting of the Board of Governors, 23 October 1978.
41 Minutes, Meeting of the Board of Governors, 19 October 1980.
42 Minutes, Meeting of the Board of Governors, 3 March 1982.
43 Canadian Council for Social Development, *Annual Report,* 1982-83.
44 Calculated from Splane, *75 Years of Community Services in Canada,* Appendix 4.
45 For a description of the CCSD's involvement with the Court Challenges Program, see Canadian Council for Social Development, *Annual Report,* 1989-90, 9.
46 The program was reinstated after the 1993 election, but it was administered by an independent corporation rather than the CCSD.
47 Splane, *75 Years of Community Services in Canada,* 102-3.
48 Ibid., 107. Chapter 7 recounts the mobilization in 1991.
49 This observation is from the interviews.
50 Panet-Raymond, "Le Conseil québécois de développement social est né!" 196-97.

51 Splane, *75 Years of Community Services in Canada,* 108.
52 Ibid., 113-15.
53 Ibid., 114.
54 As an example of the second type of explanation, see ibid., 110-11, where Splane suggests, with reference to the 1995 referendum, that "the prospect that Quebec might separate from Canada may have been a contributing factor in the decision of the Quebec members of the Council's Board of Governors to resign from the Council in 1994." For his part, Panet-Raymond explained the split to the Quebec social policy community as the result of the lack of appreciation of research models used in Quebec, at a time when the CCSD's finances depended so heavily on obtaining research grants. Panet-Raymond, "Le Conseil québécois de développement social est né!" 196-97.
55 Canadian Council for Social Development, *Annual Report,* 1993-94, 7.
56 As early as June 1994, the CQDS approached the CCSD to work out an agreement for future collaboration on projects and communication. It also offered to continue distributing the CCSD publications in Quebec for a minimal fee. In Jean Panet-Raymond, President, CQDS, to David Ross, Executive Director, CCSD, 7 September 1994.

Chapter 7: Managing Linguistic Practices in International Development NGOs
I would like to acknowledge the financial support of the International Development Research Council, which funded this research, the generous assistance of WUSC, which made available its archives, current documents, and staff for interviewing. Finally, I would like to thank my two research assistants, Rachel Laforest and Tapas Chowdhury, for their invaluable contribution.

1 WUSC, "A Narrative History of WUSC," http://www.wusc.ca/.
2 Indeed, WUSC currently houses WUS International records and documents, which remain unarchived.
3 Canadian Council for International Cooperation Policy Team, "A Profile of Canadian NGOs," in *The Role of the Voluntary Sector in Canadian ODA,* October 1995, http://fly.web.net/ccic/volsector.htm.
4 The NGO Project Facility was created in 1995 to provide support to small and medium-sized Canadian NGOs for overseas development activities. However, CIDA has been providing support to NGOs since 1968, when $5 million was distributed to fifty projects carried out by twenty agencies.
5 WUSC, *Fifty Years of Seminars,* 1997, 61, 109, 112ff.
6 See CCIC, "Who We Are," http://fly.web.net/ccic/whoweare.htm.
7 In the case of Oxfam, there is a separate Oxfam Quebec, founded in 1973.
8 World Vision now has a bilingual website.
9 Minutes, Annual Assembly, 15 July 1964.
10 Minutes, Annual Assembly, 12 May 1968.
11 Manuel Neira, *Report on Structural Reforms and Constitutional Revisions,* 1969, 3.
12 Ibid., 5.
13 CUSO also split along regional-linguistic lines but has been more successful at sustaining the viability of a Quebec chapter.
14 Minutes, Meeting of Board of Directors, 12 May 1968.
15 Minutes, Meeting of Board of Directors, 16 September 1968.
16 Ibid.
17 Moved by Mr. Davies, seconded by Mr. Agnew, ibid.
18 Annual Report of International Assembly, May 1968.
19 According to John Watson, by 1973 the annual budget of WUSC had decreased from approximately $1 million in 1968 to $120,000, onto which was added a $12,000 debt. Interview, 15 September 1999.
20 For example, in 1975 WUSC first received project funding from CIDA for the Swaziland Rural Water Supply Project.
21 WUSC, "A Narrative History of WUSC," in *WUSC Annual Review,* 1977, 6, http://www.wusc.ca/.

22 WUSC, "Long Term Bilingualism Development Program for WUSC," 30 November 1975.
23 WUSC, Annual Report, 1976, 13.
24 This task includes the registration of students and maintaining contact with the universities.
25 Incorporation of EUMC (Quebec Section), Document 2.
26 Through the 1980s, WUSC undertook projects in at least twenty-six countries (including Zimbabwe, Sierra Leone, Gabon, Swaziland, South Africa, Zaire, Bhutan, Mali, Ethiopia, Botswana, Cameroon, Malawi, Tunisia, China, Bangladesh, Burma, Indonesia, Nepal, Malaysia, Benin, the Eastern Caribbean, Costa Rica, Peru, and Guyana). It mounted water and sanitation, health, food relief and security, refugee, and agricultural projects in addition to its ongoing work in the educational sector.

Chapter 8: Two Voices for Human Rights
 1 John Meisel and Vincent Lemieux, *Ethnic Relations in Canadian Voluntary Associations*, Studies of the Royal Commission on Bilingualism and Biculturalism, Document 13 (Ottawa: Queen's Printer, 1972).
 2 Besides the translation of the minutes of AI meetings done in Ottawa, only 30 percent of documents originating from London were translated by Quebec volunteers.
 3 Amnistie international, section canadienne (francophone), and Amnesty International, Canadian section (English speaking).
 4 Even though a majority of the permanent staff of the francophone chapter are bilingual, the majority of the thirty employees of the anglophone branch are unilingual. The exceptions are Secretary General Roger Clark, originally from Britain, and the Franco-Ontarian receptionist, Louise Imbeault, who speak impeccable French. The other unilingual employees are of Anglo-Saxon origin, such as Bob Goodfellow; John Tackaberry, director of media relations; Cheryl Hotchkiss, network coordinator; Keith Rimstad, public awareness campaigns coordinator; and William Bryant, assistant responsible for resources development, who has been an active participant since the foundation of the movement. Certain employees are of multi-ethnic origins, such as Lily Mah-Sen, Lilibeth Ackbarali, and Lu Pinto. As for the members of the Board of Directors, they are also unilingual anglophones: the president, David Scrimshaw; the vice-president, Michael Bossin; the chairperson, Sharon MacGougan; the treasurer, Michael Wilkshire; the secretary, Katia Gianneschi; and the directors, John Argue, Cheryl Hotchkiss, Anne Jayne, Mark Schiml, Deborah Smith, and Seiko Watanabe.
 5 For example, the Scouts or the Optimist Clubs.
 6 Respectively, Help Age, United Nation Associations of Canada, World Association of Community Radio Broadcasters, Canadian Crossroads International, International Centre of Human Rights and Democratic Development, Social Justice Committee, Canadian University Service Overseas, Development and Peace, World University Service of Canada, Canada World Youth, Oxfam Canada, and YMCA.
 7 Solidarité, union, cooperation (SUCO) separated from CUSO in the 1970s.
 8 See the minutes of the first conference of the Canadian Amnesty International Groups, held at 348 Hickson Avenue, St-Lambert, Quebec, 12-13 May 1973.
 9 Group 7 of Montreal.
10 Besides Quebec offices, francophone bureaus have been put in place in Ottawa, Toronto, Winnipeg, and Calgary (from 1982 to 1984).
11 Cooperation at international meetings was difficult because the two groups had different views of the world and different priorities. Anglophones did not have the same sensibility regarding questions of international development; for example, francophones were in favour of the development of linguistic groups in francophone African countries. Female genital mutilation, gay rights, and Aboriginal claims are still themes perceived differently by the two sections.
12 The AI national bureau in Ottawa hired professional translators but did not have the necessary budget to do all of the requested translation. Volunteers completed the remaining translation in Montreal. Quebec volunteers translated about 30 percent of the movement's official documents.

13 That office acted autonomously as a team of francophone activists, with one representative named by the national executive who administered it. The bureau assumed the diffusion of information in French, translated urgent actions, and was in charge of the accreditation of new groups and of subscriptions, which were more or less sent to Ottawa. In 1976 and 1977, the AI-Québec office in Montreal tried to improve its structures to be recognized as a section. Its first demand was to get Ottawa to approve a regional coordination structure in Quebec within the Canadian section. This formula constituted a form of asymmetrical federalism.

14 The francophone branch often used respected artists, such as Yvon Deschamps in 1976, to promote the organization and attract new members. Since 1995, the comedian Daniel Lemire was the spokesperson for the francophone section. There is no similar counterpart in the anglophone branch.

15 In Montreal, seven permanent employees, headed by the general director, coordinate the activities of the francophone secretariat; in Ottawa, there are about thirty employees.

16 Because of the support of volunteers, the two secretariats have their own public awareness activities as well as services such as communication, support to groups and urgent action networks, government and embassy representation, as well as financing. The activities of the members of the movement result from the work of local and school groups as well as specialized groups, such as the Judicial Commission (which includes judges, lawyers, notaries, and law school students); the Health Network, composed of health professionals; the Religious Sector, composed of groups representing different Christian denominations; the Woman Sector; the Urgent Action Network; and the Refugee Committee. In addition, the anglophone section has a department of cultural diversification, which seeks greater participation of members from all ethnic origins.

17 According to Meisel and Lemieux, NGOs are composed of people socially involved who represent society's most influential groups. Voluntary organizations are in fact composed of educated people who have incomes superior to the Canadian average. The membership of AI in Canada reflects this fact. The francophone branch is composed of 20,000 members, of which 95 percent are from Quebec. The other members come from the francophone regions of Manitoba (Winnipeg), New Brunswick (Moncton), and Ontario (Toronto). There is a small percentage of allophones, such as Latinos and former residents of Africa and Haiti. After the separation of the two branches, the membership went from 300 members in 1974 to 25,000 in 1982, with a budget of $800,000. On the francophone side, membership declined by 4 percent in 1998, which resulted in a decrease of revenue of about $30,000 (for a total of $670,000 in 1998). There are between 3,000 and 4,000 active volunteers in the francophone section. Among the most active, there are as many men as women, the majority (75 percent) are more than forty years of age, more than half (56 percent) have a university degree, and their annual incomes vary between $20,000 and $75,000. There are aabout 30 local groups and 200 academic groups. This form of activism is more developed in the francophone section because of the presence of school chaplains. Their participation has contributed to the proliferation of academic groups and the regular production of educational materials. Anglophone activists are three times more numerous, with 60,625 members. Membership has gone through a phenomenal expansion: from 5,000 members in 1981, it became 29,000 in 1986 and 67,360 in 1998. The anglophone section has 6,735 volunteers. The majority of members are women between forty-five and seventy years of age, and because of the youth program there are about 5,000 young people in the anglophone branch. There are 413 groups and more than 300 academic groups coming from schools and universities. But anglophones were less successful with teachers, who are not, unlike in Quebec, part of strong union organizations that support the movement.

18 Meisel and Lemieux, *Ethnic Relations*, 11-12.

19 Janet Adams, Sackville group, to the founding members, containing the revised minutes of the first conference of Canadian Amnesty International Groups held at 348 Hickson Avenue, St-Lambert, 12-13 May 1973.

20 This council was composed of the president (John Humphrey at the foundation of the movement), the president of the Canadian Executive Committee, two elected vice-presidents

(one of which was a representative of the francophone community), the elected treasurer, the secretary, and the director of finances and public information.

21 See founding document.

22 Among them was Senator Eugene Forsey.

23 The first Canadian Executive Committee was composed of John Humphrey, John Robbins, Eugene Forsey, Vernon Nichols, Bruce Kennedy, Jane Armitage, and J.R. Beattie. The national director of AI was Robert Inch.

24 Revised minutes of AI foundation, 7.

25 Group 7 of Montreal.

26 A francophone structure (called successively AI-Québec, Secretariat du Québec, and Section québécoise) was created at the end of 1975. The office founded by the francophone activists of AI was located at 300 Carré St-Louis, in the bureaus of the Human Rights League.

27 Testimony of Pierre Dorchies, former treasurer of the francophone section of AI.

28 Proposition presented by Jean-Luc Hêtu and François Martin to the Committee for the Drafting of a New Constitution, 7 January 1978. In this proposition, it is said that "Francophone Quebeckers do not identify with a predominantly Anglophone national structure."

29 After much dispute, Quebec groups 7, 14, and 16 (as well as groups 28 and 30) finally adopted a resolution approving the principle of the establishment of two pan-Canadian linguistic branches that are autonomous, parallel, and have the same rights. Each branch is responsible for putting in place regional structures to achieve its objectives. A coordinating committee called the Canadian National Section represents the two branches at the national and international levels. See in the annex the proposition adopted by the 1977 AGA concerning constitutional revisions.

30 The francophone members of the Constitutional Revision Committee were François Martin, Pierre Dorchies, Jean-Luc Hêtu, and Robert Thibault, who represented francophones from outside Quebec. The anglophone members were John Boyle, Jean Loubser from outside Quebec, and Jean Smith, an anglophone member from Quebec.

31 Four anglophones, four francophones, and one Spanish-speaking member, including Sue Nichols, Pierre Dorchies, and François Martin.

32 Clauses 3.1 and 4.1 of the Rule Project.

33 The member designated by the anglophone Executive Committee was Phil de Gruchy.

34 The International Secretariat is composed of 300 permanent employees, and its Executive Committee meets seven times a year.

35 Francophones had their own budget for separate fundraising campaigns.

36 The francophones' strategy consisted of the accreditation of support groups that did not require, contrary to adoption groups, the authorization of London. "Francophones were fighting for a faster development and the development of their own structure ... to legitimize the creation of a francophone section," recalled François Martin in an interview conducted in 1999. In fact, they managed to penetrate the Quebec francophone clientele through the creation of support groups, especially in the educational world, because of Jeunesse du monde. Leaders of this movement contributed, in 1977, to the diffusion in the school system of a petition in favour of the abolition of torture. This initiative explains the phenomenal growth of school groups in the francophone Canadian section.

37 Messages circulating in an NGO are related to membership lists; correspondence; financial statements; programs of congress; minutes of meetings; letters of agreement, membership cards, official magazines; the Internet site; the language of simultaneous translation; and the language of origin of translated documents.

38 Membership cards, financial statements, minutes of national Executive Committee meetings (besides the minutes of special meetings concerning the division of the two groups) – everything was in English.

39 Amnesty International Canadian Section and Amnistie internationale section canadienne.

40 Published starting 1 January 1974, its name was *Bulletin Amnesty International-Amnistie international,* and it was written exclusively in English.

41 All the francophone countries, including France and Belgium, used the anglophone designation Amnesty International section française or belge.

42 That is, urgent translations, annual reports, reports of public awareness and action network campaigns, as well as press releases.

43 The translation of information sent to groups constituted significant work and limited the expansion of the francophone group, composed of about 100 members in 1975.

44 To attract new members, francophones opted for mass advertisements, with well-known spokespersons such as Yvon Deschamps, contrary to anglophones, who were sending letters only to authorities and prisoners. See "Entrevue du mois: Yvon Deschamps," *Maclean's*, mars 1976, 23-24.

45 Memorandum of Agreement between the anglophone Canadian section and la section canadienne francophone, 25 February 1978.

46 François Martin, Pierre Dorchies, and Robert Thibault.

47 Meeting of the Canadian section delegation with IEC and IS members, at Eros Restaurant, Cambridge, 22 September 1978.

48 The member designated by the anglophone Executive Committees was Phil de Gruchy.

49 For example, during the worldwide campaign on the violations of human rights in the United States, for the defence of Stanley Faulder, 1998-99, a letter in French and in English was sent to the minister of foreign affairs, Lloyd Axworthy.

50 Minutes, Meeting of the Board of Directors of the francophone Canadian section of AI, Montreal, 17 June 1979.

51 Contrary to anglophones, francophones were fighting for the establishment of linguistic entities in African francophone countries.

52 See the resolutions adopted at the special general assembly of the Canadian section of AI in London, Ontario, 2 June 1978.

53 The francophone chapter for a number of years has raised $850,000 per year and sent $250,000 in subscriptions to the London headquarters. The anglophone chapter, which managed $4.5 million per year and sends to the IS more than $1 million, has gone through major financial difficulties. It has been trying to re-equilibrate its budget through a more aggressive marketing and fundraising plan.

54 Joint committees were formed for the advent of major events, such as the International Council that was held in 1982 in Montreal, the visit of Donald Wood from the United States, and the fiftieth anniversary of the human rights declaration.

55 For example, in the case of Steve Faulder, the two chapters worked on a common plan of action to formalize their intervention. There was close coordination between the two groups on the issue of the death penalty, with a view to increasing the weight of the common actions of francophones and anglophones.

56 Even though there is constant communication between the communication directors, as well as constant exchanges of information between the two Canadian sections, the francophone section works more in collaboration with francophone countries, for example to plan events regarding the Sommet de la francophonie held in Moncton. At this event, only the francophone section participated in a parallel summit led by other francophone NGOs.

57 See the document "Philosophy and Responsibility of the Executive Committee."

58 Coordination of the activities of the Canadian section occurs without trouble between the two linguistic chapters. Following the suggestion of Michel Frenette, the annual meeting of 1997 that brought together all the section directors of AI was held in Montreal, in the francophone east end of the city. Anglophones were in charge of animation, while francophones were in charge of infrastructure, organization, and welcoming. The duality of Canada was put at the front of the event. Today the designation "section canadienne francophone" is informally accepted.

59 Roger Clark, Anglophone Director, to Gilles Corbeil, Francophone Director, 2 April 1990.

60 The current secretary general is Irene Kahn.

61 At the Montreal meeting of 1997, exchanges were in English with simultaneous translation.

62 Annual reports of the section, website, e-mails, monthly publications for the membership, bulletins, pamphlets, minutes of the meetings of the Executive Committee and General Assembly, et cetera.

63 Canada, Belgium, France, Luxembourg, Switzerland, Ivory Coast.

64 Julian Gruda, vice-president of the Board of Directors of the francophone section, was the president at that time.
65 From 1988 to 1994, according to Gilles Corbeil, the Canadian francophone section had more contact with the French and Belgian sections than with the Canadian anglophone section because of the transmission of documents.
66 Annual reports, countries' information, the different themes, press releases, or urgent actions released by London. The latter are sent by e-mail to Paris, translated, and sent from Paris to the different francophone countries, where the French version is adapted.
67 Documents for the public: general and promotional pamphlets, Internet site, action toolkit, and letters. Documents for members: the monthly bulletin *Agir*, campaign or action bulletins, and those sent to specialized networks.
68 According to Pierre Dorchies, there were significant differences in terms of the ages and social classes of the activists of both sections. The anglophone approach was politically correct and consisted of pure voluntary services. In the francophone section, there were fourteen paid full-time employees who structured the activities of the movement.
69 Francophones were in favour of sending petitions and newspaper articles to authorities to facilitate the liberation of prisoners, whereas anglophones would only write letters.
70 The membership went from 300 to 30,000 between 1974 and the end of the 1970s. In 1982, there were more than 25,000 members, and the annual budget was $800,000.
71 During the Oka crisis, in 1990, the anglophone section issued its own press release reflecting its support of Aboriginals. This action created tensions with francophones that were dealt with in the meetings of the francophone section on 23 and 30 November 1990 and at the meeting of the Board of Directors on 30 November of that year.

Chapter 9: Accommodation at the Pinnacle
1 Royal Commission on Bilingualism and Biculturalism, *Preliminary Report of the Royal Commission on Bilingualism and Biculturalism* (Ottawa: Queen's Printer, 1965), xvii.

Bibliography

Bédard, Denis. *Pacte 2000: Rapport de la Commission nationale sur les finances et la fiscalité locale (Bédard Report)*. Québec: Les Publications du Québec, 1999.

Bens, Charles, and Anne Golden. *The Federation of Canadian Municipalities: In Search of Credibility*. Toronto: Bureau of Municipal Research Paper, 1976.

Breton, Raymond. "Social Participation and Social Capital." Paper presented at the second national Metropolis Conference, Montreal, 1997.

Breton, Raymond, Jeffrey G. Reitz, and Victor F. Valentine. *Les frontières culturelles et la cohésion du Canada*. Montreal: Institute for Research on Public Policy, 1981.

Business Council on National Issues to Council of Premiers, memorandum, 15 July 1991. *Memorandum for the Honourable Frank McKenna, Premier of New Brunswick and Chairman-Designate, Council of Premiers*, 1.

Caldwell, Gary, and Paul Reed. "Civic Participation in Canada: Is Quebec Different?" *Inroads* 8 (1999): 215-22.

Canadian Federation of Independent Business, "Québec's Small Business Sector Rejects Sovereignty Option." Press release, 18 October 1995.

Chambre de commerce de Montréal. *Un siècle à entreprendre: La chambre de commerce de Montréal 1887-1987*. Montréal: Éditions Libre Expression, 1987.

Chambre de commerce du Montréal métropolitain/Board of Trade of Metropolitan Montreal. "Les services en français et en anglais à la Chambre de commerce du Montréal métropolitain: Bilan et recommandations." Juin 1995.

Chambre de commerce du Québec. "Canadian Federalism Is an Economic Failure." In *Canada, Adieu? Québec Debates Its Future*, ed. Richard Fidler, 82-89. Lantzville, BC: Oolichan; Halifax: Institute for Research on Public Policy, 1991.

Coleman, William D. *Business and Politics: A Study of Collective Action*. Montreal: McGill-Queen's University Press, 1988.

–. "Federalism and Interest Group Organization." In *Federalism and the Role of the State*, ed. Herman Bakvis and William M. Chandler, 171-87. Toronto: University of Toronto Press, 1987.

–. *The Independence Movement in Québec: 1945-1980*. Toronto: University of Toronto Press, 1984.

Coleman, William D., and Tim A. Mau. "French-English Relations in Business Interest Associations, 1965-2002." *Canadian Public Administration* 45, 4 (Winter 2002): 490-511.

Coleman, William D., and Grace Skogstad. "Policy Communities and Policy Networks: A Structural Approach." In *Policy Communities and Public Policy in Canada: A Structural Approach*, ed. William D. Coleman and Grace Skogstad, 14-33. Mississauga: Copp Clark Pitman, 1990.

Confederation 2000. "Today and Tomorrow: An Agenda for Action: Ideas and Recommendations of the Confederation 2000 Conference Participants." 3-4 May 1996.

Conseil du patronat du Québec. "The Dangers of Sovereignty." In *Canada, Adieu? Québec Debates Its Future,* ed. Richard Fidler, 114-19. Lantzville, BC: Oolichan; Halifax: Institute for Research on Public Policy, 1991.

Cook, Ramsay. *Canada, Quebec, and the Uses of Nationalism.* Toronto: McClelland and Stewart, 1986.

Della Porta, Donatella, and Mario Diani. *Social Movements: An Introduction.* Oxford: Blackwell, 1999.

Federation of Canadian Municipalities. *FCM 1937-1987: 50 Years Making History.* Ottawa: Federation of Canadian Municipalities, 1987.

Feldman, Lionel D., and Katharine A. Graham. *Bargaining for Cities: Municipalities and Intergovernmental Relation – An Assessment.* Montreal: Institute for Research on Public Policy, 1979.

Fidler, Richard, ed. *Canada, Adieu? Québec Debates Its Future.* Lantzville, BC: Oolichan; Halifax: Institute for Research on Public Policy, 1991.

Fletcher, Frederick J. "Media and Political Identity: Canada and Quebec in the Era of Globalization." *Canadian Journal of Communication* 23, 3 (1998): 359-80. http://www.cjc-online.ca/viewarticle.php?id=472.

Forbes, H.D. *Ethnic Conflict: Commerce, Culture, and the Contact Hypothesis.* New Haven: Yale University Press, 1997.

–. "Integration, Contact, and Linkages." Paper prepared for the Privy Council Office. Ottawa, Government of Canada, 2001.

Glenn, Ted. "The Calgary Declaration." *Backgrounder B-19.* Toronto: Ontario Legislative Library, Legislative Research Service, 24 April 1988.

Herring, Martin. "Consociational Democracy in Canada." 1998. http://www.archiv.ub.uni-marburg.de/sum/84/sum84-6.html.

Kymlicka, Will. "Citizenship in an Era of Globalization: Commentary on Held." In *Democracy's Edges,* ed. Ian Shapiro and Casiano Hacker-Cordón, 317-27. Cambridge, UK: Cambridge University Press, 1999.

Laponce, Jean. "The Case for Ethnic Federalism in Multilingual Societies." In *The Territorial Management of Ethnic Conflict,* ed. John Coakley, 23-43. London: Frank Cass, 1993.

–. *Languages and Their Territories.* Toronto: University of Toronto Press, 1987.

–. "Reducing the Tensions Resulting from Language Contacts: Personal or Territorial Solutions?" In *Language and the State: The Law and Politics of Identity,* ed. David Schneiderman, 125-31. Cowansville, QC: Éditions Yvon Blais, 1989.

Lazar, Harvey, and Tom McIntosh. "How Canadians Connect: State, Economy, Citizenship, and Society." In *Canada: The State of the Federation 1998/1999: How Canadians Connect,* ed. Harvey Lazar and Tom McIntosh, 3-33. Montreal: McGill-Queen's University Press, 1999.

Lemieux, Vincent. "Le conflit dans les organisations biculturelles." *Recherches sociographiques* 24, 1 (1973): 41-57.

Lijphart, Arend. *Democracy in Plural Societies: A Comparative Exploration.* New Haven: Yale University Press, 1977.

Lindblom, Charles E. *Politics and Markets.* New York: Basic Books, 1977.

Marmen, Louise, and Jean-Pierre Corbeil. *New Canadian Perspectives: Languages in Canada: 1996 Census.* Ottawa: Minister of Public Works and Government Services Canada, 1999.

McCarthy, John D., and Mayer N. Zald. "Resource Mobilization and Social Movements: A Partial Theory." *American Journal of Sociology* 82 (1977): 1212-41.

McRoberts, Kenneth. *Misconceiving Canada: The Struggle for National Unity.* Toronto: Oxford University Press, 1997.

Meisel, John, and Vincent Lemieux. *Ethnic Relations in Canadian Voluntary Associations.* Studies of the Royal Commission on Bilingualism and Biculturalism, Document 13. Ottawa: Queen's Printer, 1972.

Melucci, Alberto. *Challenging Codes: Collective Action in the Information Age.* Cambridge, UK: Cambridge University Press, 1996.

Narayan, Deepa. "Bonds and Bridges: Social Capital and Poverty." Policy Research Working Paper 2167. Washington, DC: World Bank, 1999.

Panel on Accountability and Governance in the Voluntary Sector. *Building on Strength: Improving Governance and Accountability in Canada's Voluntary Sector – Final Report.* Ottawa: Voluntary Sector Roundtable, 1999.

Panet-Raymond, Jean. "Le Conseil québécois du développement social est né!" *Nouvelles Pratiques Sociales* 7, 1 (1994): 195-98.

Paré, Jean. "Merger shows the persuasive power of money." *The Financial Post,* 16 March 1992, S2.

Pritchard, David, and Florian Sauvageau. "English and French and Generation X: The Professional Values of Canadian Journalists." In *Canada: The State of the Federation 1998/1999: How Canadians Connect,* ed. Harvey Lazar and Tom McIntosh, 283-306. Montreal: McGill-Queen's University Press, 1999.

Putnam, Robert. *Bowling Alone: The Collapse and Revival of American Community.* New York: Simon and Schuster, 2000.

Reed, Paul B., and Valerie J. Howe. *Voluntary Organizations in Ontario in the 1990s.* Ottawa: Statistics Canada, 2000.

Royal Commission on Bilingualism and Biculturalism. *Preliminary Report of the Royal Commission on Bilingualism and Biculturalism.* Ottawa: Queen's Printer, 1965.

Russell, Peter H. *Constitutional Odyssey: Can Canadians Become a Sovereign People?* Toronto: University of Toronto Press, 1993.

–. "The End of Mega Constitutional Politics in Canada?" In *The Charlottetown Accord, the Referendum, and the Future of Canada,* ed. Kenneth McRoberts and Patrick Monahan, 211-21. Toronto: University of Toronto Press, 1993.

Schmitter, P.C., and Luca Lanzalaco. "Regions and the Organization of Business Interests." In *Regionalism, Business Interests, and Public Policy,* ed. William D. Coleman and Henry J. Jacek, 201-30. London: Sage, 1990.

Skogstad, Grace. "Canadian Federalism, Internationalization, and Quebec Agriculture: Dis-Engagement, Re-Integration?" *Canadian Public Policy* 24, 1 (1998): 27-48.

–. *The Politics of Agricultural Policy-Making in Canada.* Toronto: University of Toronto Press, 1987.

Smiley, Donald. "Language Policies in the Canadian Political Community." In *Être Contemporain: Mélanges en l'honneur de Gérard Bergeron,* ed. Jean-William Lapierre, Vincent Lemieux, and Jacques Zylberberg, 270-87. Sillery, QC: Presses de l'Université du Québec, 1992.

Splane, Richard. *75 Years of Community Services in Canada: Canadian Council on Social Development, 1920-1995.* Ottawa: Canadian Council on Social Development, 1996.

Statistics Canada. "Population by Knowledge of Official Language." Ottawa: Statistics Canada, 1996.

Stevenson, Don, and Richard Gilbert. "Coping with Canadian Federalism: The Case of the Federation of Canadian Municipalities." *Canadian Public Administration Journal* 48, 4 (2005): 528-51.

Taylor, Charles. *Reconciling the Solitudes: Essays on Canadian Federalism and Nationalism.* Montreal: McGill-Queen's University Press, 1993.

Union des producteurs agricoles. "Mémoire présenté à la Commission parlementaire québécoise par l'Union des producteurs agricoles: L'avenir politique et constitutionnel du Québec." In *Canada, Adieu? Québec Debates Its Future,* ed. Richard Fidler, 150-57. Lantzville, BC: Oolichan; Halifax: Institute for Research on Public Policy, 1991.

Van Parijs, Phillippe. "Must Europe Be Belgian? On Democratic Citizenship in Multilingual Polities." In *The Demands of Citizenship,* ed. Catriona McKinnon and Iain Hampsher-Monk, 235-53. London: Continuum, 2000.

Contributors

Cathy Blacklock works as a consultant and is based in Toronto. She has a doctorate in political science (Carleton University, 1996).

David Cameron, FRSC, is the chair and a professor of political science at the University of Toronto. His professional career has been divided between public service – in Ottawa and at Queen's Park – and academic life. A long-time student of Canadian federalism and Quebec nationalism, he has recently turned his attention to ethnocultural relations and constitution making in emerging or potential federal countries, such as Iraq and Sri Lanka.

William Coleman is Distinguished University Professor at McMaster University, where he holds the Canada Research Chair on Globalization Studies and Public Policy and is the founding director of the Institute on Globalization and the Human Condition. He has written on Quebec politics and has published extensively on business-government relations, agricultural policy, and financial services policy and globalization. He is a fellow of the Trudeau Foundation.

Sylvie Dugas is a researcher and communicator from Quebec. Her radio, television, and print reporting on Canada, Latin America, Europe, and Asia – mostly about politics and the economy – has appeared in the mainstream Quebec media and in academic publications. Author of *Le pouvoir citoyen: La société civile canadienne et québécoise face à la mondialisation*, published in 2006 by Éditions Fides, she is as well the founder of Communications Confluences, a company specializing in social, economic, political, and cultural research.

Michel Duquette received his PhD from McGill University. He was professor of political science at the Université de Montréal and an associate professor at the Institut d'études politiques d'Aix-en-Provence. He has published extensively on social movements in Brazil and Canada, as well as on the social consequences of structural adjustment reforms in Latin America. More recently, until his death in September 2008, he had been working on the social dimensions of integration mechanisms in the European Union, Mercosur, and NAFTA.

Richard Gilbert, now a consultant on energy, transport, and urban issues, was a municipal councillor in Toronto from 1976 to 1991 and president of the Federation of Canadian Municipalities in 1986-87.

Jane Jenson was awarded the Canada Research Chair in Citizenship and Governance at the Université de Montréal in 2001, where she is a professor of political
science. Named a fellow of the Trudeau Foundation (2005-8), she is also a member
of the Successful Societies program of the Canadian Institute for Advanced Research. Her research interests and publications include social policy, social movements, citizenship, diversity, and gender studies in Canada and the European
Union.

Rachel Laforest is an assistant professor and head of the Public Policy and Third
Sector Initiative in the School of Policy Studies at Queen's University. Her research
areas include the voluntary sector and public interest groups, with a special
emphasis on representation, advocacy, and new forms of political activism. Her
work has been published in *Politique et sociétés, International Journal of Canadian
Studies,* and *Social Policy and Administration.*

Tim A. Mau is an assistant professor in the Department of Political Science at the
University of Guelph, where he teaches undergraduate courses on business-
government relations, local government, and public management and administration and graduate-level courses for the Guelph-McMaster Collaborative MA
in Public Policy and Administration and the collaborative MA (Leadership) program. He has published articles on topics such as public sector leadership, leadership in the Canadian military, and Quebec and Scottish nationalism.

Richard Simeon, FRSC, is a professor of political science and law at the University
of Toronto. From 2006 to 2008, he was the William Lyon Mackenzie King Visiting Professor of Canadian Studies at Harvard University. A life-long student of
federalism, his *Federal-Provincial Diplomacy* (1971) was honoured by the American
Political Science Association as a "work of lasting significance in federalism and
intergovernmental relations." His current work focuses on institutional design
for divided societies.

Grace Skogstad is a professor of political science at the University of Toronto.
Her research and publications have focused on Canadian and European agricultural and food policy, the internationalization of domestic politics and policy
making, and Canadian federalism. She served as president of the Canadian Political Science Association in 2002-3 and was a Senior Fernand Braudel Fellow at
the European University Institute in 2007-8.

Don Stevenson is a former deputy minister in the Ontario government, responsible at different times for municipal affairs, intergovernmental relations, and
resources development. He was president of the Institute of Public Administration of Canada in 1978-79.

Index

Business Council on National Issues (BCNI). *See* Canadian Council of Chief Executives

Calgary Declaration, 39, 48-49, 191n34
Canada, Government of: and Amnesty International, 162; and bilingualism, 8, 77, 105, 164, 171, 187n7; CCSD, 130-31; civil society, 10, 21; constitutional debates, 70, 87-88; and decentralization, 71, 74, 90, 92; farm communities, 52, 54, 57, 67-71, 73; multiculturalism, 171; municipal governments, 82-83, 85, 87-88, 90, 92, 94; and Quebec, 5, 75, 78, 82; voluntary associations, 181-82; voluntary health associations, 100, 104, 105, 116; and WUSC, 137, 147, 148-49
Canadian Bureau for International Education, 138, 139
Canadian Cancer Society, 99-100, 104
Canadian Chamber of Commerce (CCC): and bilingualism, 27, 33; and CCMM/BTMM, relations with, 36-37; and CCPQ, relations with, 30-32; and CCQ, relations with, 35-37; and francophones, 31; organizational structure, 28; and representation, linguistic, 32, 42
Canadian Council for International Cooperation, 141
Canadian Council of Chief Executives (CCCE): and bilingualism, 33, 39; Calgary Declaration, 48-49, 51; founding of, 25; organizational structure, 27, 29, 30; and representation, linguistic 42
Canadian Council on Fair Taxation, 24
Canadian Council on Social Development (CCSD): and bilingualism, 126-28, 130, 135; budgeting, 129-31; CQDS, relations with, 122, 134-35; as CWC, 122-26, 128-29; French Commission, 125-28; French-speaking section, 123-24; organization of, 121; Quebec office, 132-33; and Royal Commission on Bilingualism and Biculturalism, 122, 124, 126
Canadian Diabetes Association, 100, 104
Canadian Executive Services Overseas, 139
Canadian Export Association (CEA), 25, 27, 28, 40
Canadian Federation of Agriculture (CFA): and bilingualism, 60-62; decision-making process within, 59, 66-68; goals, 54-56; membership of, 56; NFU, 54; organizational structure, 58, 62, 66, 67; trade liberalization, 69-70; and UCC/UPA, 52, 56-60, 67, 69, 71-72

Canadian Federation of Independent Business (CFIB): and bilingualism, 34, 38; and constitutional debates, 47-48; organizational structure, 27, 29, 50; Quebec, 29; and representation, linguistic 35, 38-39, 42
Canadian Federations of Mayors and Municipalities. *See* Federation of Canadian Municipalities
Canadian Manufacturers and Exporters (CME): and AMEQ, relations with, 40, 41; and bilingualism, 34, 35, 40-41, 51; merger of CMA and CEA into, 25, 28; organizational structure, 27, 28-29, 50; and representation, linguistic, 42
Canadian Manufacturers Association (CMA), 24-25, 27, 28-29, 40
Canadian Pork Council, 64-66, 67, 72, 192n14
Canadian Welfare Council. *See* Canadian Council on Social Development
CARE Canada, 139
CBC, 188n15
CCC. *See* Canadian Chamber of Commerce
CCCE. *See* Canadian Council of Chief Executives
CCDM. *See* Chambre de commerce du District de Montréal
CCMM. *See* Board of Trade of Metropolitan Montreal
CCPQ. *See* Chambre de commerce du Québec
CCQ. *See* Chambre de commerce du Québec
CCSD. *See* Canadian Council on Social Development
CEA. *See* Canadian Export Association
Centre d études arabes pour le développement, 139
Centre d information et de documentation sur la Mozambique et l Afrique australe, 139
CFA. *See* Canadian Federation of Agriculture
CFIB. *See* Canadian Federation of Independent Business
Chambre de commerce de la Province du Québec. *See* Chambre de commerce du Québec
Chambre de commerce du District de Montréal (CCDM); goals, 26, 28, 44; merger into BTMM/CCMM, 24, 43-46, 50-51; organizational structure, 27
Chambre de commerce du Montréal métropolitain. *See* Board of Trade of Metropolitan Montreal

only, 164; quality of, 38, 151; simultaneous interpretation, 64
Tremblay Commission, 187n6

UMQ. *See* Union des municipalités des
Québec
UNICEF Canada, 139
Unifarm, 56
Union catholique des cultivateurs (UCC).
See Union des producteurs agricole
Union des municipalités des la province
du Québec. *See* Union des municipalités
du Québec
Union des municipalités du Québec, 75-
76, 82-84, 89, 92
Union des municipalités régionales de
comté et des municipalités locales, 83
Union des producteurs agricole (UPA):
and bilingualism, 193n41; and CFA,
relations with, 54, 57-62, 67, 69, 71-72;
and Dairy Farmers of Canada, tension
with 63; history, 56; organization of, 56-
57, 58-59, 66, 67; and Quebec sovereignty, 70-71; and trade liberalization, 69
Union générale des étudiants du Québec,
144-45
Union of Municipalities of New Brunswick,
86
Universal Declaration of Human Rights,
156, 157
UPA. *See* Union des producteurs agricole
Urbanization, 91, 187n8, 195n2
Uruguay Round negotiations. *See* GATT

Van Parijs, Phillippe, 16, 189n37

Varshney, Ashutosh, 14
Vietnam, 83
voluntary associations: and bilingualism,
5, 6, 8-11, 16-19, 20, 118-19, 175-76,
184; in Canada, 21, 138-39, 174-75,
190n43; in civil society, as part of, 4-5,
11-12; in divided societies, 14, 180; external institutional environment of, 116,
181-82; and federal government, relations with, 181-82; and international
organizations, as part of, 155, 159;
leadership, role of, 180; membership,
200n17; objectives of, 47, 173, 180, 183;
organizational structure of, 15, 17, 104,
176-78, 180-81; in Quebec, 102, 176. *See*
also civil society

Watson, John, 136, 147
websites. *See* internet
Wild Rose Agricultural Producers Association, 56, 192n25
Wilkinson, Jack, 62
women's movement, 9, 10
World Trade Organization, 69
World University Service of Canada: and
bilingualism, 142, 144, 147-49, 151, 152;
goals of, 136, 142-43, 148, 152; EUMQ,
relations with, 145-46; funding, 147-48,
150, 198n19; history of, 136-38, 139;
ID NGO community, 140-41, 150, 152;
organizational structure of, 143-44, 148;
in Quebec, 144-48, 149-51; treasure van,
138, 142-43
World Vision Canada, 139, 141

Printed and bound in Canada by AGMV Marquis
Set in Stone by Artegraphica Design Co. Ltd.
Copy editor: Dallas Harrison
Proofreader: Meaghan Craven
Indexer: Dubi Kanengisser

Marquis Book Printing Inc.

Québec, Canada
2009